Fast Fixes
and
Simple
Solutions

SURPRISING
USES FOR
ORDINARY
HOUSEHOLD
ITEMS

To Julian
Wishing you All the Best
Anne.

March, 2004

Publisher's Note

The editors of FC&A have taken careful measures to ensure the accuracy and use-fulness of the information in this book. While every attempt has been made to assure accuracy, errors may occur. We advise readers to carefully review and under-stand the ideas and tips presented and to seek the advice of a qualified professional before attempting to use them. The publisher and editors disclaim all liability (including any injuries, damages, or losses) resulting from the use of the informa-tion in this book.

The health information in this book is for information only and is not intended to be a medical guide for self-treatment. It does not constitute medical advice and should not be construed as such or used in place of your doctor's medical advice.

FC&A
103 Clover Green
Peachtree City, GA 30269

Produced by the staff of FC&A
Distributed to the trade by National Book Network

Table of Contents

Sparkling solutions for
household cleaning

Get disposable gloves for free. Need to get down and dirty? Save those plastic produce bags you tear off in the grocery store and turn them into disposable gloves. Slip the bags over your hands and hold them in place with rubber bands. When you're done, just toss them out.

Bounce odors with fabric softener. Freshen the scent of your bedroom or bathroom without throwing away money on fancy-smelling air fresheners. Just put a fabric softener sheet in your wastebasket.

Prevent toilet trouble with baking soda. To put the lid on toilet bowl backups and odors, pour in one cup of baking soda once a week.

Strike a match to strike out odor. One of the most effective ways to mask unpleasant bathroom odor is also one of the easiest. Simply light a match or two, and you'll camouflage any smells. Keep a few matchbooks in your bathroom for emergencies.

Spray away shower scum. Commercial shower cleaners can clean out your wallet if you use them every day, so make your own daily cleaner instead. Pour 8 ounces of rubbing alcohol in a 32-ounce spray bottle and top it off with water. Spray this concoction on your shower walls and curtain after every shower. You won't even have to rinse it off.

Stop mildew before it starts. Scrubbing mildew off your shower tiles can be as much fun as going to the dentist. Instead, prevent mildew from growing in the first place by running a squeegee over your tiles after every shower. Keep the squeegee in your shower stall so you won't forget to use it.

Clean your shower while you sleep. Make cleaning mildew and muck on your tub or shower tiles as easy as calling it a night. Spray bleach on paper towels and spread them on the grungy areas. The wet towels will stay in place and clean throughout the night. All you have to do is rinse off the tiles in the morning.

Fight soap scum on tiles. To clean grime off your bathroom tiles, whip up a solution of equal parts Epsom salt and liquid dish detergent. The salt adds friction, which helps the detergent scour away the scum.

Wash mildew down the drain. If your shower is becoming mildew's favorite hangout, mix three-quarters cup of bleach in one gallon of water. Rub this powerful solution on your tile and grout, and wipe down your plastic shower curtain. Once the mildew fades away, rinse with plain water.

Muscle out bathroom mildew. Cleaning your bathtub and shower regularly can stop mildew in its tracks. That's because a clean bathroom doesn't contain the things mildew thrives on, like soap scum, shampoo residue, and body oils. To deprive mildew of the moisture it needs, leave shower doors or curtains open right after you've bathed or showered. Keep the bathroom door open to dry the room out, too.

Erase dirty grout this 'elementary' way. Erase dirt between your bathroom tiles with a circular typewriter eraser. Simply roll it along the grout to rub it clean. Many of these erasers come with brushes to sweep away the eraser dust left behind.

Spray mildew away. Fighting mildew is an everyday battle. Arm yourself with an inexpensive homemade weapon. Mix one-half cup of rubbing alcohol, three cups of water, and one tablespoon of liquid laundry detergent in a spray bottle. Spray this mixture on your tiled bathroom walls after each shower.

Banish mildew easily. Here's a tip for getting rid of mildew from your bathtub that requires practically no effort. When it's time to clean your bathroom, start by dipping cotton balls in bleach and pressing them into the tub's corners, where mildew is most likely to sprout. Leave them there while you finish cleaning. When you're done, remove the cotton balls and rinse the corners with water.

Make your shower doors shine. For those water stains on your fiberglass shower doors, brush on a coat of acrylic floor finish. It will finish off those stains and put a shine on your doors.

Baby your shower doors. Baby oil can help your shower doors repel dirt, soap scum, and hard water deposits. Rub a light layer of baby oil on your shower doors to keep them crystal clear for months.

Dry your shower doors with dryer sheets. Used fabric softener sheets also come in handy in the shower. Wipe down your shower doors with them. They won't leave streaks or water spots.

Get your shower back on track. Bathe the track of your sliding shower door with full-strength vinegar to make it like new. Let the vinegar sit in the track for a few minutes and then rinse it out.

Double your shower power. It does a good job cleaning you, so it makes sense that a hot, steamy bath or shower can also loosen the dirt off your bathroom fixtures, tiles, and tub. Wait to clean your bathroom until right after you've taken a hot shower or bath. Or if you want, lather up your shower tiles while you're lathering up yourself.

Safeguard your shower with car wax. Follow this two-step tip to chase away shower grime and mildew. First, do a thorough job of removing soap and water residue from the tiles. Then rub on a layer of paste wax, like car wax, and buff with a clean, dry cloth. You'll only need to reapply the wax about once a year.

Whiten your bathroom caulking. Return your caulking to its original pearly whiteness with a solution of one-quarter cup bleach to one gallon of water. Rubbing alcohol can clean caulk, too. It's also good for getting chrome and glass to glitter again.

Teach your shower curtain to glide. If your shower curtain seems about as flexible as the Iron Curtain, try rubbing some baby oil on the shower rod. A bar of soap also works well. Either way, your curtain will slide more smoothly.

Overwhelm shower curtain mildew. Mildew can't stand salt water. So either take your new shower curtain to the beach or dip it in salt water at home before you hang it. That unsightly mildew will look for another place to call home.

Give new life to old shower curtains. If your shower curtains are already in the grimy grip of mildew, rescue them with a lemon. Wash the curtains in hot, soapy water and then rub lemon juice on the mildew. After you let them dry in the sun, they'll be as good as new.

Give shower curtains a bath. To get your shower curtain sparkling clean, soak it in warm water and baking soda.

Clobber soap scum in your soap dish. If getting rid of soap scum isn't your idea of fun, here's how you can eliminate it in the first place. Find a sponge that fits your soap dish and set it underneath the soap. That way, wet soap will seep into the sponge, not all over your soap dish. To clean up, just rinse out the sponge.

Clean your toilet while you're away. Next time you run an errand, pour one-quarter cup of bleach in your toilet bowl before you head out the door. When you get back, just flush, and you'll have a glistening bowl. But remember, don't put bleach in your toilet if you already have a tank-held cleaner, the kind that works each time you flush. It might contain ammonia. Mixed together, ammonia and bleach release toxic fumes.

Banish bathroom moisture with charcoal. To soak up moisture in your bathroom, hide some charcoal around the room. It also helps cut down on musty and unpleasant odors.

Do away with ring around the toilet. Flush toilet rings down the drain with borax and lemon juice. First, be sure the sides of your toilet bowl are wet. Then, make a paste out of the two ingredients and rub it into the ring. Let it stand for two hours and scrub it off.

Dream about a ring-free toilet bowl. White vinegar can wash away the ring in your toilet bowl while you sleep. Just pour in one-half gallon of vinegar every month and let it sit overnight. The vinegar will do all the work. All you have to do is flush.

Make your grout like new. The grout between floor tiles can get pretty grimy, especially in the bathroom. Return it to its original, bright color by gently rubbing it with folded sandpaper. To keep your grout looking like new, apply a coat of tile sealer.

Add shine to your bathroom fixtures. To remove hard-water stains on your bathroom fixtures, apply a paste of baking soda and vinegar. When you're finished, carefully drape a towel over the fixtures. After about an hour, wipe clean, rinse, dry, and marvel at the shine.

Put the squeeze on mineral deposits. Lemon juice is a powerful, all-natural corrosive that can remove built-up mineral deposits on your faucets. Try slicing a lemon in half and squeezing the juice on the metal. After waiting a few minutes, rub the faucet with the lemon slice and rinse. Repeat the process using the other half of the lemon if needed.

Get the cold facts about foggy mirrors. Keeping fog off your bathroom mirror is easy. Just run some cold water into your bathtub before you add the hot water. No more fog.

Run rings around bathtub rings. Rubbing out bathtub rings takes some serious elbow grease. But if you cut back on another kind of grease – oily bath preparations – you could save your elbow the effort. A water softener could also roll back rings if you live where there's hard water. For another all-around good idea, try rinsing out the tub every time you're done using it.

Call in a ringer for bathtub cleaning. If a ring forms around your tub no matter what you do, don't reach for the power sander. Put on your rubber gloves and get down and dirty with undiluted ammonia. Rubbing the ring with a wet sponge saturated with baking soda can work, too. In a worst-case scenario, attack the ring with automatic dishwasher detergent or a vinegar-soaked cloth. Whatever tactic you use, finish the job by rinsing the tub clean and wiping it dry.

Clean fiberglass for pennies. Gently clean your fiberglass tubs and sinks with nonabrasive cleaners, like dishwashing soaps and liquid laundry detergent. You can make your own cleaning solution by diluting one tablespoon of trisodium phosphate (Spic & Span) in one gallon of water. A baking soda and water paste is an effective cleaner, too. Just make sure to wet the surface of the fiberglass before applying the paste. Or go all-natural by rubbing a freshly cut lemon on light stains. Whatever you use, let it soak in for an hour before rubbing it off with a sponge or a brush made from a nonabrasive material, like nylon, polyester, or polyethylene. When you've finished cleaning, give your fiberglass a good rinse.

Give new life to yellowed enamel. There's hope for the yellowed enamel in your bathtub and sinks. A mixture of salt and turpentine can return it to its original pearly whiteness.

Foil grimy grills without elbow grease. You don't need a metal brush and lots of elbow grease to clean your grill. Instead, tear off a sheet of aluminum foil big enough to fit your grill. Lay it shiny-side down and turn the grill on for 10 to 15 minutes. When you take the foil off, the greasy mess will be gone.

Rescue an overworked paintbrush. If your paintbrush is ready for retirement, give it a new "haircut" and a new job. Trim its bristles very short, like a crew cut. Then use the brush to clean up some of your nastiest messes, like the gunk on your grill or the soap scum in the corners of your bathtub.

Clean your grill with newspaper. Steam clean your dirty barbecue grill while you relax. Here's how. When you're finished grilling, soak yesterday's newspaper in water and leave it on top of your warm grill rack with the lid closed. After about 45 minutes, open the lid and wipe off the greasy grime. Just remember – don't let the newspaper sit on the grill rack too long, or it will dry out and become a bigger mess.

Get your broom ready for action. A clean broom works harder than a dirty one. To keep your broom's bristles clean, dry, and straight, store it upside down or hanging off the ground. Hose off dirty or moldy bristles, and use your fingers or an old wide-toothed comb to remove dust and lint trapped inside.

Counteract kitchen stains with bleach. With a few drops of bleach and this clever tip, you can make ugly countertop stains disappear, and you won't even need to scrub. Just soak paper towels in bleach and put them over the stains. On top of this, add a layer of paper towels soaked in water. Let them sit overnight, and the unsightly stains will vanish by morning. This trick also works for white porcelain sinks. To protect your hands, wear rubber gloves when handling bleach.

Bubble your way to sparkling countertops. To make your old countertops look brand new, try washing them with club soda. This bubbly helper won't scratch your countertops, like scouring powder. Furniture polish also works well to make your countertops sparkle again.

Choose baking soda for countertop stains. It's easy to banish coffee and tea stains from your countertops. All it takes is a good rubbing with baking soda and water made into a paste.

Add sparkle to crystal. A handful of salt and some vinegar can make your crystal glassware shine like never before. Just add the two common, but amazing, ingredients to your dishwater.

Take a shine to cut glass. A dab of baking soda on a damp rag is all you need to give your precious cut glass a gentle cleaning. Afterward, rinse it with clean water and buff it with a soft cloth.

Overpower hard-water stains. If hard-water stains on your glassware are hard to deal with, dip some steel wool in vinegar and scrub them away with ease.

Make drinking glasses sparkle. Cloudy drinking glasses will be sparkling clean again if you soak them in warm white vinegar for about an hour. Then rub gently with a dishcloth to remove the film.

Rescue Corelle from ugly spots. It's easy to clean Corelle dish ware. Just get out your baking soda, sprinkle some on a damp cloth, and rub on the stains, especially metal or hard-water spots. For temporary discolorations, turn to another old favorite, vinegar. Mix three tablespoons vinegar with one cup of hot water, and let the solution bathe the stain for several minutes. Then wash and rinse as usual.

Remove china stains with baking soda. Baking soda makes a gentle but powerful stain buster for your china. Just rub a little on the stain before washing.

Stave off streaks and spots. Hard water hard to wash with? Add some baking soda to your next dishwasher load. Your dishes will come out free of those annoying mineral streaks and spots.

Freshen your garbage disposal. The baking soda in your refrigerator has worked for months getting rid of food odors. And it's not done yet. When it's time for a new box, pour the old baking soda down the drain. It will clean and deodorize your garbage disposal.

Sink drain problems with salt. Salt isn't just for adding flavor to food. It can also freshen your drain and keep it from getting gummed up with grease. Mix up a cup of extra salty water and pour it down your kitchen sink.

Drain the smells from your sink. For a fresher-smelling drain, pour half of a box of baking soda down the drain. Follow this with a half cup of white vinegar. Cover the drain tightly for a few minutes and flush with cold water.

Free your freezer from frost. If frost in your freezer has you losing your cool, here's a way to make future defrosting easier. Next time you scrape the frost out, coat the inside of your freezer with a thin layer of cooking oil.

Double your steel wool supply. To double the number of uses you get out of your next box of steel wool soap pads, cut the pads in half. As an added bonus, your scissors will get sharpened, too.

Kill germs and save money. Give germs some of their own medicine with this easy-to-make disinfectant. All you need are one cup of borax and one gallon of hot water. But remember – borax is toxic so handle and store carefully.

Guard your fridge from odor. If you're going on a long trip, place several opened boxes of baking soda in your refrigerator before you leave. When you return, your refrigerator will smell sweet and fresh.

Zap microwave smells with a lemon. If your microwave still smells like the fish you cooked last week, get out a lemon and cut it in quarters. Place the lemon and a cup of water in a microwave-safe dish. Cook on "high" for three minutes.

Make stale air disappear. You don't have to buy an aerosol spray to make your house smell better. Just put some cinnamon and cloves in water and simmer. Your house will smell good enough to eat. To make it easier to clean out the pot, put the spices in a cheesecloth bag.

Sort your silverware first. Separate your knives, forks, and spoons when you load the dishwasher, and they'll be easier to unload.

Chase away porcelain stains. Cream of tartar, a white powder that comes from old wine casks, can also clean your delicate porcelain. Just sprinkle some on a damp cloth and rub it in. It works especially well on light stains.

Rescue your skillet from distress. To get caked-on food off your skillet, fill the bottom of the pan with water and a small amount of automatic dishwashing detergent. Then put the skillet on your stove and bring it to a boil.

Shine your aluminum with apples. Restore the shine to your dull pots and pans by using them to cook apples, rhubarb, lemons, or tomatoes. You can get the same benefit by boiling one to two teaspoons cream of tartar in a quart of water. Or try two tablespoons of vinegar in a quart of water. Boil these mixtures in your aluminum pots and pans for 10 minutes.

Repel refrigerator smudges easily. For a refrigerator that's as clean and shiny as a new car, give it a rubdown with car wax, inside and out. The wax will help keep it clean, making spills, stains, and fingerprints easier to wipe off down the road.

Add sparkle to your sink. Make your stainless steel sink shine like the chrome on an old Cadillac. At the end of a hard day, pour some club soda or white vinegar on a cloth and give your sink a good rubdown. Then dry it with a clean cloth to prevent streaks.

Wipe off water spots. Why do they call it stainless steel if it can get water spots? Instead of thinking about the answer to this question, just make your steel stainless again. Dampen a soft, clean cloth with white vinegar and wipe. When you're happy with the results, dry your sink to avoid streaks.

Snuff out a rust-stained sink. Lighter fluid can rub out rust stains in your stainless steel sink. Just remember one thing. It's important for safety's sake to rinse the sink and your hands after handling the lighter fluid.

Conquer stainless steel stains. Heavy-duty stains on your stainless steel sink might need a heavy-duty fix. Try rubbing an ammonia and water solution on the stain. If this doesn't work, make your own cleanser by combining borax and lemon juice. But remember – always be careful with borax. It's toxic.

Rehabilitate a scratched sink. If harsh cleaners and chemicals have damaged your stainless steel sink, head to your local auto parts store and buy chrome polish. With a little bit of elbow grease and a dab of polish, you can return your sink to its original luster.

Shake off oven spills. Make cleaning up nasty oven spills a cinch by sprinkling them with salt before they have a chance to bake on. When you're through cooking, the stain will be a pile of ash that you can easily wipe away. Here's another salt tip. The next time you drop an egg on the floor, sprinkle it with salt and let it sit for about 10 minutes. The egg will absorb the salt, and you'll be able to wipe it up easily.

Save time taking out the trash. Always have a twist tie handy when you need it. If you dump the tie into the trash can before you put in the liner, it'll be there when it's time to take out the trash.

Ditch garbage can odor. Just because your garbage can holds garbage doesn't mean it has to smell awful. Keep your garbage can smelling fresh by emptying the trash often and cleaning the can as needed. Every month, sprinkle some borax in the bottom of your garbage can to kill odor-causing bacteria and molds. You'll find a pleasing fragrance in the most unlikely of places.

Scour with baking soda. Baking soda is a great replacement for scouring powder. It's also especially good for removing stains and odors from refrigerators and coffee pots.

Put the squeeze on stains with lemons. To clean, deodorize, and bleach away stains on your wooden cutting board and utensils, turn to Nature's unmatched bleach and odor remover – lemon juice.

Bust rust with an onion. Don't cry over a rusty knife. Use it to cut up a few onions instead. When you're done chopping, the rust will be gone.

Loosen labels with vinegar. Reach for the vinegar if you're stuck with stuck-on decals and labels. For those no-slip decals on bathtubs, soak a cloth or sponge in vinegar and squeeze it over the decal. The same tactic will work for glued-on wall hooks. Just make sure to dribble the vinegar behind the hook so it works its way into the adhesive. A price tag or label on glass, wood, or china is no match for vinegar either. Brush on some vinegar, let it soak in for a few minutes, and then rub off the label.

Clean your CDs with toothpaste. Make your CDs sound like new again by getting rid of dirt and scratches. Just rub a little bit of nongel toothpaste on your CD and wipe it off with a damp, soft cloth. Although some tiny scratches might remain, the music won't skip a beat.

Do away with messy candleholders. Sometimes your candleholder does a better job holding gobs of candle wax than holding your candle. To make it easier to get the wax off, coat your candleholder with nonstick cooking spray.

Freeze wax in its tracks. When your candles ooze wax all over your candlesticks, don't get hot under the collar. Get cold. Pop your candlesticks in the freezer for a few hours. Then simply peel off the wax.

Don't burn rubber on your tiles. Next time you pull a rug out of your dryer, don't place it on your tile floor until it cools. The rubber bottom gets very hot in the dryer, which can cause it to melt onto the floor or discolor it. Try laying the rug upside down at first.

Put the bite on pet stains. Don't worry about that dog-gone stain Sparky left on your carpet. Mix a teaspoon of a mild detergent – one without alkalis or bleaches – with a cup of warm water. Pour a bit on the stain and blot with a clean towel. Next, apply a mixture of one tablespoon ammonia in a half cup of water and blot. Now hit the trouble spot with the first mixture again and blot. Then mix one-third cup of white vinegar with two-thirds cup of water. Treat the stain with this and blot. Finally, sponge the spot with clean water, blot one more time, and the carpet should be stain free.

Choose your carpet stain cleaner. These three carpet-cleaning recipes will work against any spill under the sun. For oily messes, as well as tea, mustard, and colas, mix together one table-spoon of mild detergent, one-third cup of white vinegar, and two-thirds cup of water. For starchy or sugary spills, like blood, eggs, milk, and chocolate, mix one cup of water, two tablespoons of ammonia, and one tablespoon of mild detergent. If you don't know what the stain is, then try this old standby – one-quarter teaspoon of dishwashing soap in one cup of warm water. Whatever the stain is, always scrape off and blot the excess before applying the carpet cleaner. Then gently blot the stain with a clean towel dipped in the solution. Finish by laying several paper towels on top of the wet spot, weighing them down with something heavy, and leaving them there until the carpet dries.

Lengthen your carpet's life. Your carpet looks beautiful and fluffy. If you want to keep it that way, vacuum it at least twice a week. Always wipe up spills immediately, and get it deep cleaned every 12 to 18 months.

Wipe up wine stains. Don't whine when someone spills red wine on your carpet. Just pour a little white wine on it. This will stop the red wine from staining the fabric. If you don't have any white wine handy, shake salt onto the stain and dab with club soda. You could also blot the stain with one teaspoon of mild detergent mixed with one cup of warm water, followed by one-third cup of white vinegar and two-thirds cup of water. Finish by sponging the spot with clean water.

Send coffee stains packing. Coffee stains on your carpet can give you the jitters – unless you know how to remove them. Mix a half teaspoon of mild detergent in two cups of water. With a clean, white towel, blot the stain. If the stain is still there, continue blotting with this super solution – a half-and-half mixture of white vinegar and water. Here's another common household product that can remove coffee stains – an egg. Just rub a beaten egg yolk into the stain with a clean, white cloth and rinse with warm water.

Clean your carpet with peanut butter. Gum stuck in your carpet? Turn to the tried-and-true solution mothers have been using for years – peanut butter. Scrape up the excess gum. Then rub the peanut butter into the carpet fibers. After you wipe up the peanut butter, dab the spot with a mixture of one teaspoon dishwashing detergent and one cup of lukewarm water. Blot the area with paper towels to help it dry faster.

Put the freeze on mashed carpet. Your heavy furniture has made quite an impression on your carpet. Fluff up the flat spots by putting an ice cube in each dent. Let the ice melt, then perk up the carpet fibers with an old toothbrush, a toothpick, a coin, or your fingers. You'll be impressed with the results.

Foam away greasy carpet stains. For a cleaner carpet, spread aerosol shaving cream on your greasy carpet stains. Gently work the foam into the carpet fibers. After it dries, vacuum away the shaving cream and the stain.

Discourage dog 'accidents' on your carpet. Never clean dog urine from a carpet with an ammonia-based cleaner. Urine has ammonia in it, and your dog might think the spot has been permanently marked for his use. Try a mixture of three parts club soda to one part white vinegar instead.

Blast gum out of carpets. To remove gum in your carpet, start by heating it with a hair dryer set on warm, so the carpet fibers don't melt. When it's good and mushy, press a small plastic bag onto the gum and pull as much of it up as possible. Then rub methyl salicyclate, an ingredient in Extra Strength Ben Gay, into the remaining gum and repeat the hair dryer process again. Finally, after all the gum is up, wash the spot with a gentle detergent and rinse with water.

Perform a carpet miracle in 5 minutes. Company is coming in a half hour, and your carpet is filthy. You don't need an expensive carpet shampoo – just five minutes and a half cup of ammonia and two cups of water. Using a mop, lightly rub the mixture on your carpet. You won't need to use much. Before you begin, test the solution on a hidden area of your carpet to make sure it doesn't cause any damage. And never use ammonia on wool carpet.

Depend on diapers for spills. They don't put diapers on babies' bottoms for nothing. A diaper is incredibly absorbent. Use one to sop up large spills on your carpet or upholstery.

Add a subtle fragrance to any room. Here's a recipe for a homemade carpet freshener you can make in a jiffy. Mix together three-quarters cup of baking soda, one-quarter cup of talcum powder, and two tablespoons of cornstarch. Toss in your favorite scent and sprinkle the powder over your carpet. Let it sit for at least 15 minutes and vacuum.

Color away carpet stains with crayons. If your carpet gets a tough grease stain or bleach spot, borrow a child's box of crayons. Pick one that best matches your carpet, and color the spot with the crayon. To set the color, lay a piece of wax paper over the area, and melt the crayon into the fibers with a warm, not hot, iron. You can do this as often as needed.

Make soot stains go up in smoke. Toss a few tablespoons of salt into a roaring fire and watch the soot stains on your brick or stone fireplace go up in smoke. The salt helps loosen the soot and sends it up the chimney.

Close the door on soot. To wipe soot from your fireplace doors, spray or wipe on a mixture of one-eighth cup of white vinegar, one tablespoon of ammonia, and one quart of warm water. Scrub off the soot and finish by rinsing the door and drying it with a clean cloth.

Foil messy fireplace ashes. You can enjoy a fire in your fireplace without worrying about cleaning up afterward. Just lay a piece of aluminum foil under the fireplace grate before you build the fire. After the fire burns out and the embers cool, carefully grab the foil and fold it so the ashes can't escape.

Polish your ashtray for easy cleaning. The next time you empty an ashtray, spray it with furniture polish. Future cleanings will be a breeze because the ashes will slide right out.

Do away with dusty books. Protecting your books just got easier. All you need is Velcro in a color that matches your bookcase and clear plastic, the kind used to insulate windows. Cut out pieces of the plastic to fit your bookcase. Attach the rough side of the Velcro strips to your shelves and the soft side to the plastic. Press on the plastic to keep the dust out and take it off when you have company.

Get terrific dust cloths for free. Don't throw away used fabric softener sheets when you're unloading your dryer. Recycle them. They make great dust cloths.

Banish dust to boost brightness. Chances are you don't need new light bulbs to make your home brighter. Dusting the bulbs you have could give you 50 percent more light. Just make sure you turn off the lights and give the bulbs a chance to cool before wiping them with a cloth.

Grab hold of unbeatable dust cloths. Outdo any store-bought dust cloths with these sweet-smelling wipes you can make at home. Just stir together one cup of lemon oil and two cups of hot water. Dip lint-free cloths into this potion. Squeeze out the extra liquid and let them air dry. Store in a covered metal container until you're ready to dust.

Keep valuable trinkets behind glass. Don't let your collectibles collect dust. Keep your special dishes, figurines, and other knickknacks behind glass. Without a doubt, cleaning glass is much easier than cleaning your valuable collections.

Paint your collectibles clean. A soft, dry paintbrush makes an excellent duster for your precious collectible pottery and figurines. To get dust and loose dirt out of hard-to-reach cracks, give the collectible the once-over with a hair dryer.

Spruce up your glazed pottery. If your collectible pottery needs more than a dusting, give it a bath. First, make sure it's completely glazed. Only glazed pottery can take a dunking. Next, lay terry cloth towels in your sink. Fill it with warm, sudsy water and dunk your collectibles for a few seconds. Wipe them with a soft cloth and rinse with warm water. Let them dry on newspapers that have been covered with paper towels.

Treat unglazed pottery with special care. Take extra care when cleaning cold-painted or unglazed pottery and collectibles. Clean them using only a damp cloth. Never soak ceramic or porcelain pieces or wash especially precious items, like Hummels. Display your works of art in any room – but the kitchen. This will help keep them clean and grease free.

Enjoy dust-free curtains and spreads. Freshen heavy curtains and bedspreads at home by placing them, one at a time, in your dryer on the delicate setting with a damp towel.

Rescue your ceiling from dust. Ceiling fans cool you off, but in the process, they spread not-so-cool dust all over your ceiling. You can chase away dust in no time using a clean paint roller with an extended arm.

Discourage dust from settling down. Here's a two-in-one technique to keep your lampshades clean. Wipe them off with a fabric softener sheet, not a plain old cloth. The fabric softener sheet whisks away dust and zaps static electricity. Your lampshades will be clean after the first swipe, and a lot less dust will settle on them afterward.

Lights out for dirty cloth shades. The first step to washing cloth lampshades is to dust them – inside and out – with a vacuum brush or a clean, soft cloth. Remove any nonwashable trim and check to see if the shade is glued to the frame. If it is, sew it to the frame with the same colored thread. Then fill a washtub with a mild soap and warm water and whip it into bubbles. Scrub these suds into any stains on the shade with a soft brush. Follow this by dipping the shade into the water repeatedly until the water gets dirty. When it does, replace it with clean, sudsy water and repeat. Refill the basin with fresh water again – this time without soap – and rinse the shade with two to three dippings. Dry the frame by tying a string to the frame and hanging the whole thing upside down. Or you can pat the frame with a clean towel to remove most of the moisture, put it back on the light, turn the light on, and let the bulb's heat dry it out. Don't worry if the shade looks stretched out at any point during this process. It'll bounce back to normal when it's dry.

Renew a dirty lampshade. To clean plastic, parchment, or fiberglass lampshades, mix one-quarter cup of hand dishwashing liquid with a tablespoon of water. Whip the mixture with an egg-beater or an electric mixer until it has the consistency of whipped cream. Apply it to a cloth or sponge and clean your shade carefully. Remove the suds with a damp cloth, making sure to avoid touching any glued-on binding. This trick will also work for plastic-coated or laminated shades.

Kiss tarnish goodbye. Use a tangy salad ingredient and salt to shine tarnished brass and copper – not harsh chemicals. Salt and vinegar, mixed into a paste, make an excellent metal cleaner.

Polish your copper with ketchup. Ketchup makes your copper gleam better than expensive polishes. Simply mix ketchup and water in equal parts. Apply it to your copper with a soft cloth and wipe off. It's that simple.

Double your cleaning power. Kill two birds with one spray can. Use air freshener to clean all of your mirrors. It will keep them crystal clear and also wipe out any bad odors in your house.

Banish permanent marker stains quickly. You can remove permanent marker stains from appliances and counter tops by using rubbing alcohol on a paper towel.

Shield your cooler from musty odors. You better hold your nose when you open that ice chest or cooler you haven't used since last summer. It could be a Pandora's box of smells – unless you put newspaper inside it before you stashed it away. Newspaper will absorb any leftover moisture and banish musty odors from your cooler.

Subdue dust and odors with vinegar. To keep a handle on dust and odors, place a small container of vinegar in front of, or on top of, your heating vents. The vinegar absorbs dust and makes the air smell fresher. Just remember to change it every week.

Try a bright idea for a fragrant room. Make a room smell better with the flick of a switch. Just squirt a bit of perfume or cologne near a light bulb. When you turn on the light, the bulb will heat up and spread the fragrance throughout the room.

Clear the air with cotton and cologne. Make your own air freshener with a cotton ball and some perfume or cologne. Just soak the cotton ball with your favorite scent and put it in a glass jar without a lid. When the fragrance fades away, replace the cotton ball with a new one.

Freshen your clothes with ease. Your clothes smell great when they come out of the dryer. Preserve that fresh scent by placing unused dryer sheets in your dresser drawers and closets.

Refresh the air with wintergreen. You can deodorize your house for pennies. Just put a few drops of wintergreen oil on cotton balls. Set them in several open glass containers, and your house will smell clean and fresh for months.

Keep track of your accomplishments. Even if you find cleaning boring, you can make it more satisfying by writing a checklist of your cleaning tasks. Each time you finish one, check it off your list. That will make you feel good about yourself, since you can see you've accomplished something.

Get a jump on tomorrow. Tidy up the family room and start the dishwasher before you go to bed. You'll wake up to a cleaner house.

Enjoy yourself while you clean. If you would rather be reading than cleaning, here's a great idea – books on tape. Just visit your local library or bookstore and look for a tape of that great romance or suspense thriller you've been meaning to read. Pop it into your tape deck, and you'll be too caught up to notice how long you've been mopping.

Save a minute one room at a time. To save time when you clean, carry all your tools, sprays, and detergents with you when you move from room to room. Then you won't have to backtrack to get what you need to clean.

Start at the top for better cleaning. When you clean, start at the top of the room and work your way down. It makes sense. You'll take care of all the dirt and dust that's fallen from the rest of the room when you finish with the floor.

Spend less and clean more. Never be without these five household super heroes – ammonia, white vinegar, baking soda, bleach, and liquid dish detergent. These super solutions can clean your house from top to bottom.

Divide and conquer cleaning chores. For just 15 minutes each weekday, attack one part of your house with the broom, mop, and sponge. You'll be surprised how little cleaning you have left once the weekend rolls around.

Cut to the clutter. If you're short on time and company is coming, spruce up your tables, shelves, and counters first. A tidy home is more appealing to the eye than one that's dusted and vacuumed but littered with magazines, mail, and knickknacks.

Stay one step ahead of your guests. Keep your guest bathroom stocked with a clean rag, paper towels, and an all-purpose cleaner. That way, when your in-laws show up unexpectedly, you can excuse yourself for a moment and tidy up the place.

Safeguard your vacuum with magnets. Bits of metal can damage your vacuum if they get sucked up into the bag. To stop that from happening, attach a strong magnet to the front of your vacuum or to the nozzle.

Rev up your vacuum. To get the most dirt-sucking power out of your vacuum, wipe its brushes with a wet paper towel before hitting the carpet.

Vacuum delicate items through a screen. If you want to save a buck cleaning your delicate area rugs, tapestries, wall hangings, and upholstery, pull out your vacuum and a clean window screen. Start by placing the screen on top of whatever you want to clean. Next, use the brush attachment to vacuum through the screen. Use extra care if the valuable has long fibers.

Be patient with vinyl floors. To get the best results when cleaning a vinyl floor, mop on a mild detergent and let it soak in for a while before you mop it up.

Give new life to dull, greasy floors. A half cup of vinegar added to a half gallon of plain old water makes a great everyday cleaner for vinyl and linoleum floors. Best of all, it removes dull, greasy film easily and quickly.

Give the boot to scuff marks. If scuff marks on your kitchen floor are bugging you, grab some baking soda and rub them out. With this everyday wonder, a little elbow grease, and some water, the smudges will be gone in no time.

Restore a shine to wood floors. Bring back that old shine to your finished wood floor with vegetable oil and white vinegar. Just mix equal parts in a pump-spray bottle. Squirt it over the floor and rub it in with a cotton rag or a wax applicator. Make sure to wipe up any leftover solution with a clean cloth. Then buff your floor until it won't shine any more.

Blow away candle wax. The heat blast from your hair dryer can soften candle wax that has spilled on your wooden floor. Wipe up the softened wax with a paper towel, and clean the spot with vinegar and water.

Side step scratches on your floor. Here's a simple way to protect your wood floors from scratches and scuffs. Put down decorative rugs in hallways, entryways, and other places that get traveled the most.

Dust and wax your floors easily. If you want your wood floors to shine but you don't have the time, rely on this simple, but effective, technique. Place a small piece of wax paper under your dust mop. The mop will sweep up the dirt, while the wax paper shines the wood.

Say scram to floor nicks. To contend with scratches and scrapes on your wood floor, rub the mark gently with fine steel wool dipped in a wood floor cleaner. Next, dry the spot and polish it with a clean cloth. If your floor has a wax finish, reapply the wax to that area.

Erase crayon marks on walls. Even if your little one is a future Picasso, her artwork is best done on paper, not on your wall. Next time she uses her crayons on the wrong canvas, dip a damp cloth in baking soda and scrub the crayon mark lightly. It should come right off your wall.

Refresh tired wallpaper. For a really clean house, dust your wallpaper regularly. A vacuum cleaner wall brush does the best job, since it won't fray or shred the edges of your paper. But if you don't have one, wrap a clean cloth around a broom or mop. Just remember to change the cloth once it gets dirty. Otherwise, it could smudge your wallpaper. No matter what you use, always work your way down the wall, starting at the ceiling.

Do away with unsightly fingerprints. To keep the wall around your light switches and electrical outlets from getting dirty, fasten rectangles of clear acetate on the wall around the faceplate. Just make sure the acetate is several inches larger than the faceplate.

Do away with dirty windows. Try this nifty trick to gain the upper hand on your dirty windows. Next time you clean your windows, wipe the outside of the pane with vertical motions and the inside with horizontal ones. Then you'll be able to see which side the streaks are on.

Master the art of cleaning mini-blinds. For the cleanest mini-blinds in town, slip an old sock on each of your hands. Dip one sock into warm, soapy water and rub the mini-blind between your fingers. Dry the blind with the sock on your other hand.

Try these recipes for cleaner windows. Make your own window washing liquid with common household products. Mix two tablespoons sudsy ammonia with one quart water. For a window cleaner that's least likely to freeze, mix together one-half cup sudsy ammonia, two cups rubbing alcohol, one teaspoon hand dishwashing liquid, and one gallon water.

Add sparkle to your windows. Believe it or not, an ordinary coffee filter can make your windows sparkle better than a cloth or paper towel. They will leave lint streaks on glass, while a coffee filter will leave nothing but shine.

Grab hold of dirty mini-blind cords. To clean the pull strings on your blinds, mix together one tablespoon of bleach and one quart of cold water in a jar. Yank up the blinds to expose as much of the cord as possible, and dunk it in the mixture. Put the jar on a shelf or ladder, but don't spill the cleaner on your carpet or furniture. Soak the cord for several hours, rinse in a jar of clean water, and let dry.

SOS – save old sponges. Bring an old sponge back from the dead. Rinse it out and soak it in cold salt water.

Mop up marble stains. You don't need fancy chemicals to clean marble. Just make a paste using baking soda, water, and lemon juice. Scrub the stain, rinse, and dry. Amazingly, the same mixture works for slate, too.

Grab hold of dirty doors. Close your home to dirty doors forever. Just rub them down with a rag and soapy water, making sure to clean the really dirty spots with a brush. Remember to hit one of the most-often-missed dirty spots in your entire home – the top edge of the door frame.

Give your garage a facelift. Treat your garage like your bedroom closet and go through it regularly. Donate things you don't use anymore, and rearrange everything that's left so it's organized and easy to find. If you come across something valuable, take it inside. Your garage won't protect it from cold, heat, and dampness.

Say goodnight to sloppy beds. Want to make your beds look neater? Stitch a thread in the center top of your sheets, blankets, and bedspreads. When you make the bed, line up the stitches with the center of the headboard. Perfect results every time.

Quick & easy fixes for
the kitchen

Get rolling with refrigerator cookies. Refrigerator cookies will turn out beautifully if you follow this advice. You'll need the inner cardboard from a roll of paper towels. Cut the roll lengthwise, so you can open the tube. Line the inside with wax paper, then pack your cookie dough inside. Close it up, securing it with rubber bands, and chill the dough according to your recipe. When it's time for slicing, you'll have a perfectly shaped roll.

Bake cookies that stay fresh. Do your homemade cookies turn into rocks before they can all be eaten? Substitute honey for the recipe's sugar and your cookies will stay moist longer. For every cup of honey you use, decrease other liquid in the recipe by one-fourth cup.

Cut classy cookies. Want refrigerator cookies that look like you got them from a bakery? Use a cheese slicer to cut uniform pieces from the roll. And for angels and gingerbread men with all their limbs intact, dip plastic cookie cutters in warm oil before using.

Score one for bar cookies. You can have perfectly cut bar cookies instead of jagged pieces if you score the cookie dough as soon as it comes out of the oven. Let it cool completely, then cut the bars along the lines you made.

Use flour power for cookies. You dropped them by rounded spoonfuls, and they looked perfect when you put them in the oven. So why did your cookies turn out like pancakes? Try adding a thin sprinkling of flour to your cookie sheet after greasing it. The flour will keep the cookies from spreading out too much, and it will also keep chocolate chips from sticking and burning.

Crush cookies for creative pie crusts. Tired of graham cracker crusts? Add variety to your pie crusts by using all sorts of delicious ingredients. Each of the following when crushed will make approximately one cup of crumbs – 20 chocolate wafers,

30 vanilla wafers, or 15 gingersnaps. Your family will think you're a genius.

Make your pies shine. Ever wonder how professional bakers get that glossy shine on their pies? It's really quite simple. Beat an egg white and brush it over the crust before baking, and your pie will shine like a star.

Fashion a fabulously flaky pie. If you want your pies to be light and flaky, sneak a teaspoon of vinegar into the cold water used to make the dough.

Bake beautiful fruit pies. Use a glass baking dish when making fruit pies. Metal pans can react with the acid from fruit and discolor the pie. Just remember to reduce your oven temperature by 25 degrees when switching to glass.

Grease pans with ease. Save stick margarine wrappers in a plastic bag in your refrigerator. The bit of margarine clinging to the paper is perfect for buttering a cake pan or casserole dish without getting your hands greasy.

Flour cake pans with cake mix. When a cake mix recipe calls for flouring the baking pan, use a bit of the dry cake mix instead of flour, and you won't get a white mess on the outside of your cake.

Give cakes the slip. Your cakes will slip easily from their pans if you grease them with solid vegetable shortening instead of butter, which contains more water. For best results, line the bottom of the pans with parchment paper. Don't forget to grease and flour the sides of the pans. A cake won't rise properly if the pan is greased but not floured. The flour gives the batter something to cling to as it expands.

Put the heat on a stuck cake. You baked it to perfection, but now your masterpiece of a cake is stuck to the bottom of the pan. Don't panic. You need to heat the bottom of the pan to soften the hardened sugar and oil that are making it stick. You can do this by filling a large bowl with hot water and dipping the bottom of the pan in it. Or, if you have an electric stove, heat a burner then turn it off. Wait until it's warm but not hot, and place the cake pan on it for a few minutes. Either way, your cake should willingly exit the pan.

Cut kitchen time measurably. If you do a lot of baking, you'll appreciate this time saver. When you buy flour and sugar in bulk, separate them immediately into one-cup portions. Store the portions in resealable plastic bags and keep them in a cool, dry place. When you begin your next baking project, you won't be slowed down by measuring these common ingredients.

Measure without the mess. Use coffee filters to separate ingredients you've measured for a recipe, or to weigh food on a kitchen scale. You'll save yourself the trouble of washing several bowls.

Serve sun-kissed biscuits. Coax a golden-yellow glow from your biscuits by tossing in a teaspoon of sugar with the dry ingredients. The sugar crystals caramelize on the crust to give the biscuits a lovely tan.

Slice time making bread. Maybe your mom had time to wait for bread to rise, but you've got places to go and people to see. To speed up the process, exchange a packet of regular, dry active yeast for a packet of fast-acting yeast. True to its name, the fast-acting yeast will go right to work making those bubbles in the dough that cause it to rise. Also, make sure all your ingredients are at room temperature. You'll be slathering butter on homemade bread in no time.

Bake a can of bread. Save small coffee cans to bake round loaves of bread. Using your favorite bread recipe, put the dough in a well-greased coffee can. If you're making a yeast bread, use two cans and fill each only half full. Grease the lids, too, and place them on the cans. When the rising dough pushes the lids off, it's time to bake the bread. Place the coffee cans – without lids – upright in the oven to bake.

Cap your dough to keep it moist. Use a clean, plastic shower cap to cover a bowl of rising dough. A large cap will allow enough room for the dough to rise without becoming uncovered. The cap can be washed and used again and again.

Leave leaky blueberries on ice. Don't bother to thaw frozen blueberries for pies, cakes, muffins, or any other baked goods. Thawing them will cause blueberry juice to run all over your creation.

Pour batter easily. For little hands that want to help with baking, mix the batter in an extra-large measuring pitcher. That way, little ones will have a handle and pouring spout when it comes time to fill the cake or muffin pan. And the next time you're in the mood for waffles or pancakes, transfer the batter into an empty milk jug before hitting the griddle. You'll pour just enough batter each time, and if you have leftovers, just put the jug in your refrigerator.

Test your cake with spaghetti. Don't have a wire cake tester to test for doneness? Do what grandma did. Grab a piece of uncooked spaghetti and gently poke the center of the cake. If the batter sticks to the pasta, it needs to bake a little longer. But if it comes out clean, your cake is done.

Drizzle chocolate like a gourmet chef. Decorate cakes or brownies like a pastry chef. Place half a plain chocolate bar in a small, microwavable plastic bag. Heat in the microwave until the chocolate melts. Then snip a tiny bit off a corner of the bag and squeeze as you drizzle a design on your creation.

Protect yourself from batter splatter. Look out! Mom's mixing a cake with the electric mixer, and that means cake batter everywhere. Here's how you can prevent batter splatter. Simply spray the beaters with vegetable oil before powering up, and the batter will stay in the bowl.

Slice a beautiful cake perfectly. Is there anything more frustrating than a beautiful cake that sticks to your knife and falls apart when you try to cut it? Serve perfect pieces for your friends and family by dipping your knife in a glass of cold water between slices.

Bake a potato in a flash. Cut the baking time on baked potatoes by choosing medium-size potatoes and placing them on end in a muffin pan. Bake as usual, only check back in half the normal time. You'll be amazed by how fast and well they cook.

Scare off baked-on food. No need to break down crying at the sight of a casserole dish with baked-on food. Add two table-spoons of baking soda and enough boiling water to cover the mess. After an hour or so, the food will loosen up and wash off easily.

Keep bread fresh longer. Is your bread stale before you can enjoy it all? Try storing it in a plastic bag with a piece of fresh celery. Your bread will stay fresh much longer.

Say 'so long' to soggy bread. Bread is on sale, and you'd like to stock your freezer. But you're afraid you'll get soggy loaves when you thaw out the bread. Go ahead and buy several loaves. Simply tuck a paper towel into each bag before you pop them in the freezer. When you defrost a loaf, the towel will absorb the moisture, and your bread will be free of dampness.

Cube bread quickly. You love making bread stuffing and croutons from scratch like your mom did, but you hate cutting up all those little bits of bread. Next time, try using a pizza cutter. It cuts bread quickly and neatly.

Cream cold butter quickly. When creaming butter and sugar, you want the butter soft, but not melted. On those hectic days when you've forgotten to take the butter out of the refrigerator in time to soften up, try heating the sugar instead. It should warm the butter enough to do the trick.

Tenderize tough meat with vinegar. Does your inex-pensive stew meat turn into shoe leather after cooking? Try this. Add a tablespoon of vinegar to the water while boiling. The vinegar will tenderize even the toughest meat so you can cut it with a fork.

Tenderize meat with a tropical fruit. Try something exotic to tenderize your meat tonight. Kiwi – that cute, little green fruit – contains the enzyme actinidin, which works great on tough meat and lends an interesting flavor.

Warm buns while saving energy. Don't waste energy warming hot dog buns in the oven while you boil the wieners. Just use a double boiler and put the buns in the top. They'll stay cozy until the dogs are hot.

Marinate meat in your fridge. You're going to cook that marinating meat in a couple of hours so it's fine left on the counter, right? Wrong. Put marinating meat in the refrigerator to keep bacteria from multiplying. And never reuse marinade after it's been on raw meat or fish.

Protect meat from pineapple peril. When you're following a recipe that calls for pineapple on any meat, wait until just before serving to add the fruit. An enzyme in pineapple will make the meat fall apart if it's on too long.

Ban bacteria from grilled food. You carefully carry the seasoned hamburger patties outside to the grill and cook them to perfection. Now it's time to bring your masterpieces to the table. Hold everything! You aren't going to put them back on the same plate, are you? If you do, your wonderful burgers could become contaminated with bacteria from the raw meat. The same goes for your utensils. Use clean plates and utensils to remove cooked foods from the grill, and wash your hands often. You and your loved ones will be glad you did.

Roast a juicy chicken. If your roasted chicken makes people gasp for water, try juicing it up with an apple. Just stuff a whole apple inside the chicken and roast as usual. Throw the apple away and serve your moist and tender chicken with pride. Or try a lemon. Start with a large roasting chicken, and season it with salt and pepper inside and out. Cut a lemon in half and squeeze the juice over the chicken, then pour a quarter cup of water on it. Toss the lemon halves inside the chicken for extra juiciness and place the bird in a greased baking dish. Bake in a 300-degree oven for about three hours, basting it with water as needed.

Prevent roasts from sticking. Don't settle for roasts and poultry getting stuck to your roasting pan. Prop it up with a few stalks of fresh celery before cooking. The celery will lend a bit of flavor and make cleaning up a breeze.

Make your roast cook your vegetables. Why waste time, extra pots, and energy cooking vegetables separately from your roast? Use a roasting pan with a good lid, and place the vegetables around the roast. Cut potatoes and onions into small pieces and throw in some baby carrots. Add half a cup of water and about 10 minutes to the roast's cooking time. Your entire meal will be done at once.

Tenderize tough meat with tea. A tough cut of meat will soften up nicely if you braise it in black tea. Place four tablespoons of black tea leaves in warm – not boiling – water and allow to steep for about five minutes. Strain the leaves from the water and stir in a half cup of brown sugar until dissolved. Season 2 to 3 pounds of meat with salt, pepper, onion, and garlic powder, and place it in a Dutch oven. Pour the mixture over the meat and cook in a preheated, 325-degree oven until tender. Because the meat cooks slowly, it will take about an hour and a half, but it will turn out so tender you'll be able to cut it with a fork.

Organize your recipe clippings. Put an end to scraps of recipes sticking out of books by making your own cookbook. Simply place your favorite recipes in a photo album. The albums in which you lift the plastic sheet and insert your clipping work great. Arrange them into categories, such as entrees, side dishes, salads, and desserts. When you clip a new recipe, you'll know exactly what to do with it and where to find it later.

Baby your blender with a straw. To save your blender from unnecessary harm, use a plastic straw – not a metal utensil – to push food down toward the blender's blades.

Stain-proof recipe cards. Your recipe calls for a cup of flour and a half cup of huh? The mystery ingredient on your worn recipe card has been blotted out by a food stain. You can prevent this from happening again by rubbing your recipe cards with a white candle. The wax lends a protective coating so spills wipe off like magic. Best of all, your recipes will be preserved for future generations.

Dish out a homemade index card. You found a delicious-sounding recipe and want to copy it on an index card to put in your recipe box, but you don't have any index cards. Instead of running to the store, make your own sturdy index card by cutting a rectangle from the center of a paper plate.

Keep little hands busy with magic butter. Does your grandchild want to help when you're preparing a holiday meal? Give him a very special job. Fill a plastic jar half full of heavy whipping cream and secure the lid. Explain to your little one that you're counting on him to make "magic" butter for the meal, but it will take a lot of work. Show him how to shake the jar with a rhythm, and suggest a magical chant such as, "Milk is for cookies, butter is for bread. Milk go away, send butter instead." Before long you'll have creamy "magic" butter for your meal.

Outsmart a boiling pot. A watched pot never boils – until the phone or doorbell rings! To keep water in the pot and off the floor, insert a toothpick between the pot and its lid or rub a small amount of butter around the inside rim. For an uncovered pot, place a wooden spoon across the top. To boil water quickly, be sure to cover the pot. Uncovered, a gallon of water on a gas range takes approximately 35 minutes to boil, but a covered gallon only takes 23 minutes.

Make an organic marinade brush. Need a marinade brush for your meat? Don't run to the store and spend money. Just grab a green onion from your refrigerator and use the stem. Throw it away when you're finished and start fresh the next time you grill.

Save sauce from garlic overkill. Were you a little heavy-handed with the garlic in your sauce or soup? Don't throw it out. Put a few parsley flakes in a tea infuser and place it in the garlicky brew for a few minutes. The parsley will attract and absorb the garlic, and your sauce will be saved.

Doctor a bitter sauce. If your spaghetti sauce tastes bitter, try adding a pinch of sugar. Sugar brings out the flavor of cooked tomatoes.

Save gravy flavor, ditch the fat. If you've got delicious beef or poultry broth to use for soups or gravies, don't worry about the fat. Simply strain it through a paper coffee filter, and you're left with flavorful, fat-free broth.

Rescue salty soup with a potato. There's no need to throw your soup out if you accidentally added too much salt. Simply cut a raw potato into medium-size chunks and toss them into the pot for about 10 minutes. The potatoes will soak up much of the salt. Remove them when they start to soften, and your soup will be saved.

Peel a perfect egg. Ever make a hard-boiled egg only to have half of it stick to the shell? Here's a simple solution. Add a pinch of salt to the boiling water, and the shell will come off easily.

Shell hard-boiled eggs the easy way. Yes, yes, you know when eating hard-boiled eggs with the queen you should daintily tap the egg with your spoon and carefully remove the shell. But what about when you're making egg salad for 20? First, be sure the queen is nowhere in sight. Next, roll the hard-boiled egg on your counter while pressing down a bit. Finally, insert a teaspoon between the egg and its shell and gently move the spoon around the egg. The shell should easily fall off.

Save your eggs from a crackup. Save energy and make perfect hard-boiled eggs. Using a pot with a tight lid, cover your eggs with water, add a pinch of salt, and bring to a rolling boil. As soon as the water is boiling rapidly, turn off the heat and allow the pot to stand, unopened, for 10 minutes before removing your eggs. This allows the eggs to finish cooking without cracking and breaking.

Warm eggs for better blending. Eggs will combine better with other ingredients if they're at room temperature. To warm them quickly, put them in a bowl of warm water and wait 10 or 15 minutes before using.

Keep eggs under cover. Never mind those cute egg holders that are built into your refrigerator door. Eggs are better off kept in their padded cartons where they can't soak up odors from other foods.

Root out rotten eggs. Sometimes eggs lay around in your refrigerator for eons before you realize they're past their prime. To test an egg for freshness, fill a cup with water and add two teaspoons of salt. Gently place the egg in the water. If it sinks, it's still fresh. If it floats, toss it.

Color code your eggs. Add a drop of food coloring to the water when boiling eggs. That way, when you put them back in the refrigerator, you'll immediately know which ones are hard-boiled and which aren't.

Make your eggs a star. Have your breakfasts become less than "egg-citing?" Surprise your family with something new. Place metal cookie cutters in your frying pan and spray with cooking spray. Use stars, bells, trees – whatever shapes you have – and break your eggs directly into them. When you've finished cooking, step back and enjoy your works of art.

Scramble scrumptious eggs. Grandma knew how to stretch her food budget and make food taste good, too. Try her secret for delicious, fluffy scrambled eggs. Simply beat bread crumbs into the eggs before scrambling. You'll get more great-tasting servings per egg.

Beat eggs to a fluffy finish. Whip up unbelievably fluffy omelets and scrambled eggs with this secret. For each egg, add one-quarter teaspoon of cornstarch and beat well.

Plump up your deviled eggs. Want your deviled eggs to have plenty of filling? Mash the boiled yolks with some cottage cheese, then season and stuff as usual. Your eggs will taste and look super.

Lengthen the life of cooking oil. Store your cooking oil in colored, plastic bottles made for condiments. They're easy to pour, and the oil will last longer than in clear plastic or glass because light can't penetrate the container. Just be sure to label the bottles with a permanent marker so no one accidentally squirts oil on a hot dog.

Get the scoop on scoops. Why throw away the scoop that comes with your box of laundry detergent? You can wash it out and use it to scoop your flour, sugar, or coffee.

Save bread ends for breakfast. Don't throw away those bread ends that are too dry for sandwiches. They're perfect for making sturdy French toast. Keep them in a plastic bag in the freezer until you have enough for breakfast.

Enjoy delicious orange juice anytime. If you live alone, a carton of orange juice probably goes bad before you can drink it all. Try buying a can of frozen orange juice and keeping it in your freezer. When you want a glass of juice, pop off the metal lid and mix enough concentrate and water for just one serving. Keep the covered can in your freezer, and you'll be all set for a refreshing glass of juice the next time you get a craving.

Boycott smashed sandwiches. Do you hate to throw anything away? Now you'll know what to do with those boxes your sticks of butter come in. They're perfect for keeping a sandwich from getting smashed by the other food in your lunch bag. Wrap your sandwich in plastic, then slide it into the box. Come lunchtime, your sandwich will look freshly made.

Put bad bananas on ice. Don't worry about bananas that are too ripe. Just hide them in your freezer – peel and all. They'll turn a brownish color, but it won't affect the taste of your banana bread or muffins. Pull them out to thaw a few hours before you need them for a recipe. They'll mash nicely with a fork.

Squirrel away nuts in the freezer. Go ahead and buy a pile of nuts on sale. They'll keep for years in a freezer if you put them in a coffee can with a plastic lid. When you want nuts for baking or nibbling, just remove some from the freezer and leave them at room temperature for a few hours.

Keep frozen meat frost free. Freezer burn can ruin perfectly good meat. To keep it from chipping away at your food budget, store meat in plastic freezer bags, and carefully press all the air out of the bag before storing. Frost is less likely to form without air. In addition, label everything you put in the freezer, and be sure to note the date.

Freshen up frozen fish. Do your frozen fish fillets taste like they've been in your freezer since the ice age? They'll taste fresher when you serve them if you place them in a cup of milk to thaw.

Learn this great way to grate cheese. If you place your cheese grater in the freezer for several minutes before grating, cheese won't stick to the metal. Running it under cold water will work, too, but be sure to dry it completely before grating.

Whip cream into shape. Why won't your whipped cream ever stand up for you? Maybe it's not cold enough. Try using a metal bowl and putting it and your beaters in the freezer for a while. If your cream and utensils are icy cold, you'll soon have whipped cream standing up to salute you.

Communicate with your freezer. To avoid food poisoning, don't eat food that has been thawed and refrozen. But how can you know if your freezer ran continuously while you were on vacation? Easy. Place a plastic bag containing a few ice cubes in the freezer before you leave. If the power goes off for any length of time, the ice cubes will melt and refreeze into a block. If you come back to ice cubes, all is well. But if you return to a frozen block of water, throw out your frozen food.

Nix this in your gelatin

There's a good reason why you've never had a gelatin dessert containing fresh pineapple. An enzyme in fresh pineapple called bromelain prevents gelatin from setting properly, but canned pineapple works just fine.

Store strawberries carefully. Keep strawberries fresh in an uncovered colander in your refrigerator. And don't wash them until you're ready to use them. Strawberries are like little sponges. To keep them from soaking up too much water after washing, toss them in a salad spinner and spin them around a few times. After most of the water is gone, go ahead and cut off the tops. Use your cleaned strawberries at once for best flavor.

Bring out your berry best. If you want your berries to be their best, pull them out of the refrigerator an hour or two before you serve them. Room temperature brings out a berry's best flavor.

Keep kiwi for months. Unripened kiwi, which are very firm, can keep in your refrigerator as long as six months if they haven't started to ripen. When you want them to ripen, leave them at room temperature until they soften.

Prevent apples from turning brown. Go ahead and make fruit salad hours before your company arrives. And don't worry about the apple slices looking rusty. Simply squeeze a little lemon juice on the apple pieces, and they'll stay snowy white.

Squeeze more juice from a lemon. When life hands you lemons, you're supposed to make lemonade. But don't ruin the opportunity by wasting juice. Take lemons, or other citrus fruit, out of the refrigerator a few hours before squeezing to get them to room temperature. If you forget to take the fruit out early, simply run them under warm water for a minute. Then roll them back and forth on a hard surface under the pressure of your palm. Now when you squeeze your lemons, you'll get plenty of juice.

Peel citrus rind with precision. Don't grate lemon or orange rinds when your recipe calls for zest. You might accidentally add the bitter white pith. Instead, use a potato peeler to evenly remove a layer of rind. You can then mince the rind into tiny pieces with a knife.

Keep grapefruit fresh and juicy. You can keep grapefruit in a fruit bowl on your counter for about a week. If you want them to last longer, put them in your refrigerator in a plastic bag or in the fruit and vegetable bin.

Downsize fruit for one. You can enjoy melons and pineapples even if you live alone and can't use a whole one. Just ask the produce clerk to cut one in half for you. Most grocery stores are happy to oblige.

Make a honey of a fruit salad. Ever made a beautiful fruit salad only to have it turn brown before you could serve it? A bit of light-flavored honey mixed into the fruit will take care of that. The small amount of natural acid in honey keeps fruit looking fresh.

Crack a coconut with confidence. Opening a coconut is a delicate operation. If you just smash it with a hammer, you'll be in for a surprise. Coconuts contain a whitish juice called milk, which will make a mess if you don't drain it first. Find one of the "eyes" of the coconut by looking for round, hairless areas that are slightly indented and softer than the rest of the shell. Poke a hole in one of the eyes and drain the milk into a bowl. Now you're ready to crack it open – almost. Coconuts crack better when they're cold or hot. You can put it in the freezer for an hour, or heat it in a 350-degree oven for 20 to 30 minutes. If you heat it, be sure to let it cool before cracking. Cover the coconut with a towel and use a hammer to gently whack it all over. It will eventually break open, allowing you to cut out the meat. Enjoy.

Soften hard sugar with an apple. Has your bag of brown sugar turned into an unusable mound of rock candy? Place a slice of apple in the bag and reseal it. In no time, your sugar will be soft.

Oust stains with a potato. Potatoes will take food stains off your fingers. Just slice a raw potato, rub it on the stains, and rinse with water.

Put an apple in your potato bin. If your potatoes start sprouting buds before you have a chance to use them, toss an apple in your potato bin. The apple will slow down the sprouting process.

History of the potato

America's favorite vegetable, the potato, didn't originate in Ireland, as many people think. In the 16th century, Spanish explorers found Indians growing potatoes in South America and brought the food back to Europe. Farmers in Europe began growing the tuber, and it soon became the main crop of Ireland. Historians believe Irish immigrants are responsible for bringing the potato to America, where it now enjoys great popularity.

Wake up wilted asparagus. Fresh asparagus is so expensive you can't afford to let it wilt in your refrigerator. To keep it fresh, and to perk up wilted asparagus, cut off a half inch from the bottom of the stalk and stand the vegetable in an inch of warm water. Be careful not to get the tips wet. Your asparagus will look and taste great when you cook them for dinner.

Microwave tender asparagus. Why bother with pots and pans when you can microwave a pound of asparagus to perfection in less than 10 minutes? Using a large, microwavable container, lay the asparagus in a single layer with the tips facing the center. Cover and microwave on high for a total of six to 10 minutes or until tender. Rearrange the asparagus after half that time, exchanging pieces on the outer edges of the container with ones in the middle. Cover again and finish cooking. Watch out for steam when you remove the cover from your cooked asparagus.

Serve artichokes with 'gourmet' dips. Don't get stuck in a rut dipping artichoke leaves in butter. After steaming the vegetables until tender, try dipping the leaves in Hollandaise sauce, light mayonnaise blended with lemon juice, or plain yogurt mixed with Dijon mustard.

Prevent cauliflower from turning brown. Don't serve cauliflower that has turned brown from boiling. Squeeze a teaspoon of fresh lemon juice into the water, and your cauliflower will stay white.

Keep your mushrooms in the dark. If you want your mushrooms to last as long as possible, don't wash them before storing. Put them in the refrigerator in a paper bag or colored, plastic container that keeps the light out. Wash them just before you use them. Mushrooms last longest when they're cool, dark, and dry.

Get spinach squeaky clean. Ever wash spinach carefully only to have your family complain that it's gritty? Next time, wash it with salt water, and say goodbye to grit.

Foil limp celery. Don't let your celery get limp in the refrigerator. Wrap it in aluminum foil as soon as you get it home, and it will keep for weeks.

Freshen carrots with a haircut. Want your carrots to stay fresh in the refrigerator? Cut the leafy tops off before storing. Otherwise, the tops will continue to pull moisture from the carrots, making them dry and bitter.

Sweeten the pot for sweet corn. For deliciously sweet corn on the cob, add a bit of milk or a pinch of sugar to the boiling water. But never salt the water. The calcium in it will make your corn tough.

Serve a classy salad. Want to impress your friends with a fancy asparagus salad? Steam the vegetable early in the morning and toss them with a bit of red wine or balsamic vinegar. Refrigerate the asparagus for several hours until they're completely chilled. Just before serving, add a dusting of chopped, toasted almonds. Serve, sit back, and enjoy the compliments.

Treat tomatoes tenderly. Even if you love tomatoes, you can only eat so many from your garden. Leave what you can use in a few days on the counter for everyone to admire, but don't put any in the refrigerator. Tomatoes don't take kindly to cool temperatures and quickly lose their flavor. Yet, they freeze just fine. Spread them out on a cookie sheet and put it in the freezer overnight. Once frozen, store them in your freezer in freezer bags. When you need tomatoes for cooking, simply thaw a few.

Freshen food with salt water. Keep your apples, pears, and potatoes from turning brown as you slice them. Just drop them straight into lightly salted, cold water. They'll look freshly cut until you serve them.

Keep refrigerated veggies crisp. Vegetables and fruits can get soggy in the refrigerator, and often have to be thrown out before you have a chance to use them. But if you place a dry sponge in your vegetable bin, it will absorb some of the moisture and leave your strawberries, onions, carrots, and other produce crisp and fresh days or weeks longer.

Ripen an avocado with a banana. Avocados go all the way back to the 9th century – almost as long as you've been waiting for the one on your counter to ripen. To speed up the process, seal the avocado in a plastic bag along with a ripe banana. Keep the bag at room temperature until the avocado becomes soft and ripe.

Steer clear of food poisoning at picnics. You could take a chance that the potato salad you brought to the picnic won't spoil and make everyone sick. But there's a better way. Place the potato salad in a larger bowl filled with crushed ice. You'll be able to enjoy the picnic without worry.

Be hip to hot peppers

Do you like a little heat with your peppers, but don't want a three-alarm fire in your mouth? Before you drench your enchiladas with a bottle of hot sauce, check out the ingredients. Here's how peppers rank from mildest to hottest.

El Paso (Very mild)
Anaheim
Jalapeno
Hidalgo
Serrano
Cayenne
Tabasco
Red Chile
Chiltecpin
Tabiche
Bahamian
Kumataka
Habanero (Very hot)

Give your garlic bulb a bath. Mincing garlic can be a sticky situation. To keep the pieces from sticking to your fingers as you chop, first soak the garlic bulb in a bowl of water.

Overpower garlic with lemon. Your hands will smell lemony fresh after chopping garlic if you rub a cut lemon on your fingers.

Banish onion odor. You love the taste of onion in your food, but you could do without that lingering scent on your hands. Here's what to do. Rub your hands with salt before you wash them, and the onion smell should vanish into thin air.

Banish tears with a candle. Does slicing onions make you weep for happier meals? Try slicing the onion under running water into a colander in your sink. Or light a candle next to your work area before you begin slicing. The gasses that make your eyes water will burn off before they reach you. Besides, your spouse will think it's romantic.

Cut tears when chopping onions. Try these tricks for slicing onions without regret. Push a small piece of bread onto the point of your knife and carefully work it down toward the handle. Now when you cut your onion, the bread will absorb the fumes that bring tears to your eyes. Or try freezing the onions for about 15 minutes before you slice them. The cold will keep the eye-watering fumes at a minimum.

Season your cast-iron skillet. You've finally gotten your hands on a great cast-iron skillet like your grandmother used. But you'll have to learn to care for it like she did, or it could drip brown liquid into your foods – not an appetizing thought. First, wash and scrub the pan with a fine cleanser and steel wool. Dry the skillet completely, then rub cooking oil all over the inside. Place it in an oven set at 300 degrees for two hours. When you remove the skillet, wipe out any extra oil and wash with dishwashing liquid. Always dry your skillet completely after washing. Repeat this process, called seasoning, from time to time if it starts looking dry or dull.

Cast out rust from cast-iron skillets. What kitchen is complete without an old-fashioned cast-iron skillet? Protect yours from rust by storing it with a paper coffee filter inside. Or, if you stack smaller iron pots within larger ones, leave wax paper between them. The wax paper leaves a thin coat of wax on the pan and prevents air from interacting with the metal and any moisture. Your cooking skills might get rusty, but your pots and pans won't.

Bag bacon grease. You just fried a pan of bacon and need to get rid of the excess grease before serving it. Reach for a brown paper bag. They're sturdy enough for hot, oily food, and the paper will soak up the drippings. You can also use paper bags to cool cookies hot from the oven.

Free french fries from grease. Love homemade french fries but hate the grease and extra calories? After frying, put the french fries in a brown paper bag and shake. The bag will absorb much of the extra oil. If you like your fries salted, add a bit to the bag before shaking.

Freeze meat for stir-fry. A stir-fry dinner means quick cooking and cleanup. Streamline the process even more by freezing beef, pork, and boneless, skinless chicken breasts for 10 minutes before slicing. They'll cut neatly, making your job that much easier.

Fry without fear. Hold the salt before frying food. Because salt attracts moisture, salted food collects water on its surface. That leads to spattering when you place it in hot oil. So shake your salt at the table instead.

Dodge hot grease. Worried about hot grease spattering you and your kitchen when you fry food? Try placing a metal colander over your frying pan. It allows steam to escape so your fried food won't be soggy. But best of all, it keeps bits of food and grease from flying out.

Cook with less oil

If you want to cut down on the fat you eat, buy nonstick cookware. Regular pans require you to use oil to sauté food, but with nonstick pans, you can use a nonfat cooking spray or just a bit of oil. Think of all the fat calories you'll save by cutting down on vegetable oil, which has an average of 100 calories and 14 grams of fat per tablespoon.

Spread this butter secret. Looking for ways to cut down on fat? Used whipped butter or margarine instead of sticks.

Although you can't use it for cooking or baking, the whipped variety will spread better on bread and rolls, making it easier to use less. That should keep your waist from spreading, too.

Jog memory to save money. Coupons are great for saving money – if you remember to hand them over at the checkout counter. To jog your memory, bring a large paper clip with your coupons. As you find an item, clip the appropriate coupon to the front of your purse. When you go to check out, your coupons will be ready to save you money.

Open a tight lid with gloves. If you have a jar lid that's giving you fits, try this tip before you start banging the jar on your countertop. Just slip on your latex dishwashing gloves. They'll help you pop that top without the strain.

Get a grip on jars. If it seems like jars are getting harder and harder to open, try wrapping a rubber band around the lid or donning a pair of rubber gloves. Either way, it will help keep the lid from slipping out of your grasp.

Loosen tight lids with a nutcracker. Nutcrackers don't just crack nuts. They also crack down on a common kitchen problem. If you're having trouble removing a jar's tight lid, try loosening it with a nutcracker. Nutcrackers come in handy because they adjust easily to the size of the jar.

Watch out for messy charcoal. Oh no! Your guests just arrived for your cookout and you're covered with charcoal soot from your grill. Next time you buy charcoal, fill paper grocery bags with enough charcoal for one fire each. When it's time to fire up the grill, just toss in one of the bags and light it. It will quickly burn and ignite the charcoal without getting your hands or clothes dirty.

Kiss boring barbecues goodbye. Add a touch of exotic flavoring to your grilled food by placing fresh herbs on your hot coals. Try using rosemary, dried basil seedpods, and savory. As the coals heat up, the aroma will cling to your food and send a pleasing fragrance through your yard.

Breathe new life into charcoal. Make a tiny bellows for your barbecue coals by using an empty plastic squeeze bottle. If your coals start to go out too soon, a little well-placed air should do the trick.

Brush and floss your meat. You probably brushed your meat with a sauce, but have you flossed it? Dental floss is the best material to use for trussing up meat to be grilled. It's strong enough to do the job, and it won't burn over the coals. Plus, it comes in a handy little dispenser. What more could you ask for?

Protect yourself from microwave mishaps. Liquids heated in microwaves can "superheat" and erupt. That's because your microwave can heat inner layers of liquid to a boiling point while the surface remains calm. When you move the container, the inner layer can explode and cause serious burns. To make sure this doesn't happen to you, use a conventional stove for heating liquids whenever possible. When microwaving, always use a container at least one-third larger than the liquid being heated. Before heating a liquid in the microwave, stir it well, and place something in the container to spread out the heat energy. You can use a tea bag or stirring stick. Break up heating time and stir the liquid at least twice while microwaving, and again when it's done. Never exceed the recommended heating time.

Defrost meat safely with your microwave. A big problem with defrosting meat is not knowing if the center is thawed. If it's still frozen, your meat won't cook evenly, and even worse, the still-cold center could harbor bacteria. That's where your microwave comes in. Microwaves heat from the inside out, which is not good for cooking a roast, but it's great for defrosting one. Use the "defrost" setting, and microwave about 10 minutes for each pound of meat. Be sure to turn the meat regularly for even thawing. If you don't have a "defrost" setting, check your microwave's manual for recommendations.

Steam vegetables with ease. Save time cooking and cleaning pans by steaming vegetables in your microwave. Using a plastic bag made for use in the microwave, add fresh, cut vegetables and a few teaspoons of water. Don't completely seal the bag so steam can escape. Microwave for two or three minutes or until the veggies are tender.

Free yourself from potato peeling. It's no surprise that peeling potatoes is considered a punishment in the Army. But potatoes can easily be coaxed to remove their jackets without all that elbow grease. Wash them, pierce with a fork in several places, microwave for 10 minutes, and let cool. The skins will become wrinkled, and you'll be able to pull them off easily under cold water.

Make your microwave work smarter. Arrange food carefully in your microwave so everything will be finished at the same time. Place thicker and larger pieces of food on the outside edges of a plate, and smaller pieces toward the middle. For example, when you microwave stalks of broccoli, put the heads pointing toward the middle, and aim the thick stems toward the rim of the plate.

Peel chestnuts easily. Chestnuts roasting in the microwave. It's not the stuff songs are made of, but it helps their skins fall right off. Here's how. Make a small slit in the round end of each of several chestnuts. Place them in a bowl of water and heat on high for three to four minutes or until boiling. Allow the water to boil for another minute, then turn off the microwave. Let the bowl cool for five to 10 minutes. When the water is cool enough, remove one chestnut at a time and peel. The water will keep the others soft until you get to them.

Toast nuts quickly and easily. Toast nuts and seeds quickly in your microwave. Coat a microwavable plate with a thin layer of oil or butter. A spray works well. Scatter sunflower, sesame, or pumpkin seeds on the plate and microwave on high for three or four minutes. Stir every minute or so. When they begin to turn brown, they're toasted.

Crack nuts in your microwave. Don't use a sledgehammer to crack nuts open. There's an easier way. Put hard nuts, like walnuts, Brazil nuts, and pecans, in a bowl of water and cover. Heat on a high setting until the water boils. Let the bowl stand in your microwave until the water cools a bit, then drain. You should now be able to open the shells easily. Crack them over a bowl to catch excess water.

Freeze your own treats. The cost of convenience snacks can quickly eat up your grocery money. Fight back by making these frozen gelatin treats your kids will love. Add orange soda instead of water to a large box of orange gelatin. In addition, mix in the contents of a small box of orange gelatin without any more liquid. Stir until the solids are dissolved, then pour the mixture into clean, plastic, single-serving yogurt containers. Cut a small slit in the top of each container and insert a popsicle stick. Pop these in your freezer, and several hours later you'll have delicious treats that only cost you pennies to make.

Unhand sticky marshmallow treats. Run your hands under cold water before pressing marshmallow treats into the pan, and the marshmallow won't stick to your fingers.

Become a chocolate expert. Mmmm. Homemade chocolate candy is so good – if you know what you're doing. For starters, cut chocolate into small pieces for quick melting. Place the pieces in the top of a double boiler, and keep the water hot but not boiling. If the temperature is too high, the flavor and consistency will be off. Be sure the top pan is not touching the hot water in the lower pan, since that could burn the chocolate. Stir it constantly to keep the heat evenly distributed. For a quick melt, use your microwave. Dark chocolate can be heated on medium heat at 50 percent power. Heat milk and white chocolate on low heat at only 30 percent power. Stop the microwave every 15 seconds to stir, and stop heating just before it's completely melted. Continue stirring until the remaining heat finishes melting the chocolate. If you need to soften hardening chocolate, add a bit of vegetable oil until it's liquefied. Never add water to chocolate, which is oil-based. It won't mix, and your batch will be ruined. Beware of drops of moisture on utensils and bowls that could spoil your hard work.

Perk up your coffee with salt. If your coffee has been warming on your automatic coffee maker for over an hour, chances are it will taste less than fresh. Don't throw it out. Toss in a pinch of salt to improve the flavor and neutralize the bitterness.

Increase shelf life with plastic lids. Don't throw out the plastic lid from that empty coffee can. Slip it on the bottom of your new coffee can to protect your cabinet shelf from scuff marks.

Cook pasta like a pro. Cooking pasta to perfection is a delicate operation, so don't be heavy-handed. Use a lightweight pot, and the water will boil faster and return to a boil quickly after you add the pasta. Best of all, your spaghetti won't clump together or stick to the bottom of the pot.

To rinse or not to rinse pasta. Experts say you shouldn't rinse pasta destined for sauce since its slightly sticky starch helps hold the sauce on your spaghetti. But if you're making lasagna, go ahead and rinse the wide noodles for better handling. Also, rinse any pasta you'll use in a cold salad. Cold, starchy pasta doesn't taste so hot.

Protect pasta from hidden peril. You'd never know by looking at it, but the pasta you have in pretty glass jars on your counter is under attack. Once fortified pasta is exposed to light, its vitamins start to break down. You'll have to use it within a month or two to get the benefit of the vitamins. For long-term storage, hide pasta in airtight containers in a dark place. You can keep it up to 18 months when stored properly.

Keep spaghetti out of sight. Once you use some spaghetti from the 1-pound box, you're left with dry pasta falling out in your pantry. Next time, put the rest of the uncooked pasta in one of those cartons that stacked chips come in. Just be sure to label it so you don't accidentally take dry spaghetti to a picnic.

Boil beautiful pasta. If you place a spoon in a pot of pasta before boiling, it won't boil over. Another trick is to treat the pot with nonstick spray before adding the water, or adding a dash of oil and salt to the water. Whatever you do, never add the pasta before the water boils. If you do, you'll slow down the boiling process, and your pasta will stick together.

47

Wake up plain pasta. If your kids won't eat sauce but are tired of plain pasta, try this. Add a bouillon cube to the boiling water then toss in the pasta. You'll get a new flavor and a new lease on serving spaghetti.

Freeze leftover wine for cooking. If you're not much of a drinker, you might be tempted to throw out wine left over from a dinner party. Resist the urge, and freeze it in an ice cube tray instead. You can use it later for casseroles and sauces that call for a splash of vino.

Let your wine recline. Ever wonder why wine racks are built so the bottles can be laid on their sides? There's a good reason. If you don't store corked beverages lying down, the cork will dry up and won't fit properly when you try to re-cork the bottle. Alcoholic beverages without a cork can be stored standing at attention.

Don't let cream sour your holiday. Yikes! It's a holiday and you need sour cream for your recipe. But the grocery stores are closed, and the convenience stores have been picked clean. Here's an easy substitution. Mix one tablespoon of lemon juice into a cup of evaporated milk. Leave the mixture at room temperature for 40 minutes, and you've got sour cream. No evaporated milk in the pantry? No sweat. Just mix three-fourths cup of buttermilk or sour milk with five tablespoons of melted and cooled butter.

Flip fluffier flapjacks. Your family and friends will wonder what magical recipe you've stumbled across when you serve them pancakes lighter than air. The secret? Simply substitute club soda for the recipe's liquid ingredients.

Design fancy finger sandwiches. Impress your friends with rolled sandwiches so fancy they look catered. First, trim the crust off half a loaf of thin sandwich bread. Next, mix cream cheese with various shades of food coloring and spread a different color on each slice of bread. Stack them in groups of four or five layers. Finally, use a cheese slicer to cut dainty sandwiches as you would a jelly roll.

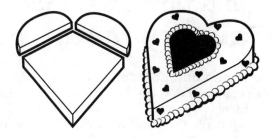

Wow your valentine with a special cake. That fancy, heart-shaped cake in the bakery window is really a cinch to make. You'll need two cake pans – one round and one square. Divide the batter between the pans and bake. Once the cakes have cooled, cut the round cake in half. Now turn the square cake on an angle so it looks like a diamond and add the half-circle pieces to each top side. Frost with pretty pink icing, and proceed to melt the heart of a loved one.

Stop throwing out salad. Make a crisp, tossed salad the day before your holiday gathering and spend time mingling with your guests. Here's the secret. Choose a large bowl and add lettuce, celery, cucumbers, cabbage, radishes, broccoli, cauliflower, green and red peppers, carrots, and green onions. Don't add any tomatoes. Cover the salad completely with water and refrigerate. When it's time to serve your guests, drain the salad well and add tomatoes. Your salad will be as fresh as if you just made it.

Top tips & time savers for
the laundry room

Spend less on soap powder. You'll get your clothes clean and save money, too, when you make your own laundry detergent. First, grate a bar of Fels Naptha or Ivory Soap. Mix one cup of these homemade soap flakes with a half cup each of washing soda and borax. Use one-and-a-half cups of this mixture to wash a regular load of clothes.

Wash away itching and sneezing. If you are allergic to laundry detergent, try washing your clothes, towels, sheets, pillowcases, and blankets with baking soda instead.

Get the scoop on soap

Soap and detergent aren't the same thing. If the label says use soap, be sure that's what you choose. Ivory liquid, for example, is a soap, while most dishwashing liquids are detergents.

Chase away overflowing suds. Too much laundry detergent can cause your washer to overflow. Counteract the excess suds with two tablespoons of white vinegar or a capful of fabric softener.

Increase your towels' drying power. If you want towels that really soak up moisture, it's important to get out all the laundry detergent. Just put a cup of white vinegar in the rinse water about once a month.

Soften clothes at a great price. With a few inexpensive items from your kitchen cabinet, you can make a fabric softener to rival the popular brands. All it takes is two cups white vinegar and two cups baking soda. Slowly stir these into four cups of water. Be sure to mix it in a container in the sink because it will fizz. Store in a plastic bottle, and shake well before adding one-quarter cup to the final rinse. These same ingredients may also do the job when used individually. Try adding half a cup of white vinegar or one-quarter cup of baking soda to the last rinse.

Make your own fabric softener sheets. You can replace expensive fabric softener sheets with a homemade version. Just mix a cup of liquid fabric softener with two cups of water. Keep a bottle of the solution in your laundry room. When it's time to dry your clothes, dampen an old washcloth with a small amount and toss it into the dryer with your wet clothes.

Size up fabric finishes

In doubt about which fabric finish to use? Starches work best on cottons and cotton blends. Save fabric finishes and sizings for synthetic fabrics.

Give droopy permanent press a boost. Over time, permanent press items can become limp and shapeless. Give them body again by adding a cup of powdered milk to the final wash and wear rinse cycle.

Save wear 'n tear on your wash 'n wear. Keep several threaded needles handy in your laundry room. Mend holes, rips, and weak seams to prevent additional wear and tear in your washing machine. If you don't have time for on-the-spot repairs, use safety pins to control the damage. If an article is too far gone to be saved by repairs, hand washing may give you a few more wearings before tossing it in the rag bag.

Hang it up to air. Washing clothes as soon after wearing them as possible helps get out odors and stains before they set. But if washing has to wait, turn the items inside out and put them on hangers. This allows the perspiration to dry and prevents mildew and the permanent mingling of odors that can occur in laundry hampers.

Wipe out smelly dishcloths. Don't wash another dish with a sour-smelling dishcloth. Soak away the odor in a solution of water and baking soda.

Oust tobacco odors and stains. The best way to rid your clothes of odors and stains from cigars and cigarettes is to add some baking soda, along with your regular detergent, to the wash cycle.

Arm yourself against mildew. You forgot to open a bag of dirty, damp clothes right after your camping trip, and now they are mildewed. You may be able to save them if you apply a paste of vinegar and baking soda, and then wash as usual. Or moisten the mildewed areas with lemon juice and salt and place in the sun to dry.

Brighten dark colors with salt. If you buy brightly colored towels to perk up a dull bathroom, you don't want them fading after just a few uses. So add a cup of salt to the water the first time you wash them. It will set the color, and they'll stay pretty longer. Salt in the wash also helps dark clothes retain their deep colors, and it perks them up again when they start to fade.

Avoid the washday blues. It's a good idea to wash new blue jeans by themselves to avoid staining other garments. And after you dry them, check inside the dryer for dye that could ruin your next load of clothes. If you do find traces of dye, wipe out the drum with soapy water. Then swab it again with a clean, wet cloth to remove any soap residue.

Don't let detergent fade your duds. Did you know that if detergent comes in direct contact with fabric it can cause it to fade? That's why it's a good idea to add it as the washer is filling with water and wait until it is dissolved before adding your clothes.

Restore the color in faded cotton. Black cotton garments and lingerie look sharp when they are new. But it doesn't take long for them to look dull and brownish. Restore that shiny black sheen by adding two cups of strong black coffee to the rinse water.

Keep the blue in blue jeans. Some clothes, especially jeans and other denim items, will fade less and last longer if you turn them inside out before washing.

Save water when you wash. If you don't have a full load of dirty clothes, adjust the water level appropriately or wait until you have more. Also, if you presoak heavily soiled clothes, you won't need to rewash them. This will save even more water.

Oil your woolen sweaters. When hand washing wool or cashmere sweaters, add a tiny drop of bath oil to the final rinse. The fabric will be easier to smooth into its original shape, and your sweater will keep just a hint of the fragrance.

Make a case for less fuzz. To keep sweaters from pilling, wash them in a pillowcase that's tied closed with string.

Do away with melted decals. Don't let heat melt the decals on T-shirts or other clothing. Wash them inside out in cold or lukewarm water, and line dry or use the dryer's air-only setting.

Control corduroy's lint and wrinkles. Clothing made from corduroy should be washed inside out so it doesn't pick up lint. Wash it in warm water and dry on a normal setting, but take it out of the dryer before it's completely dry. Smooth the pockets and seams by hand, and hang to finish drying.

Pin down delicate lace. To keep fragile lace from getting tangled when you wash it, pin it to a clean, white cloth. Gently hand wash in cool or lukewarm water using a soap or detergent designed for delicate fabrics. Squeeze out excess water – don't rub, wring, or twist. Then spread it on a towel to dry. Baste a large item, like a table-cloth, to a white sheet. Wait until both are dry to separate.

Stuff your sneakers. Fabric tennis shoes will hold their shape better if you fill them with paper towels and air dry them after washing.

Balance bulky items in your washer. If the label says it's safe to machine wash your pillows or stuffed toys, go ahead. But wash two at a time and place them on opposite sides of the agitator for balance. To clean your nonwashable "cuddly" things, shake them in a closed pillowcase containing some baking soda.

Rid hand washables of soap residue. When hand washing any fabric except silk, remove the residue of soap or deter-gent by adding a capful of white vinegar to the next to last rinse.

Clean and fluff blankets easily. If your woolen blankets need refreshing but you don't want to dry clean them, use your washer's gentle cycle and a mild dishwashing soap. Then dry them using the air-only setting on your dryer. They'll come out nice and fluffy.

Handle 'down' with care. Before washing a down-filled garment, check to be sure the outer material is washable. Then make a bag twice as big as the garment from tightly woven, white fabric and put the item securely inside. Close the bag using strong thread and stitches small enough to assure no feathers will escape if there is a loose seam in the garment. Always machine dry down-filled pieces. Use a low-temperature setting, and toss in a few clean tennis balls to fluff the garment and make sure it dries evenly.

Slip on a damp slipcover. To prevent shrinking, remove slipcovers from the dryer while still damp. And if you put them back on your couch or chairs immediately, they'll dry smoothly and won't need ironing.

Give white gloves a hand. Don't use soap and water on your pretty white gloves. Keep them clean by rubbing them with white flour. They'll retain their shape, and they won't shrink.

Make a tiny sweater big again. If you wash a woolen sweater and it shrinks, soak it in the same kind of cream rinse you use for your hair. By relaxing the fibers, you might be able to carefully stretch it back to its former size.

Take a bite out of food stains. Denture tablets are a natural choice for removing stains from false teeth. But did you ever think of using them on your clothes? You might be surprised by the results. Just put the stained item in a container of warm water and plop in several denture tablets. Let soak for the amount of time recommended on the package for dentures, and then wash as usual.

Say 'so long' to longtime stains. Use a solution of two cups warm water and a half cup white vinegar to remove stains that have been hanging around in colored clothing for a long time. Soak the clothes for about an hour. Rinse, rub the stains with Fels Naptha Soap, and wash as usual.

Make sorting socks simple. If you have trouble deciding which socks are dad's and which belong to your teenage son, here's a simple solution. Buy a zippered mesh bag for each member of your family. Ask them to put their dirty socks in the bag. Tie a different colored yarn on each zipper pull so it will be easy to identify whose socks are in which bag. When it's time to wash, just toss the zipped bags into the washer and then the drier. No more lost or mismatched socks.

'Pin' socks with a plastic top. Don't pin socks together before you wash them. Pins can rust or come open in the washer and get too hot in the dryer. The plastic top of a milk jug offers a better alternative. With a sharp knife cut an X in the middle of the top – just big enough to push a bit of the two socks through for a snug hold.

Get white socks dazzlingly clean. Even those dingy sweat socks come out white when you soak them in a solution of a half cup lemon juice or two tablespoons automatic dishwasher detergent in a gallon of super-hot water. Soak for 30 minutes, or overnight if they are very dirty.

Knock out smelly socks. Sweeten smelly feet by washing your socks in a solution of one-quarter cup baking soda and a gallon of water. Dry without rinsing.

Brighten your whites. You won't believe how bright your white clothes will be when you add a bit of cream of tartar to the wash water.

Be kind to your dress shirts. If you carefully launder dress shirts, they'll last for years. Wash your shirts each time you wear them so perspiration stains won't have time to set in. When you find a fresh stain, soak the shirt in ammonia. For an old stain, use vinegar and soak the shirt for 30 minutes. Pretreat any spots with a stain remover and wash in the warmest water recommended for the fabric. Avoid starch, which can damage fabric. To avoid shrinkage, take shirts out of the dryer while they're still damp. And for best results, iron them while they're slightly damp.

Stop clothes from yellowing. Use half the bleach you've been using, and still make your favorite white clothes bright again. Just add half a cup of baking soda, a time-tested whitening agent, to a regular wash load to give your bleach a boost.

Turn wash-and-wear white again. White, permanent-press clothes often turn yellow with wear. When this happens, soak them for half an hour in a solution of one-quarter cup liquid bleach and a half cup automatic dishwasher detergent mixed into two gallons of hot water. Then wash as usual, but add a half cup white vinegar to the rinse water.

Take the zing out of static cling. Winter time can make you feel like a giant ball of static electricity. Clothes made with nylon become charged, causing skirts and blouses to twist and ride up. But you can fight static electricity by adding a tablespoon of white vinegar to your washing machine's final rinse cycle. That way, when you take off your coat, your skirt will be right where you expect it to be.

Get a leg up on lint. A leg from an old pair of pantyhose, tied up in a knot, makes a great lint catcher in your dryer.

Don't set fire to your dryer

Never put fabric that has come in contact with paint, machine oil, gasoline, or any other flammable liquid or solid in your dryer. Their fumes can catch fire.

Toss off wet tissue. You make it a point to empty pockets before you do the laundry, but every now and then a tissue slips through unnoticed until you're ready to empty the dryer. It's hard to miss that white lint on your clean, dark clothes. You can solve this problem quickly. Just put a little fabric softener on a handkerchief and toss it in with the load for about five minutes on the delicate cycle.

Make post-wash wrinkles vanish. If you interrupt the cycle to take slightly damp clothes out of your dryer and hang them up immediately, they shouldn't need ironing. But what if you can't get to them in time and wrinkles set in? Hang them up anyway and mist them lightly with water from a spray bottle. Or hang them in the bathroom while you take a shower. The wrinkles should disappear as your clothes dry.

Save money by drying at night. Do you wait all day to call your loved ones during the cheaper evening hours? Use the same logic to time your dryer cycles. Electricity is cheaper in off-peak hours, so plan to load your dryer between 10 p.m. and 9 a.m. Don't forget to clean out your filter before flipping the switch. Your clothes will dry faster, and you won't have to battle lint.

Chase away cat odor. If your slip covers or throw rugs are soiled with cat urine, add a cup of vinegar to the wash cycle to get rid of the odor. In addition, vinegar in the rinse cycle reduces lint – another major benefit, especially if you have a Persian or other long-haired cat.

Give wrinkled clothes a tumble. If you are one of those people who still irons your clothes, you'll be amazed to learn that your dryer holds the secret to a wrinkle-free wardrobe. Just throw your rumpled items into the dryer with a damp towel and a fabric softener sheet. Using a low temperature setting, toss for a few minutes and take out immediately. Hang them up – or put them on – while still warm and wrinkle free.

Stop ironing your curtains. You can save money, energy, and time if you hang curtains while they are still damp. If you like, toss them in the dryer for a few minutes to shake out the wrinkles. But in most cases, the weight of the fabric will straighten them out just fine.

Decrease creases without ironing. If your pants or skirt has a crease from where you were sitting, don't get out your iron. Just moisten the wrinkle slightly with warm water using a wash cloth or sponge. Then smooth out the crease and hang it to dry.

Air dry a sweater faster. If you want to shorten a sweater's drying time, stuff it with a paper bag before you spread it out to dry.

Quick-dry your lingerie. In a hurry to dry a delicate item? Use your hair dryer. It will dry even faster if you slip a dry cleaner bag over the item and trap the hot air inside.

Hang up your clothes with paper clips. What should you do if you want to hang up small items to dry, but don't have any clothespins? Try using paper clips, bobby pins, pen caps with pocket clasps, or clip-on earrings. To prevent rust from the metal, put wax paper or plastic wrap between the clip and the cloth.

Hang a rain-or-shine drying rack. Your garage is a good place to dry clothes, no matter what the weather. Suspend an old refrigerator rack or oven rack from the ceiling, and hang your wet clothes on hangers from the rack.

Make a window screen drying rack. Use a nylon mesh window screen to make a portable drying rack to hang in your laundry room. Punch holes in the corners of the screen and insert shower curtain rings. Suspend four chains from the ceiling. When you need to use the screen, slip the shower curtain rings through the end links of the chains. When not in use, you can store the screen flat against a wall or stand it between your washer and dryer.

Foil a dirty iron. Don't you just hate it when the face of your iron gets coated with burnt starch or residue from polyester fabric? Fortunately, you can remove it easily. Rub it with aluminum foil, or apply a baking soda paste with a soft cloth. Even an iron with a nonstick coating can get a buildup of starch. To get rid of it, scrape it away gently with a scrubber made for cleaning nonstick cookware when your iron is cool.

Encourage your iron to let off steam. If mineral deposits have clogged the vents in your steam iron, fill it with equal parts vinegar and distilled or filtered water. Turn on the iron and let it steam or spray until all the water is gone.

Turn up the steam. Get your iron good and hot before you start ironing with steam so you won't get water spots on your clothes.

Prevent stretching when ironing. You are less likely to stretch your garments if you iron them with lengthwise strokes. On the other hand, ironing from side to side or with a circular motion could change the shape of some fabrics.

Don't flatten pretty stitches. The raised texture of embroidery and eyelets on a dress or blouse gives them their charm. To avoid flattening them, place a fluffy towel underneath and press lightly with a steam iron.

Press without puckers. It is possible, believe it or not, to iron collars, cuffs, and hems without puckers and creases. Just press them on the underside first. Begin ironing collars at the points and press toward the center.

Help acrylics keep their shape. Take your time when pressing acrylic knits to avoid stretching them out of shape. Press one part completely and let it cool before moving on to the next section.

Fluff up flattened fabrics. If the nap of a velvet or corduroy garment has gotten flattened, here's a clever way to plump it up again. Lightly press the fabric, right side down, against a piece of the same kind of material. Then again, a different kind of fabric with a higher pile, like a fluffy towel, may work even better.

Hold your pleats with a paper clip. To iron a pleated dress or skirt, secure each pleat with a paper clip. Begin ironing on the underside, removing one clip at a time. Iron a pleat, replace the clip, and move to the next one. When you finish, turn it right side out and repeat the process.

Getting the most from your iron

Do you know the difference between ironing and pressing? To iron, you generally go over the entire garment with long, smooth strokes. Pressing involves short lifting and lowering motions just where there are wrinkles.

Cut ironing time in half. You can cut your ironing time in half by ironing only one side of your clothes. But how do you get the wrinkles out of the underside? Place aluminum foil beneath the ironing board cover. It will absorb heat and reflect it back up, allowing the pressure of the iron to smooth both sides at once.

Use your bed as an ironing board. Use your bed as an ironing board the next time you iron a large tablecloth. You won't have to worry about keeping it off the floor as you iron. An extra-firm mattress works best.

Dab away deodorant stains. To remove a deodorant stain from a washable shirt or dress, dab it with white vinegar. If that doesn't do the trick, sponge it with denatured alcohol and wash it in the hottest water the fabric can stand.

Clean ring-around-the-collar with cornstarch. You don't need to buy new shirts. Just get rid of those oily ring-around-the-collar stains on your old shirts. It's easy and inexpensive with cornstarch and water. Make a paste, apply it to the collar, let it dry, and brush it off. Another economical way to get out these stains is to rub in a little white chalk before laundering, or dab it with a moist cloth dipped in borax.

Remove ring-around-the-collar. Get out the perspiration and grime that settles on the insides of shirt collars with a paste of vinegar and baking soda. Just scrub it in before washing.

Squirt away stains with vinegar. Those fruit, beverage, and grass stains in your washable clothes won't stand a chance against a mixture of equal parts white vinegar, dishwashing liquid, and water. Squeeze on this solution from a plastic squirt bottle and work it in. Let it stand for a few minutes, rinse, and say good-bye to stains.

Remove spots right before your eyes. For a general, all-purpose stain remover, add one-quarter cup of borax to two cups of cold water. Soak the stained garment in the mixture before washing with laundry detergent and cold water.

Do away with costly stain removers. You don't have to use a costly commercial stain remover. Just keep a spray bottle filled with equal amounts of white vinegar and water in your laundry room. Spray spots on clothes right before adding them to the wash.

Pretreat stains away from home. Dealing quickly with stains is the key to removing them, but when you are away from home, this can be hard to do. If you keep a small stain stick with you to treat a new spot immediately and launder it as soon as you get home, chances are good the stain will disappear.

Tenderize a tough blood stain. Like all stains, blood comes out better if you treat it while it's fresh. Soak it in cold water, changing the water frequently as it turns pink. To get out the tougher stains, mix unseasoned meat tenderizer with cold water to form a thick paste. Using a damp sponge, apply it to the stain. Let the garment dry for about 30 minutes, and rinse with cold water.

Beat blood stains with club soda. You cut yourself while shaving. Now you have a blood smear on your white T-shirt. To remove it, try soaking it in club soda.

Cover a coffee stain with coffee. Can't remove that stubborn coffee stain from your white tablecloth? Soak it in a bucket of strong, black coffee to transform it into a lovely earth tone tablecloth instead.

Wash out coffee stains. Coffee can leave some tough stains on your clothes. Fortunately, you can get them out. Using a white cloth, work in either beaten egg yolk or denatured alcohol, and then rinse with clear water. Or stir a half teaspoon mild detergent into two cups of water. Dab it on the stain and blot with a white towel. If the stain still isn't gone, apply a mixture of equal amounts of water and white vinegar.

Cut grass stains easily. Get those grass stains out of your favorite white shorts with bar soap. Wet the stain, lather with soap, and give it a brisk rubbing. Repeat if necessary. Apply soap once more before you add it to the normal wash. Another solution for grass stains is a few drops of household ammonia mixed with a teaspoon of 3 percent hydrogen peroxide. Apply to the stain and when the green is gone, rinse with plain water. You can also remove grass stains with toothpaste, and the ideal tool for rubbing it in is a toothbrush. Or soak the stain in molasses, leave it overnight, then hand wash using dishwashing liquid.

Remove mystery stains with soda. When you have no idea where a strange stain came from, club soda or seltzer is probably your best shot at getting it out.

Keep up a stain-free tradition. Your grandmothers knew the secret to getting out stains – Fels Naptha Soap. This 100-year-old laundry product is still doing the trick today, especially on oil-based stains. It's also good for getting makeup, baby formula, and even poison ivy resin out of your clothes. Just wet the bar, rub the stain, let it sit for a bit, then wash as usual.

Rub out red stains with alcohol. Stains from red drinks, ices, or berry juices can be removed with rubbing alcohol. Just pour it over the stain before laundering.

Kiss off lipstick stains. You can remove a lipstick stain from a washable fabric with vegetable shortening. Just work it into the stain and launder using borax. If you get lipstick on a woolen garment, rub the stain gently – but firmly – with white bread.

Wash away ink spots. You just discovered ink stains on your favorite shirt. Don't write it off as a lost cause just yet. Wet the stain with cold water, and work in a mixture of cream of tartar and lemon juice. Leave it for one hour, and launder as usual.

Scrub away spaghetti stains. Getting spaghetti stains out of your clothes can be almost as tricky as trying to eat this popular pasta gracefully. But here's a method that's worth a try. Wet the fabric, cover the stain with powdered automatic dishwashing detergent, and brush it in with an old toothbrush. Rinse away the powder and wash as usual.

Get the red out of your blues. You can't believe your eyes. Your new red flannel shirt bled on your jeans in the wash. Should you just throw them in the dryer, assuming they'll be your painting or gardening pants from now on? Not yet. The heat will set the stains permanently. Try soaking them in rubbing alcohol. You may have to soak and wash them a few times before the dye comes out, but don't throw them in the dryer until the stain is gone.

Add soda to suds for cleaner duds. Your clothes, especially those with oil or grease stains, will come out fresher and cleaner when you add a half cup of baking soda to the wash cycle.

Make grease disappear like magic. If you get a grease spot on your favorite blouse while cooking, quickly open your pantry and get out some baking soda, cornmeal, or cornstarch. Rub it into the spot to absorb the grease. Then let it dry, brush away the remaining powder, and wash the item as soon as possible.

Don't cry over scorched fabric. You may be able to remove a scorch stain by rubbing it with grated onion. If it's really stubborn, soak it for a few hours in onion juice. Vinegar is another possible scorch remover, and peroxide might work on a cotton garment.

Attack stubborn stains from behind. When you're trying to remove a stain, avoid working it deeper into the fabric. Here's how. Place the item, stained side down, on a white cloth or paper towel. Apply the stain remover and push the stain out from the back. With a particularly resistant spot, you may have to replace the cloth or towel several times.

Face the truth about cosmetic stains. A makeup stain might be easier to remove than you thought. Dip the spot in cool water, rub on some white bar soap, rinse, and wash as usual.

Create your own stain removal kit

Save money by creating a do-it-yourself stain removal kit for your laundry room. Include some baking soda, lemon juice, vinegar, and hair spray. Add a few clean, white cloths; a roll of white paper towel; and a toothbrush.

Give shoe polish stains the boot. If you get shoe polish on a colored fabric, treat it with a mixture of one part rubbing alcohol to two parts water. If the fabric is white, use only alcohol.

Conquer tough iodine stains. Removing brown iodine stains can be tough, but you might be successful using a water and baking soda paste. Work it in, wait 30 minutes, rub gently, and wash as usual.

Remove rust or tea stains. To get rid of tea or rust stains, treat the fabric with lemon juice, then with salt. Let the fabric dry in the sun, and then wash as usual. A paste of lemon juice and cream of tartar may also do the trick. And here's another good idea. Check the drum of your washer to be sure that's not where the rust came from.

Pre-spot grease stains with dish detergent. Keep a bottle of liquid dish detergent in your laundry room for pre-spotting grease stains before washing. The degreaser in the formula makes it an effective greasy stain remover.

Wash away suntan oil. If you get suntan oil on your clothes, gently work in some liquid detergent and rinse under cold water at full force.

Work magic on wine spills. As you watch spilled wine spreading across your white tablecloth, all you can think of is a big cleaning bill. But if you act fast, dry cleaning won't be necessary. Grab enough salt to cover the stain and soak up the liquid. Place the cloth in cold water for 30 minutes and wash as usual.

Neutralize sour baby odors. The sweet smell of a baby is quickly replaced by an unpleasant odor if he spits up on his clothes after feeding. Just sprinkle some baking soda on a moistened cloth, and dab away at the sour spot until the odor is gone.

Douse diaper pail smells. No need to hold your breath each time you open the diaper pail. Just pour in half a cup of vinegar to each gallon of water. Not only will the urine smell disappear, the vinegar will reduce stains as well.

Unstick gum with egg whites. There is more than one way to remove chewing gum from fabric. Try using a toothbrush to scrub the gum with egg whites. Leave it for 15 minutes, and then wipe away remaining traces and launder as usual. Or cover it with wax paper and press it with a warm iron. Just peel off the paper, and the gum should come off with it. You can also remove gum by soaking it in warm vinegar.

Squeeze a lemon to loosen adhesive. The next time adhesive tape or gum sticks to your clothes, grab a lemon and squeeze some juice on the sticky spot. Wait a few minutes while the lemon juice does its thing. Then rinse with warm water.

Move quickly to remove paint. If you act fast, acrylic, latex, and other water-based paints can be washed out of fabric with warm water. But if you let them dry, you'll probably find them impossible to remove.

Dispose of doodads in your dryer. Nickels and dimes rattling around in your dryer. Lint building up in the filter. Dollar bills hiding in pockets. Take care of these annoying problems with a plastic newspaper bag. Clip it to the side of your dryer with a magnet. Then dump the lint, coins, and other laundry leftovers into it.

Surefire strategies for
getting organized

Hang onto hair care products. Don't let scattered toiletries turn you into a basket case. Buy one of those three-tiered, hanging basket sets that people usually fill with fruits and vegetables. Hang it in the bathroom and use it to hold your hair supplies. Put your sprays and styling gels in one basket, your brushes and picks in another, and your hairdryer and curlers in the third.

Flush reading material from your floor. Your bathroom looks like a library – without any bookshelves. Here's an easy way to get those books, magazines, and newspapers off your bathroom floor. Hang an extra towel rack and drape your reading materials over it.

Jot down ideas in the john. Experts say the bathroom is one of the top 10 places to think. Keep a pad of paper and pen there just in case you feel inspired.

Provide a place for toilet paper. Pedestal sinks are both trendy and classic, but they don't come with a cabinet to store toilet paper. If you have a pedestal sink, keep toilet paper rolls in a decorative basket in the bathroom.

Bag your messy bathroom. If you're like most people, your bathroom is one of the most cluttered rooms in your house. Fix the problem by hanging a shoe bag on the inside of your bathroom door. The bag's little pockets can hold toiletries and anything else that might be crowding the room.

Equip your sink for stylish storage. Take advantage of otherwise wasted space under your freestanding bathroom sink. Cut the sides and bottom of a king-size pillowcase with pinking shears. Then string a length of ribbon or elastic through the hemmed pocket at the top. Wrap your new curtains around the lower edge of the sink, and tack the ribbon to the wall on both sides. Now you have a place to store beauty luxuries – while hiding plumbing necessities.

Get a grip on your next manicure. You can use a magnetic knife holder to keep a handle on the nail clippers, tweezers, and scissors in your bathroom.

Shelve old toiletries. Surprisingly, toiletries and makeup have a shelf life. Make sure to look for an expiration date on the package. If you can't find one, toss out anything you've had for more than six months.

Rack up more closet space. Recycle your old dish rack and unclutter your closet – all at the same time. Store your extra hangers in the dish rack. It holds a whole closet's worth of hangers and keeps them from getting tangled.

End hanger hunts. As you're dressing, always return an empty hanger to the end of the clothes rod. When you put your garment back in the closet, you'll know exactly where its hanger is.

Construct a new closet. Make your own closet using two old doors. Grab the ones you have lying around the house or pick some up at a yard sale. Hinge the doors together and stand them at a 90-degree angle in a corner of your room. Use one door as the closet door and the other as a wall on which you can hang shelves or a curtain rod. If you get really adventurous, you can use four doors to create a freestanding closet in the middle of your room.

Rejuvenate your closet. Motivate yourself to clean out your closet. Buy a can of your favorite color paint, empty the closet, and repaint the whole thing. As you refill the closet, you'll have the chance to throw out unnecessary items and reorganize the things you keep.

Reach new heights in organization. Create extra storage space for things you don't need that often, like seasonal clothes, holiday decorations, and photo albums. Add a new shelf to your closet between the present top shelf and the ceiling. That way, the stuff will be out of your way but easy to find.

Brighten your closet with batteries. Nowadays, you can buy a cheap battery-powered light to stick on the wall of your closet if it doesn't have a light fixture.

Hats off to this idea. Attach a pegboard to the back of your clothes closet to make a home for your handbags and hats.

'Shoe' chaos from your closet. Tired of rummaging through your front hall closet for mittens, scarves, or caps? Here's a neat solution. Hang a shoe bag on the inside of the closet door and place your winter items in the pockets. Find one made of clear plastic so you can see everything at a glance.

Mix and match your closet. Spend a little time reorganizing your closet, and spend much less time searching for clothes and coordinating outfits. Hang the same types of clothing together – skirts in one section, blouses in another, and so on. Do the same thing with colors, and dressing will be a snap.

Make the most of your closet space. Besides building a new closet, the best way to gain closet space is through better organization. For instance, you could hang all of your shorter garments – like shirts and folded slacks – on one end of the closet. That gives you room for another bar or a small chest of drawers. Another space-saving strategy is to remove all the clothes you haven't worn in a year. If you're not ready to toss some of these, put them aside for six months. You'll know it's time to give them up if you haven't worn them by then. Lastly, drop a shower curtain ring over each of your hangers and place another hanger through the loop. This gives you twice the closet space.

Store special things in a special box. The partitioned boxes that liquor and wine bottles come in also make great nonalcoholic containers. They can handle rolled up artwork, holiday ornaments, umbrellas, and even shoes. If you cut the bottoms out of two boxes and stack them on top of a third box, you can also store long garden tools, like rakes and shovels.

Battle the box buildup. You want to save some boxes for your next big move. But in the meantime, don't let boxes take up all your closet space. Break them down, stack them flat, and keep them in an out-of-the-way place, like your attic.

Clear your closet of clutter. Don't let your closet and drawers fall prey to clutter. Once or twice a year, go through your wardrobe and separate your clothes into three piles. One pile should be clothes that are keepers. These should fit you well and be in good repair. Make another pile of good clothes that need mending. In the third pile, place clothes you no longer want or no longer fit you. Mend the second pile, donate or sell the third, and enjoy the extra space.

Store seasonal clothes in a suitcase. When winter rolls around, pack your summer clothes in a suitcase. Not because you're going on vacation – although that would be nice – but because suitcases make great storage containers. Put your folded clothes inside pillowcases or sheets before putting them in the suitcase. That way, you can remove them easily if you need the suitcase for a trip.

Put together a portable clothes rod. Build your own clothes rod with a chain, a plastic pipe, and curtain rings. The plastic pipe should be skinny enough to fit clothes hangers and short enough so the chain hangs out at either end. Run the chain through the plastic pipe and attach the rings on either side of the chain. You can hang your new rod wherever and whenever you need it.

Draw up better drawer plans. If your underwear and sock drawers are so crowded you can't find anything, build dividers in them. Cut old shoeboxes in half, and stick the open end of each half against the front of the drawer.

Stack your slacks on a rack. For a handy place to hang your pants, fasten a towel rack to the back of your closet door. It can also hold scarves, shawls, skirts, and other flat garments.

Trim a coat tree. Your coat tree can hold more than just coats. Drape necklaces, hats, belts, or scarves on it. In your kitchen, attach little hooks to the end of each arm and hang coffee mugs on your tree.

Store extra belts in a coffee can. If you have more belts than you have loops, roll up your spare belts and store them in a cleaned-out coffee can. The clear lid will let you find your belts easily, and the can's perfect size will prevent your belts from getting creased.

Tie your neckwear together. Save the plastic Z-shaped hooks that come with men's dress socks. You can use them to make a handy tie holder. Just hang a tie on each "Z," then slip all the hooks onto a clothes hanger.

Dangle – don't tangle – your jewelry. Keep your costume jewelry from becoming a giant spider web. Line a hanger with plastic shower curtain rings. From each ring, hang several necklaces or bracelets. Then display the hanger on a hook in your closet. Or you can invest in a corkboard, and use pushpins to hang pieces. Either way, you'll finally be able to see all your jewelry and get to it easily.

Simplify your search for earrings. If you're like most women, your earrings are in a jumbled mess in your jewelry box, and finding a matching pair is a daily challenge. Solve that problem by lining a small drawer with a piece of Styrofoam or corkboard. Match each earring with its mate, and poke each set into the material.

Tool your jewelry around in this. Jewelry doesn't have to go in a jewelry box. Choose a spacious toolbox with many levels and drawers instead. You'll get lots of handy compartments that are perfect for storing earrings, bracelets, rings, and pins. In addition, you'll have a handle for easy lifting and carrying.

Sink jewelry worries. Screw a small hook into the wall near your kitchen sink, and you won't have to worry about washing that family heirloom down the drain. When you do the dishes, just put your rings, watch, or other jewelry on the hook until you're done.

Liberate your linen closet. Break up your crowded linen closet by storing sheets and pillowcases in the bedrooms where they'll actually be used.

Put storage worries to bed. Hang extra bedspreads, blankets, pillowcases, and other spare linens in the back of your clothes closet or on a towel rack on the back of your bathroom door.

Decrease tablecloth creases. Cut a lengthwise slit in a paper towel tube and then squeeze it onto the straight edge of a clothes hanger. This new "padded" hanger is perfect for table linens, because it won't leave a crease.

Tuck blankets into bed. The most convenient place to keep extra blankets is in your bed. Just lay them between your mattress and box spring.

Discover a 'vintage' spot for towels. Just because you don't drink wine doesn't mean you can't use a wine rack. Keep one around to store spare towels.

Stash your stuff under the sofa. The space underneath your sofa isn't just for dust bunnies. It's a great place to store board games and plastic bins filled with your videotape and photo collections.

Pack your bags for more storage space. Just because you're not going anywhere doesn't mean your suitcase gets to take a vacation. Suitcases are made to hold things, so use them to store holiday decorations, last season's clothes, spare towels and sheets, or anything else you can think of.

Kick out your kids' stuff. Don't let your grown-up kids use your home as their personal storage center. Ask them to remove their stuff, and give them a deadline to come get it. If they don't, tell them you'll send them to their rooms without supper.

Scoop up a new carrying case. Turn leftover laundry detergent boxes into convenient carrying cases for all sorts of things. They can hold toiletries in the bathroom, cleaning supplies under the kitchen sink, toys in the kids' room, sewing supplies in your living room, or even emergency supplies in your car trunk. Just make sure to clean the box thoroughly before you use it.

Have a method to your storage madness. Save time by keeping things where you last used them or where you plan to use them next. Instead of storing bed sheets in a hall closet, put them in the laundry room or bedroom closet. Keep your silverware and plates near the dishwasher or in the dining room.

Make a two-point basket. Add a window seat and some extra storage space with a pillow and a large wicker basket. Just put the pillow on top of the basket's lid. It can work with a trunk, too.

Pin up some storage space. Glue spring-loaded clothespins to the inside of your closets or cabinets. The clothespins can hold plastic bags filled with rubber bands, stamps, twist ties, or other small items you need on a regular basis.

Picture a tidy home. Collect the loose stuff lying around your house and put it in plastic bins. You can store the bins underneath the sink, in a hall closet, or anywhere you have the space. To keep track of what's in them, snap an instant photo of each filled plastic container, put the lid on, and tape the picture to the lid.

Maintain your stuff's status quo. If your home is filled to the brim with stuff, follow the "one in, one out" rule. For instance, if you pick up a new magazine, get rid of an old one to make room.

Rake in the benefits of a tidy garage. Hang a sturdy rake on your garage wall, and its fingers will make great hooks for your smaller pieces of gardening equipment.

Put the brakes on a messy car. Movie rentals, magazines, clothes, cleaning supplies, mail, and other random items can really clutter up your car. Put a plastic crate or laundry basket in your trunk or backseat to hold all your stuff.

Get the message with carbon pads. If you never seem to get your phone messages, don't get mad – get even. An even better message system, that is. It could be as simple as a carbon message pad. You and your family could still pass each other phone messages by tearing off the top sheet of the pad. But if the note gets lost, you can always check the carbon copy for the message. Make sure to keep pads near all the phones in your house.

Hang up on pricey cell phone cases. You carry a small cellular phone in case of emergencies. But it shouldn't take an emergency spending plan to pay for your cell phone case. To protect your phone – and your pocketbook – use a simple cloth eyeglass case instead.

Open a gallery for your kids' artwork. Budding young artists can bring a ton of artwork home from school. To make sure every picture gets its turn on the refrigerator, start a rotating exhibit. Let your children pick which of their masterpieces should get first billing each week. Keep the rest in clean pizza boxes. Just make sure to go through the boxes every year.

Deliver yourself from menu mayhem. You want to order a pizza, but the take-out menu is nowhere to be found. You hunt for your second option, Chinese, but that menu doesn't turn up either. If this sounds familiar, get yourself a simple manila envelope. Fasten it to the inside cover of your phone book for an easy-to-find menu holder.

Close the door on cluttered countertops. Keep your kitchen appliances on the counter but out of the way. Attach small, hinged doors to the bottom of your overhead cabinets, and hide the appliances behind them.

Double your cabinet space. Screw hooks into the bottoms of your cabinet shelves, and hang coffee mugs from them. Your kitchen cabinets will hold twice as much.

Start your own meals on wheels. Save yourself the trouble of lugging dishes back and forth between your kitchen cabinets and the dinner table. Stack your everyday dishes and silverware in a wheeled cart so you can push your dishes to dinner.

Keep an extra cutting board. Create some spare counter space in your kitchen with a heavy-duty hardwood board. Just lay it across your sink or an open drawer whenever you need more room to chop, dice, or peel.

Customize coffee cans for your kitchen. Transform old coffee cans into personalized kitchen counter canisters. Simply wrap the cans in contact paper that matches your kitchen wallpaper or paint. Then fill the cans with beans, rice, sugar, flour, or other kitchen essentials.

Make essentials easy to reach. It makes sense to store things you use every day – like coffee mugs, medicine bottles, and phone books – in easy-to-find and easy-to-reach places. That means shelves, cabinets, and drawers that are no higher than your shoulder and no lower than the middle of your thigh. Keep your first aid kit there, too. Guest sheets, extra toiletries, spare pillows, and anything else you don't need very often can be stored on out-of-the-way shelves.

Add an extra 'room' to your house. Turning a closet into a laundry room is like adding an extra room to your house. Just follow these five easy solutions, and you'll have an organized laundry room at little or no cost. First, make sure to keep the original closet shelves above the washer and dryer. They can hold detergents and stain removers. Set up a rod or dowel to hang clothes that need to be ironed or pre-treated. Next, install towel racks on the back of the closet door to hang clothes that need drying. For clothes that need to dry flat, like sweaters and knits, set up wire shelves. And for a convenient spot to iron, hang a drop-down ironing board on a side wall.

Tidy up your tiny items. Need somewhere to stash paper clips, safety pins, loose coins, extra keys, and other small items? Try a muffin tin.

Divide up your desk drawer. Keep track of all your pens, pencils, erasers, and other items in your desk drawer. Put them in a cutlery tray or drawer organizer with several compartments.

Tidy your desk with baskets. Unclutter your workspace by attaching hooks to the bottom of your desk's bookshelf. Hang small baskets from the hooks and stash sticky notes, pens, pushpins, and other little loose items in them.

Wipe out your weekly grocery list. Here's a tip if you sometimes forget to buy what you need at the supermarket. Hang a small chalkboard or wipe-off board in your kitchen. When you run out of something during the week, write it down on the board. Then, on shopping day, copy the list onto a piece of paper. Add anything else that you're running low on or that you'll need for meals.

Pop plastic bags in tissue boxes. Plastic grocery bags come in handy, but they also tend to accumulate in large piles. Take control of your plastic bags by filling old tissue boxes with them. Insert one bag at a time, making sure to leave the handles of the last one sticking out of the box. When you insert each bag, thread it through the previous bag's handles and then push it into the box. That way, when you remove one bag, the next bag's handles will pop out for easy access.

Keep tabs on your rubber bands. You know you have dozens of rubber bands in your house – but when you actually need one, they all seem to disappear. Don't let this problem stretch the limits of your patience. Use the plastic tabs from old bread bags to keep your rubber bands together.

File away extra furniture. Put a file cabinet in your bedroom, and cover it with a decorative tablecloth. Not only can it store your important papers, it can also moonlight as a nightstand.

Protect prized papers. To save valuable papers from dust and creases, roll them up and stash them in cardboard tubes.

Bind your warranties. Save your appliances' warranties and manuals by punching holes in them and filing them all in one three-ring binder.

Take inventory with index cards. A few index cards could be all you need to keep track of everything you have in storage. Start by labeling each box with a number. On an index card, write this number and then list everything you packed in that box. Keep all your index cards together, and make copies just to be safe. It's a convenient system – and it comes in handy for insurance purposes.

Pocket your reading material. Stitch together a "pocket protector" for the newspapers and magazines cluttering your den. Using slipcover fabric, make a handy pouch for the side of your reading chair. Design the pocket so you can attach a long flap underneath the seat cushion with fabric fasteners. You can even make a smaller version for your remote control.

Free yourself from a book bind. When your private library outgrows your bookshelves, start double-parking your books. Stack one row of paperbacks in front of another, placing your favorite books in the front row. If you're a real book hound, you can even stack books on top of each other to quadruple your shelf space. Organize your books by subject, author, title, or even cover color – whichever way is easiest for you.

Leave your table leaves alone. Store the leaves from your dining room table in the back of your clothes closet. They will be safe from scratches and out of your way until you need them.

Export china from dining room. Store your extra china on an out-of-the-way shelf or in a closet. Just keep enough settings for daily family meals in your dining room.

Tame those tangled cables. If your computer or stereo cables are out of control, try this handy tip for getting them neat and organized. Buy a coiled telephone cord in the length you need or cut an old one to the right size. Then gather the unruly wires together and wrap the phone cord around them.

Round up your electrical cords. Here's another handy use for those cardboard tubes inside toilet tissue rolls. Use them to tidy up all those electrical cords on your bathroom counter. Stuff the cord for your hairdryer, curler, or electric razor inside the roll, leaving out just enough cord to reach the outlet.

Put a lid on container confusion. If you have more plastic containers than you do patience, try one of these simple ways to organize your collection. Divide a shoebox into compartments with cardboard slips, then sort your lids by size and shape. Or store lids and containers on an old dish rack. You could also use a color-coding or numbering system to match lids with bottoms. Whatever you choose to do, make sure everyone in your home knows the new plan.

Find new jobs for lidless containers. Containers with missing lids are much more useful than you might think. Place one underneath a hanging plant to catch water or put them in drawers to keep small items organized. You can even attach them to closet or cabinet walls to boost your storage space.

Write an autobiography in every album. While you're putting together a photo album, make sure to write a little story on the back of each picture. Who are the people in the picture? What are they doing? Where are they doing it? It will take a little longer, but it will make your album a true keepsake.

Preserve your pictures. Acid-free archival binders are the safest place to store your photographs. Always have a few handy.

Piece your photo life together. Sort through all your loose photos, pull out the best, and organize them by theme – like vacations, holidays, and birthdays – or by year. Then put each set in a labeled folder inside one of those accordion-style files.

Get positive results from negative storage. Here's a tip to keep all your photograph negatives together. Punch holes in the side of the plastic sleeve that they usually come in. Of course, make sure not to punch holes in the negatives themselves. Label each sleeve with the date and occasion. Then store the plastic sleeves and negatives in a three-ring binder.

Give your sitter a six-pack. Tired of searching all over the place for misplaced baby bottles? Keep track of your bottles and carry them in style with this simple device. Just use a cardboard six-pack drink holder. When you're done with the drinks that came in it, decorate the holder with some cute designs and turn it into a baby bottle carrier. It's perfect for when you drop your child off at a baby sitter's. Just ask the sitter to replace the empty bottles in the carrier, and pickup time is a breeze.

Create containers for your candles. You can never have too many candles, but you do need somewhere to stash them. For your long candles, try a cleaned-out potato chip can. If your candles are too long for that, put them in a paper towel roll. Seal the ends by taping paper over them.

Box up your CD collection. Shoeboxes make perfect storage containers for your compact discs. Arrange your CDs with the titles facing up. That way, you can easily find the one you want to play.

Color code to escape the moving blues. Make your next move a colorful experience. Assign each room a color, and label each packed box with a matching marker or sticker. For instance, if you decide your kitchen color is purple, make a purple mark on every box with kitchen stuff in it. That way, you'll have a much easier time unloading things in your new house. If you hire movers, post colored sheets of paper or stickers in every room so they'll know where each box belongs.

Pack with precision. When packing your stuff for a move, keep all related items together. Cable cords should stay with the television, lids with their pans, and remote controls with the stereo. Prevent small items, like screws, from getting lost by putting them in a sandwich bag and taping the bag to a larger item, like a bookshelf. Or you could keep all little things like cords, cables, controls, nails, and screws in a separate, labeled box.

Shrink your stuff before you move. Size does matter when you're packing for a big move. That's why it's a good idea to use trash bags instead of bulky boxes. Just toss your pillows, sheets, or clothes into a trash bag. Suck the air out of the bag with a vacuum nozzle, and seal the end with a rubber band. Without the air, the bag will take up much less room.

Fast fixes for
home appliances

Freshen refrigerator while you move. Tie some charcoal in a pantyhose foot, and put it inside a refrigerator or freezer before you move. Even if the appliances are closed up for some time, they'll come out smelling sweet and fresh.

Eliminate refrigerator odors. Pour some vanilla extract on a cotton ball and place it in your refrigerator to remove unpleasant odors.

Add a lemon scent to your refrigerator. The next time you clean out the inside of your refrigerator, add some lemon extract to the rinse water to give it a pleasant citrus scent.

Peel away refrigerator odors. Here's another tip to kill odor and absorb moisture in your refrigerator. Cut an orange or lemon in half and remove the fruit. Put a heaping amount of table salt into each citrus "bowl" and put them in the back of your refrigerator, one on each side. When the salt becomes damp, dry it out by putting the fruit cups on the back of your stove when the oven is on. You can then reuse them.

Unblock refrigerator drain tube. The drain in your frost-free refrigerator might be clogged if you notice water underneath the crisper and meat drawers. Try removing the drain cup and washing it. Then, using a meat baster, shoot hot water through the drain tube into the drain pan.

Round up mold in your refrigerator. Rinse down the walls and shelves of your refrigerator with vinegar after every washing. The vinegar's acid will kill mold and mildew before it has a chance to grow.

Take a stab at refrigerator mold. Scrub black mold off your refrigerator gaskets with an old toothbrush and some bleach. If mold is embedded into the cracks and crevices of the rubber, wrap a bleach-soaked cloth around a blunt knife and slide it into the cracks.

Check your refrigerator gasket. Every so often, check the condition of your refrigerator gasket. It's the rubber lining around the door that seals in the cold. One way to check it is to close the door on a newspaper page. Try to pull the paper out. If it rips, the seal is good. Or leave a dollar bill in the door. If it's difficult to pull out, the seal is tight. Here's another quick test. Leave a flashlight turned on in your refrigerator. Point it so the light shines to where the door closes. Your seal is good if you can't see the light when the door is shut. If the gasket fails any of these tests, have it replaced.

Master refrigerator moving. Give yourself a hand moving your refrigerator. Underneath the lumbering giant, slide a carpet remnant, pile side down. You won't need Hercules' strength to push the refrigerator where you want it, and it won't scratch your floor.

Move appliances with ease. For any appliance that's too heavy for you to budge, use dishwashing liquid to make it glide across a hard floor, like it's on ice. Just squeeze some around the base of whatever you're trying to relocate.

Watch out for sneaky refrigerator grime. Don't forget the greasy dirt that's been gathering on top of your refrigerator. Stir together a simple cleaner of one part ammonia to 10 parts hot water. Pour it on the grimy mess, and let it work its magic. After several minutes, wipe off the grime in one fell swoop with a cloth or rag.

Ward off yellow stains. Unsightly yellow stains on any appliance don't stand a chance with this homemade cleaning solution – one-half cup of bleach and one-quarter cup of baking soda mixed with four cups of warm water. After you wash the appliance with this solution, wait 10 minutes and rinse with clean water.

Detail the dings on your appliances. The touch-up paint for your car could also cover up scratches and dings on your appliances. If you don't have a matching color at home, pay a visit to your local automotive parts store. They're sure to have a rainbow of shades to pick from.

Line your crisper for easy cleaning. Lining your refrigerator's crisper drawer with Bubble Wrap can protect your produce from bruises. On top of that, the Bubble Wrap makes cleanup easier because you can just throw it out when it gets dirty.

Snap a lid on refrigerated liquids. Cover that open can of soda before you stick it in the refrigerator. Otherwise, you'll overwork your refrigerator. Refrigerators remove humidity to help keep food cold. An open container of liquid keeps your refrigerator busy constantly.

Arrange your appliances to save money. Help your refrigerator and stove last years longer with this simple tip – make sure the two appliances aren't next to one another. Putting a "cold" appliance next to a "hot" one makes them both work harder to maintain their temperatures. Moving them apart will save you big bucks over the years.

Save money with a full freezer. A freezer runs more efficiently when it's at least two-thirds full. If you don't keep your freezer well-stocked, fill plastic milk jugs or food containers with water and put them in your freezer. This is also a great way to keep your food frozen longer during a power failure.

Defrost your freezer quickly. If your freezer reminds you of the ice age, it's time to defrost. The quickest way is to turn off your freezer and unleash your hair dryer on the ice inside. For stubborn chunks stuck to the freezer walls, use a plastic or wooden pancake spatula. (Don't use metal since it can scratch.) After you've removed the ice, wash the freezer with soap and water and spray it with nonstick cooking spray. The next time icebergs show up in your freezer, you'll be able to slide them out quickly.

Turn up the temperature on sweaty freezer. Your freezer could be too cold on the inside if it's sweating on the outside. Just remember – it doesn't have to be set below zero degrees to get the job done. If you adjust the temperature to zero degrees and your freezer is still sweaty, it could be the humidity in the air. Blow a fan across your freezer to help it cool off.

Fight fish smells in your microwave. Get rid of fishy smells in your microwave fast and easy. Pour a bit of vanilla extract in a bowl and microwave on "high" for one minute. Repeat if necessary.

Throw in the towel for a dirty microwave. A wet paper towel is all you need to clean your microwave. Place the towel inside and "cook" it for four minutes. Let it sit for another minute or two, and then use it to wipe down the inside of your microwave.

Scrub-free way to a clean microwave. Don't boil with anger over a messy microwave. Fill a bowl with four tablespoons of baking soda and two cups of water. Let that boil in your microwave for five to six minutes. Then remove the bowl and wash the inside with soap and water.

Run a dish through the microwave test

Before using a casserole dish in your microwave, give it this fail-safe test. Place the empty dish in the microwave, side by side with a microwave-safe glass measuring cup. Fill the measuring cup with a half cup of water, close the microwave, and run it on "high" for one minute. Touch the casserole dish. If it's cool, you can safely use it in your microwave.

Brighten your microwave's window. To clean your microwave's window, get a damp rag and head for the fireplace. Wood ashes dabbed on the rag can work wonders on a dirty microwave window. When you're happy with the results, wipe off the ashes with newspaper.

Zap microwave spills with a lemon. Hardened microwave spills wipe away with ease when you use this fragrant solution. Combine three tablespoons of lemon juice and one-and-a-half cups of water in a microwave-safe dish. Heat the solution for five minutes on "high," and wipe away the softened splatters with a damp rag.

Dispose of garbage disposal goofs. If you've ever scared yourself silly by turning on the garbage disposal when you meant to flip on the sink light, here's a tip that could save your ears and your nerves. Dab colored nail polish onto the disposal's switch, and you'll never get the two confused again.

Double your kitchen cleaning power. Clean your dishes and your garbage disposal at the same time. If your dishwasher drains through your disposal system, turn your disposal on when your dishwasher is pumping out sudsy water.

Clobber garbage disposal gunk. No bones about it, you can really clean out the food buildup on the inside of your garbage disposal by running chicken bones through it. Just be sure to run plenty of cold water at the same time.

Keep your disposal running smoothly. Fatty foods can clog your garbage disposal. To keep yours running smoothly, throw in a few ice cubes, and let it run until the ice is gone. The cold will help the fat congeal to a point where the disposal can deal with it. You can also grind lemon or orange rinds with the ice cubes. You'll have a clean, smooth-running disposal with a citrus-fresh scent.

Clean gas burner with a pin. If a hole in one of the burners on your gas stove is clogged, turn it off and poke a straight pin into the clog. You can also try a pipe cleaner to clean the hole, but never use a toothpick since it could break off inside the burner.

Don't peek for better baking. Be patient when cooking food and keep your oven door closed. Every time you open it to check your food, the oven temperature drops about 50 degrees. That adds up to extra minutes in cooking time and extra dollars in energy bills. So wait until you really think the food is done to peek in.

Release grease from oven fans. That disgusting, greasy buildup on the fan filter above your oven isn't hard to clean. All you need to do is take the filter out, put it on the top rack of your dishwasher, and run it through a full wash cycle.

Fight kitchen grease. White vinegar is a safe, economical cleaner for cutting the grease buildup on your stove top. It also prevents grease from building up on the inside of your oven. Just wipe down your oven walls with a cloth dipped in water and vinegar.

Encourage finicky oven racks. Grease and grit can build up on your oven racks, and this causes trouble sliding the racks in and out. Clean the racks by rubbing their edges and guides with a soap-filled steel wool pad. For extra slide, grease the edges with vegetable oil after they've dried.

Give oven cleaning a head start. Cleaning your oven doesn't have to be a time-consuming chore. Just set your oven at 250 degrees. After five minutes, turn it off and put a small, glass bowl of ammonia on the top shelf. On the bottom shelf, put a large pan and fill it with boiling water. Close the oven door and let it stay overnight. By morning, cleaning your oven should be a cinch. But remember – don't use this tip if you have a continuous-clean oven.

Steer clear of oven spills. The best way to clean oven spills is to prevent them in the first place. Always use a casserole dish or roaster big enough for the food you're cooking. And, just in case, put a cookie sheet or drip pan underneath to catch those messy spills.

Let your dishes dry themselves. The heated drying cycle of your automatic dishwasher saps a lot of electricity. To save energy and money, turn off your dishwasher right before the drying cycle starts and leave the dishwasher's door open. The dishes will dry overnight on their own.

Wash half your dishes at half the cost. Save money on your water and energy bills and use the forgotten cycle on your dishwasher – the rinse-and-hold cycle. If your dishwasher isn't full, this is perfect. The rinse-and-hold cycle will wash food off your dishes before it gets caked on, but it won't waste the hot water and the electricity of a full cycle.

Deal with a musty dishwasher. Your dishwasher could start to smell like your basement if you keep it closed most of the time. Flush out that musty odor with two tablespoons of baking soda and a run through the rinse cycle.

Dampen your dishwasher's smells. A dishwasher can smell a little musty if you don't use it every day. Baking soda can prevent this by soaking up odors. Just toss a handful of baking soda in the bottom of your dishwasher between loads.

Get grease and grime out of your dishwasher. If you want your dishwasher sparkling clean and smelling as fresh as a grove of citrus trees, put powdered lemon or orange drink mix in the detergent dispenser and run it through a whole cycle. Rusts stains will vanish, too.

Enhance your dishwasher's performance. A safety pin can help you get maximum performance from your dishwasher. That's because it's great for de-clogging the spray holes in your dishwasher's arms. Usually the bottom arm has the most clogs since it sits in the water, but make sure to clean the top arm's holes, too. For a complete cleaning, give the arms a bath under a sink faucet. Take the arms out of the dishwasher by removing the racks and then undoing the hubcap that holds them in place.

Remove dishwasher film with vinegar. Adding a cup of white vinegar to an empty dishwasher and running it through a full cycle will remove soap film.

Doom hard water deposits. The battle against hard water deposits never ends. Take the offensive in your dishwasher every week by adding one-half cup of vinegar to the rinse cycle.

Refresh your dishwasher. One good cleaning deserves another. Treat your hardworking dishwasher to a super cleaning by running it through a full cycle using baking soda instead of detergent.

Tie up loose items in dishwasher. Small, loose items, like plastic lids, can bounce around in your dishwasher. Secure them by putting them in a small, mesh bag closed off with a rubber band. Then use the rubber band to attach the bag to one of the hooks on the top rack.

Fend off glassware film. To make your glassware sparkle, stop your dishwasher after the rinse cycle. Open it up and remove all metal objects. Then, on the bottom rack, place a glass dish filled with two cups of vinegar and run your dishwasher through a full cycle. You can prevent this dull film from coming back by changing detergents or using more of your current brand.

Give your dishwasher a facelift. Remodeling your kitchen doesn't mean you have to buy a new dishwasher. Your old dishwasher might come with its own remodeling kit. Just inspect inside its door. Sometimes the door panel has another color on the other side, or other panels are stored behind the door. If these colors still don't match your new kitchen, take the door panel to an auto body shop and have it repainted to match your new decor.

Serve great-tasting coffee. Save your coffee maker – and your taste buds – from foul-tasting mineral buildup. Mix a quart of water with one-quarter cup of baking soda. Run it through your coffee maker and follow with a pot of plain, cold water.

Don't throw money down the drain

Your old washing machine could be cleaning more than your dirty clothes. It could be cleaning out your wallet. An old machine uses up to 50 gallons of water a load, while newer machines use only 11 to 30 gallons. That difference adds up to a lot of money.

Silence a clunky washer. If your washing machine often acts like a Mexican jumping bean, a remnant of flame-retardant carpet could settle it down. Just lay the carpet underneath the washer, and it should stop its vibrating racket.

Brighten wash by cleaning washer. If your clothes come out dull and faded, don't reach for extra-strength detergent. Your washing machine might need cleaning. Once a year, run a half gallon of vinegar through a wash cycle. It's an easy, all-natural way to clean out dirt and soap residue.

Give your washing machine a bath. After working so hard washing your clothes, your washing machine deserves a bath. Just wet a sponge with warm water and sprinkle on some baking soda. Wipe down the entire outside of the machine, adding more baking soda if needed. Rinse with clean water.

Make old appliances look like new. Buff your washer, dryer, and other metal appliances with car wax at least twice a year. The wax will preserve the finish and make them shine like new.

Water down your energy bills

Washing clothes gobbles up a lot of energy. According to the U.S. Department of Energy, about 85 percent of this energy is used by your hot water heater. You could save a load of money on your next energy bill by washing your clothes in warm or cold water. These temperatures work just fine in getting out most stains, especially if you use a detergent made for cold-water washing. Only wash full loads to cut down on the water you use. And if you wash less than a full load, remember to change the setting on the water level.

Tame your lint trap. To get every little piece of lint and dust off your dryer filter, use an old fabric softener sheet as a brush.

Dry your clothes faster. Your clothes will dry faster if you throw in a dry hand towel with your load of wet laundry.

Unclog your steam iron. Return your clogged iron back to its old, steamy self with a half-and-half mixture of vinegar and water. Pour the combo into the water chamber, sit the iron upright, and select the "steam" setting. After five minutes, unplug your iron and let it cool. Empty out the water chamber, and your iron should be clog free.

Unclog iron vents easily. Use a toothbrush on a cool iron to really clean out the vent holes.

Refill your iron without creating a flood. Pouring water into your iron can be a messy chore, but it doesn't have to be. Just use a clean condiment dispenser or meat baster to do the job.

Pulverize melted polyester on your iron. Don't throw out your iron just because polyester melted onto the bottom. Instead, use a block of wood, a wooden spatula, or a wooden clothespin to carefully scrape off the plastic. If this doesn't work, try nail polish remover containing acetone. A few drops should make the polyester easier to scrape off. Be sure to clean your iron with a damp cloth before using it again.

Recycle water from dehumidifier. Recycle the water from your dehumidifier by using it in your steam iron.

Get a good peep at your pilot light. Put a mirror on the ground under your heater to see if the pilot light is lit. It's also a bright idea when you need to relight the pilot.

Overpower humidifier's damp smell. Add one tablespoon of strained lemon juice to the water in your humidifier to get rid of that musty smell.

Make your own humidifier. If you need a makeshift humidifier, get out your electric skillet, fill it with water, and turn it on "low." If someone is sick in bed, the best place to put it is on the floor near the bed. Remember to fill it with water every eight hours.

Think safety when using a space heater. Here are two safety tips to keep your space heater working and your tootsies warm. First, clean the dust out of the heater with a shop vac if you haven't used it in a while. Then inspect its cord for wear and tear, making sure the plug is firmly attached and the insulation is intact. To be sure, recheck the cord after your heater has been on for more than 15 minutes. If the cord is hot, turn it off. It could have a problem that requires a service call.

Blow away grime from your fan. Your window fan needs a thorough cleaning every year. Start by removing the grills and vacuuming them with a shop vac. Next, wipe the dust off the blades. If they're really dirty, use an ammonia or an ammonia-based cleaner – not a petroleum-based one. Then attach the pointy nozzle on your shop vac and use it to get into the slots in the back of the fan engine, where a lot of dirt, dust, and hair can build up. When you can see clearly through the slots, they're clean. Finish the job by checking to see if there are oil holes on the top of the engine case, or in a dimple in the front or back. If there are holes, squeeze in 10 to 20 drops of three-in-one oil. If there aren't any oil holes, the motor is self-lubricating, and you're finished.

Clean your hair dryer with a toothbrush. If your hair dryer smells like burning hair, it usually means hair and lint is trapped in the air intake. Rubbing an old toothbrush over the holes of the intake will get rid of the problem.

Lengthen the life of your appliances

Today's appliances have an average life span of 30 years. Yet, they can't live to that ripe old age without a little help from you. To keep them blending, toasting, and whipping, you'll need to carry out routine maintenance, cleaning, and minor repairs. Check your owner's manuals.

Protect small appliances from dust. If you have an appliance you don't use very often, like a juicer or a coffee grinder, cover it up so it doesn't collect dust. For a decorator look, use the cover from an old throw pillow. If you want an old-fashioned look, use a clean, cloth sack that rice or flour comes in.

Unbend a bent beater blade. If a beater blade on your electric mixer is bent, lay it on a cutting board and press down on it with the round side of a teaspoon.

Pick apart a dirty beater. When your electric beater feels like it's grinding or vibrating too much, unplug it and clean out its sockets with a toothpick. With all the food it whips up, the beater sockets could get clogged with hardened food.

Spray away can opener grunge. Spray your clean electric can opener with nonstick vegetable spray. Dirt and food won't stick, making cleanup a snap.

Take aim at melted plastic. A little nail polish remover comes in handy if you accidentally melt a plastic bread bag, or other plastic, on your toaster oven. Wait until the toaster is cool and wipe off the plastic using a rag dipped in nail polish remover.

Conquer a crusty crock pot. A crock pot encrusted with burned on food might seem like a lost cause. But, surprisingly, you only need hot water and dishwashing detergent to clean it. Fill the pot with the mixture and set it on "high" for about an hour.

Avoid costly, unnecessary purchases

The best money-saving tip you can follow is to consider these things before making a major purchase. First, make sure it's something you need. Is it the best buy for the money? Think about the emotional reasons you might be buying it, like overcoming sadness or showing off. Will it improve your life? You might find that you can get along without it. Look at the price to figure if it's a good value. Some luxury items lose their value quickly. Is this one of them? What would happen if you don't buy it? Lastly, gauge how costly the upkeep will be. You might have to give up a lot to own it. Whether it's worth it, of course, is up to you.

Unstick toast with chopsticks. It's not exactly shocking news, but wooden chopsticks are your best bet for removing bread stuck in your toaster.

Amplify your alarm clock. If you're immune to your alarm clock's ring, set the clock on a tin plate, a metal dish, or a ceramic tile. That'll make the ring louder and a wee bit harder to ignore.

Foil a noisy food processor. If your food processor makes a racket every time you turn it on, put it on a large, plastic pad. The best pads are those used in offices to keep printing and copying machines quiet. Look for them at office supply stores.

Clean recharging contacts with eraser. Use a pencil eraser to wipe off the metal recharging contacts on the handset and base of your cordless phone. Your phone will get a better recharge. Try this also for the battery contacts on your TV and stereo remote controls.

Exercise caution with warranty. Wait to send in your appliance's warranty card until you're sure it works properly. Most stores will let you return a "lemon" within 30 days if it doesn't work. If you already mailed in the warranty card, you might have to send your appliance to the manufacturer to be repaired. That could be a bigger hassle than it's worth.

Organize your electrical cords. Keep your electrical cords from getting tangled with ponytail hair bands. You can buy them at any discount drugstore for a few cents apiece. They'll help keep your cords in neat little bundles.

Study up on new appliances. Before you use any new appliance, it's important to read the owner's manual from cover to cover. Once you've done that, store it in a zip-lock bag with the warranty information.

See your reflection in your appliances. It's easy to get that showroom shine back on your kitchen appliances. Polish the chrome trim with a cloth dipped in rubbing alcohol.

Regain control over broken remote. You push and push the buttons on your remote control, but it still doesn't work. Instead of mashing the buttons senseless, get a sheet of aluminum foil and tear it into small squares. You'll need one small square for each broken button. Then remove the face of your remote and its circuit board. With a little bit of contact cement, attach the foil to the broken buttons. Reattach the board and the remote face, and you're ready to channel surf.

Hit 'PLAY' to vanquish VCR troubles. You might not be able to figure out how to program your VCR. But chances are you can fix it if it starts acting up. About one-quarter of all VCR problems stem from dirty heads. Too many particles on the heads can cause your TV screen to turn blue suddenly while you're trying to watch a video. One easy and effective way to clean the VCR heads is just to play an ordinary tape for about an hour. Eventually, the tape will remove the gunk from the heads, and your picture will return to normal.

End TV and VCR interference. If a snowstorm seems to hit your television any time you turn on your VCR, try this tip before you call in a repairman. Lay a sheet of aluminum foil between the TV and the VCR. The static could be caused by interference between the two appliances. If this is the problem, the foil will help control it.

Keep your remote under your control. Leave your TV remote control where you need it – right where you're sitting. Stick a strip of fabric fastener, like Velcro, on the back of your remote, and the other half on the arm of your couch or chair. It's best to stick the hooked half of the fastener on your remote and the soft half on your furniture.

Vacuum smells away. Spread a fresh smell throughout your house every time you vacuum. Leave a scented fabric softener sheet in the bag of your upright vacuum. Just remember to replace the sheet every few weeks. For a change, you could also try whole cloves, carpet freshener, baking soda, or potpourri.

Recycle a vacuum bag. If your vacuum cleaner bag fills up and you don't have a replacement, don't empty it through the little hole in the front. Instead, take the whole bag out and cut a slit in the back, down the middle. After you've emptied it, hold the edges of the slit together, fold them closed, and seal the opening with strong masking or duct tape. This recycled bag won't hold as much dirt as before, but you'll be able to continue vacuuming.

Get more vroom from your vacuum

Vacuum cleaners push out air at an amazing speed — up to 60 to 70 cubic feet per minute. That's why it's important to empty your vacuum bag regularly. A clean bag filters air as it gets blown out of the vacuum. But a bag that's too full can't filter air fast enough to keep up. The vacuum ends up pushing dirty air back onto your carpet.

Uncommon ways to
care for & repair furniture

Use ashes to erase water marks. If you follow this tip, you might have trouble explaining why you bought a pack of cigarettes, but it's all for a good cause – removing water marks from your table. Gently sand the rings with #000 steel wool pads. Next, mix some cigarette ashes with vegetable oil to make a dark paste and rub the paste into the rings. They should vanish quickly.

Clobber water marks with coasters. The best way to deal with water marks on your furniture is to prevent them in the first place. Have coasters handy on your buffet, dining room, and coffee tables so your guests won't be tempted to set a glass on a bare wood surface. For the best protection for your furniture, buy coasters lined with absorbent material inside and felt underneath.

Dry wet wood with care. You accidentally left a window open while you went shopping, and a thunderstorm soaked some of your wood furniture. What should you do? First, don't try applying intense heat, like a hairdryer, to dry it out. Too much heat at once could cause the wood to crack. But too little heat can cause mold to settle in. Keep the wet wood in a room temperature environment – approximately 70 degrees – and put a fan in the room set on "low" to keep the air moving.

Attack water marks with toothpaste. When water damage leaves white spots on your furniture, try this simple solution before calling in the big guns. Mix equal amounts of toothpaste and baking soda to form a mildly abrasive paste. Dampen a cotton cloth with water and rub the paste into the spots. Now buff the area with a soft, dry cloth. If the damage is not too serious, this should restore your furniture.

Beware of potpourri. Potpourri smells great and looks pretty, but don't put it directly on your wood furniture. The ingredients in the mixture can take the finish off, even through a plastic bag. Put potpourri in a glass jar instead.

Remove stuck-on paper from wood. Did you get a piece of newspaper stuck to your expensive dining room table? Take a deep breath. Now go get some vegetable oil. Soak the paper with oil, and soon you'll be able to pull it right off.

Shield dining table from trauma. Keep your dining room table looking new by using table pads under tablecloths. The pads protect your table from water marks, dings from dropped silverware, and damage from hot plates. You can order table pads through many department stores. If you have a rectangular table, you can even use a twin-size mattress pad – a cheaper alternative to a custom made table pad.

Shield furniture legs from wet carpet. If you don't plan to move all your furniture before shampooing your carpet, slip small plastic bags over the legs of couches and chairs. This will keep wood stain and rust from seeping into your wet carpet. In addition, the bags will protect the furniture's wooden legs from the shampoo chemicals.

Make your wood glow. Dirt and grime can build up on furniture and leave it looking dull. You can wash finished furniture, but you must do it carefully. Use only a mild, oil soap designed for wood. Squirt a bit in a clean bucket of warm water and stir up some suds. Use only suds on a damp sponge to gently clean the surface of the wood. Dry the wood immediately with a soft cloth. Then with another soft cloth, buff in the direction of the wood's grain.

Don't mix wood and nails. Never, never, never polish your nails or remove nail polish at a wooden table. It's almost impossible to get nail polish off wood without damaging the wood's finish. And one drop of nail polish remover can eat through varnish and cause an expensive repair bill. Keep all solvents, including rubbing alcohol and paint thinner, away from your furniture.

Rock without ruining your floor. Do you have a rocking chair on a hardwood floor? If you use it often, the finish on your floor might start wearing away. Before that happens, place a piece of weather-stripping tape on the bottom of each runner. Now you can rock away without ruining your floor.

Check the finish before you polish

Don't just grab the nearest can of furniture polish. First, find out the type of finish on your wood so you can choose wisely. Buy some linseed oil at the hardware store and place a few drops on your furniture. If the oil is absorbed, you have an oil finish. If it beads up, you have a protective coating, such as varnish or shellac. For oiled wood, buy a liquid polish specifically for that finish. For protected surfaces, use a multi-surface polish. Once you're polishing with the correct formula, don't switch brands. Different brands can interact with each other and dull the finish.

Touch up scratches with shoe polish. Don't spend a fortune having dings and scratches in your furniture repaired. You can use a variety of ordinary products to camouflage those scratches, but be sure to test a hidden area first. For scratches in dark wood, use shoe polish just a bit lighter than the finish. For light wood or cherry, use iodine diluted with denatured alcohol until the color matches. For a nick, use a matching crayon or marker.

Restore wood this nutty way. You know that quality furniture is made from trees. So why not use part of a tree to restore it? Use the meat of a pecan nut to erase scratches and nicks in your wood furniture.

Find scratch mender in your pantry. For a small scratch on varnished wood, use a soft cloth dipped in cooking oil. The oil will darken the scratched area and help it blend in.

Lift a dent out of wood. Believe it or not, you can lift dents out of wooden furniture without an expensive repair bill. First, check to see if the wood has broken apart under the dent. If not, your chances of removing the dent are excellent. Place a damp cloth over the indentation and hold an iron on a medium setting over the cloth. When the iron dries out the cloth, rewet it and repeat the procedure until the dent disappears.

Repair cigarette burns on wood. Someone dropped a lit cigarette on your beautiful table, and now you're stuck with a cloudy spot on the finish. But as long as the burn mark didn't go all the way through to the wood, you can fix it. Grind up a bit of pumice stone and add it to boiled linseed oil to make a paste. Gently work the paste into the burned area, then wax or polish over it in the direction of the wood's grain. The cigarette mark will be a distant memory.

Make your own furniture polish. Don't spend a bundle of money on expensive wood furniture polish. Make your own polish by mixing three parts olive oil to one part vinegar and start polishing. Or try this recipe. Mix one part lemon oil to three parts olive oil. Your furniture will look beautiful, and your house will smell great.

Treat dry furniture to a drink. For an inexpensive furniture polish that works wonders and smells good, too, mix one cup of baby oil with one-half cup lemon juice. Your furniture will drink it down and ask for more.

Prevent cracks in wood. Don't let the finish on your fine furniture crack. Clean it during early fall and late spring with naphtha, an oily liquid you can buy at most hardware stores. After cleaning with naphtha, treat your table to a coating of lemon oil. Let it soak in for about a week, wipe off, then polish as usual.

Stop waxing polyurethane finishes. Good news! You can stop waxing any furniture that has a polyurethane finish. This type of finish is like a layer of hard plastic covering the wood. Waxing it actually causes it to attract dirt and dust. Instead, find a furniture polish made for polyurethane finishes.

Make fingerprints disappear like magic. You've polished and polished that table, but those fingerprints just keep coming back. Here's what to do. After polishing, sprinkle a bit of cornstarch on the table. Using a soft cloth, buff until the cornstarch is absorbed. Like the cornstarch, your fingerprint problem will vanish.

Respect your antique's charm

Don't ruin the value of an antique you're trying to restore by coating it with something like polyurethane. Since high-gloss finishes didn't exist until modern times, your antique will no longer appear old or authentic. Your best bet is to contact a professional antiques restorer with good credentials. A professional might actually decide your antique is more valuable the way it is.

Polish nooks and crannies. You can make an old piece of furniture come alive by applying furniture polish with a toothbrush to all its lines curves, and scrollwork.

Clean and restore wood with tea. Remember that old piece of furniture your Aunt Ethel gave you a million years ago – the one you keep hidden in the attic because you hate the color it's stained? You can easily re-stain it with an item that costs only pennies and is probably already in your kitchen – tea. With tea, you can remove old furniture polish, dirt, and grime and restore the original look to wood furniture. In a quart of water, toss in two tea bags and boil until the water is a brownish color you like. Let it cool, then test the back of the piece or another unseen area with a soft rag soaked in the solution. The first pass should remove old polish and strip the wood. Then you can apply some as stain. If you're pleased with the way it looks, finish the whole piece. But remember, tea is a permanent stain. When it's dry, buff it and follow up with polish if you want a finished look.

Uncover the beauty of old furniture. To clean an old, grimy piece of furniture, dip a cloth in pure ammonia, wring it dry, and give the piece a good rub down. Rinse the cloth with water as it gets dirty. Before long, you should see your furniture's original beauty.

Outsmart mold on old furniture. When old furniture develops a damp, musty smell, it's tempting to spray it with something that smells good, like furniture polish. But that would only cover up the real problem – mold. Spores of mold can take hold in any wood that absorbs moisture and is left in a relatively dark place. To get rid of the mold, remove all drawers and wipe the inside with denatured alcohol. Now move the furniture to a dry, sunny area for a week or so. If a hint of mold still exists after that, buy a wood sealer and paint it on the inside of the piece.

Create a new look with vintage furniture. Are you building your dream home or remodeling? Build in some older pieces of furniture to give your house a cozy, unique look. Scour used furniture stores and flea markets for deals on old furniture. A classic dry sink can be modified by your builder to house a kitchen sink. And with a few alterations, an antique buffet can hold your bathroom sink while lending an air of elegance to the room. You'll save yourself the expense of custom reproductions, and guests will notice you have the real thing.

Dress up your kitchen with a dresser. Who says bureaus have to stay in the bedroom? If your kitchen has an old-fashioned charm, use an antique bureau as a server. You can fill the drawers with napkins, tablecloths, and other kitchen supplies, and use the top when serving food buffet style. Not only will an antique bureau look classy, no one will see your clutter.

Treasure that old look. Be very careful when refinishing an old piece of furniture. If you don't know much about antiques, ask someone who does. Sometimes the aged, worn appearance of an old wooden piece – called the patina – makes it more valuable to antique collectors. So before you strip the finish and redo a table or other item, get some advice.

Make an old trunk smell like new. You found a gorgeous, old wooden trunk at a thrift store, and you couldn't wait to get it home. But once you got the lock off and opened it, you weren't so excited. Seems that someone stored clothes in it with mothballs, and that terrible smell is in the wood to stay. But you can get rid of that awful odor. Sand the inside of the trunk with sand paper, then give it a coating of polyurethane. Your trunk will smell brand new.

Move heavy furniture with ease. You've decided to move the antique armoire from one end of the room to the other. There's no way you could lift it, but how can you slide it without leaving deep gouges in your beautiful hardwood floor? Easy. Grab some empty, waxed cardboard cartons of milk, flatten them, and slide one under each leg of the armoire. Now you'll be able to move the heavy piece of furniture easily with no damage to your floor.

Battle dust with a vacuum. You dust wooden surfaces, blinds, and books, but what about your upholstered furniture? Dust falls there, too. Once a month, use your vacuum cleaner attachments to give your upholstery a good cleaning. But don't vacuum down-filled furniture unless you know it has down-proof ticking. Otherwise, the down feathers might start coming out.

Demolish dust with cheesecloth. Cheesecloth makes a good dust rag, but only after you've washed it. If you use it right out of the package, it still contains the starchy sizing the manufacturer adds to the material. This could scratch your furniture as you polish or dust. After washing the cheesecloth, be sure to polish with the grain of the wood. That way, any accidental scratches will be less noticeable.

Lift – don't slide – to prevent scratches. It's easier to just push things around when you're dusting, but go the extra mile and lift lamps, vases, and other objects resting on your furniture. Moving them across the wood can cause scratches that you'll regret.

Baby your furniture when dusting. Wiping dust off furniture seems like a no-brainer – just grab a rag and attack. But if you want to protect your wood, there's a bit of science to it. For best results, use a soft cloth made of flannel, cotton, or terry. Synthetic materials, like polyester, won't absorb the polish you spray on it, and you could end up getting too much water on your wood surface. Whatever you do, never dust with an unwashed piece of cloth. The sizing in the material can scratch your finish.

Dust your furniture with feathers. Not all feather dusters are created equal. Synthetic feathers can scratch wood and cause static electricity, which will invite the dust back just as soon as you swipe that table. So what's a housekeeper to do? Buy an ostrich feather duster. They contain no oils to gum up the surfaces of your furniture, and they don't create a static charge. Ostrich dusters are especially good for dusting your computer and other electrical equipment, which should be protected from static electricity.

Don't sleep through this seasonal sale. Need a sleeper sofa? Hold off buying one until autumn. Because many people require an extra bed for holiday guests, furniture stores compete with each other by offering sleepers at a discount in the fall.

Spring for a new recliner. For some reason, people love to picture their parents in big, comfy chairs relaxing at the end of the day. At least that's what furniture stores think. That's why recliners go on sale starting around May – just in time for Mother's Day and Father's Day. If you're planning to buy a recliner, wait until spring for the best sales.

Dine in style for the holidays. Leaves aren't the only things falling in autumn. Dining room furniture prices take a nosedive, too. That's because furniture marketers know during autumn, you're likely to start eyeing your dining room set and wondering if it's big enough or nice enough for your expected holiday guests. And they're hoping a sale will help you decide to replace the old one with something nicer.

Replace that lumpy mattress. You can get a great deal on mattresses starting in late spring and all the way through the summer when manufacturers advertise special offers. Do some investigating of prices and brands, and compare sales on the brand and style you want.

Stretch your furniture budget. Stretch your furniture-buying dollars as far as possible. Wait until January or July for the best overall sales. Twice a year, furniture stores have clearance sales, which should save you a bundle of money. But if you want to visit furniture-buying Mecca, High Point, North Carolina, is the place to be in April and October. High Point is home to many furniture factories and showrooms, and their twice yearly clearance sales are among the best in the industry.

Uncover solid wood's shady past

The furniture you picked out is expensive, but the tag says it's solid wood. That must mean it's worth it, right? Don't be so sure. "Solid wood" can mean particleboard and fiberboard, neither of which will stand up to heavy use or repairs. Unless it says "solid oak" or some other type of real wood, don't assume it's high quality.

Shop tent sales for good buys. Tent sales aren't what happens when camping gear is discounted. It's a sale many furniture stores have once a year to clear out slightly damaged and slow-moving merchandise. And because the store managers are anxious to get rid of the stuff, you can sometimes even haggle over a price to get a super buy. But check everything over carefully. Tent sale items are generally not returnable.

Polish glass to perfection. Make a glass table top picture perfect by squirting on a little lemon juice and rubbing it in. Use paper towels to dry the glass, then rub it with newspaper to get rid of streaks.

Cover tables with glass this clever way. It makes sense to protect a nice wooden table with a glass top, but be careful. The glass could trap moisture on the surface of the wood and ruin your beautiful table. To make sure this doesn't happen, place a small piece of cork or felt between the table and the glass so air can circulate between them.

Absorb moisture with charcoal. To keep glassed-in bookcases and your books free from dampness and mildew, toss in a piece of charcoal. No library is complete without one.

Keep your mattress from sliding. Keep your mattress from moving every time you make your bed. Get some nonskid mats – the kind you put under rugs – and place them between your mattress and box spring. Your mattress will stay exactly where you want it.

Silence a squeaky bed frame. Does your bed squeak every time you turn over? Your bed's metal frame is likely the culprit. Take the mattress and box spring off and spray all the fittings and wheels with a silicone spray. Your bed should be a lot quieter, and you'll wake up feeling refreshed.

Try this bright idea for stuck drawer. If you have to fight with your dresser drawer to get it open, the wood has probably swollen from trapped moisture. To dry it out, empty the drawer and place a small lamp with a 60-watt bulb in it for about 20 minutes. The heat will dry the wood, and your drawer should glide open and shut like it once did.

Unstick a stuck drawer. Why fight with a stuck drawer every morning when you're trying to get dressed? Fight back with a bar of soap. Simply rub the soap wherever the drawer is scraping and soon it will glide gracefully in and out. You can also use a candle or paraffin wax to do the job.

Give wobbly chairs a leg up. Don't let guests get seasick in those wobbly old chairs. Experiment with buttons and coins until you find something that closes the gap on the short leg. Fasten the object with a glue gun, and cover it with a small circle of felt to keep it from scratching your floor.

Remove candle wax from your sofa. All is not lost if you accidentally drip candle wax on your upholstered sofa or chair.

Lay a brown paper bag over the hardened wax and slide a hot iron over the bag. The wax will soften and transfer itself to the bag.

Whip up a powerful cleaner. You can save the never-ending cost of upholstery cleaning by doing it yourself. Mix one-quarter cup hand dishwashing liquid in a cup of warm water. Use an egg beater to whip up lots of suds. To be sure the fabric is colorfast, rub a bit of the suds on a hidden part of the furniture and gently scrub with a soft brush. Let the upholstery dry. If it looks cleaner, but not as if the colors are running together, continue cleaning. Work on one small area at a time, being sure not to soak the fabric. Carefully remove dirty suds with a clean spatula. After you finish a small area, wipe it with a clean, damp cloth. Allow the furniture to dry completely before using it.

Don't slip up on slipcover care. If you take good care of a slipcover, it'll serve you well for years. Vacuum before taking it off your furniture, and wash in warm water if the label says it's washable. Soak first if it's very dirty. The fabric will keep its shape better if you use a cold rinse and take it out halfway through the spin cycle. Let it partially dry on a clothesline or on a low-heat setting in the dryer. Put it back on your furniture while it's still damp, and smooth out wrinkles and any ruffles. You can speed up the drying process with a fan, or open windows on a nice day. Just be sure the pollen count is low, or you'll have to start all over again. Keep everyone off the furniture until the slipcover is dry.

Baby upholstery stains. If a stubborn stain refuses to leave your upholstered furniture, don't give up. Dampen the material with warm water, then sprinkle a little baby powder over the spot. Gently rub it in with a soft brush, and the stain will fade away.

Toss on a throw in summer. Oils from skin and hair can cause dirt to build up on your upholstery. That's why some sofas and chairs come with extra coverings for arms and headrests. You can take that idea one step further by covering your furniture with absorbent terry cloth throws in the summer. You'll be amazed by how much dirt ends up on the terry cloth – and not on your furniture.

Give furniture a new lease on life. Your couch and chairs will last longer and wear more evenly if you regularly turn the cushions. And if you have matching chairs, switch their positions now and then if one gets more use than the other.

Outwit dirt with fabric protector. Keep your furniture looking new longer by choosing upholstery treated with a fabric protector. But even if your furniture isn't treated at the factory, you can buy the stuff in spray cans and apply it yourself. You'll still have to spot clean stains and vacuum dirt, but it should be easier to keep clean. If it does get stained, follow the manufacturer's instructions for cleaning the material.

Slip into 'new' furniture. Redo your living room or den without breaking the bank. Invest in slipcovers. You'll get a whole new look for a fraction of the cost of new furniture. If you haven't shopped for slipcovers lately, you'll be surprised by the variety of attractive fabrics they now come in. And if you can sew your own, your savings will be even greater.

Move furniture with the seasons. Notice how much sun falls on your upholstered furniture during different times of the year. Try to rearrange your pieces so no one chair or couch gets all the sun. If you don't, one piece of furniture will fade faster than the others, making your set look old before its time.

Get the lowdown on leather. Always check for manufacturer's instructions before cleaning leather furniture. Leather that has not been treated with a protective coating should be dusted regularly to keep dirt from building up. But if it does get dirty, use an artist's gum eraser on the trouble spot. Treated leather can usually be wiped clean with a damp cloth and occasionally washed with mild soap. Dry it immediately and buff it with a soft cloth. Once or twice a year, polish it with a leather cream.

Chase blood from leather furniture. Did you get a gusher of a paper cut while sitting in your leather chair? Run for peroxide to clean off your finger. Now take the peroxide and a cotton ball back to the chair and pour a bit on the blood stain. As soon as it starts bubbling, wipe the spot with the cotton ball and watch it disappear.

Spray ink spots off leather. Before calling in the pros, you might be able to remove those ink spots from your leather chair yourself. You'll need a soft cloth and a can of hair spray. Spray a bit on a hidden part of the chair before you get started. If the color isn't affected when you wipe it off, you're all set. Now spray some on that pesky spot and wipe it immediately with the soft cloth. Many types of ink will come off easily.

Baby your leather furniture. Don't let your beautiful leather furniture dry out and age prematurely. Every month or so, wipe it down with a solution of two parts linseed oil to one part vinegar. If you follow this routine faithfully, your leather will look new for years to come.

Whiten your dreary wicker. Has your white wicker furniture turned brown with grime from being outside? To make it look new again, vacuum it with a brush attachment to loosen the dirt. Then wash it with a few tablespoons of ammonia in a gallon of water. Scrub dirt out of crevices with an old toothbrush, then rinse with plenty of water. Let it dry in a shady place, and soon your wicker will again be an inviting place to relax and enjoy your yard.

Help outdoor wicker last longer. Your wicker furniture will last longer if you bring it inside during the harsh, winter months. Clean it with a damp rag, and wipe off any mildew with a mixture of three-quarters cup of bleach in a gallon of water.

Give parched wicker a drink. If you can't get any rest in your wicker furniture because of all the squeaking, it's time to give it a drink. Squeaking is a sign that your wicker has dried out and needs moisture. Go over it with a sponge dipped in water, and soon you'll be able to hear crickets again.

Tighten sagging cane chairs. Do you have some old woven cane-seat chairs that you don't use because the cane is sagging? You can tighten up the seats with very little work. Start by pouring a cup of salt into a cup of boiling water. Let the solution cool, then sponge it onto the sagging seat, being careful not to get any on the wood. Place the chair in the sun to dry, and don't put any weight on it for a few days. The woven cane should tighten up nicely, and you'll have useful chairs again.

Pay attention to patio furniture. Hose off washable patio furniture regularly to keep soil from building up. If dirt does accumulate, use a squirt of dishwashing liquid in a gallon of water to pretreat stains on cushions before rinsing with the hose. Use a brush on stubborn marks, but don't try any harsh chemical cleaners. These could ruin your furniture.

Perk up PVC furniture. If your outdoor furniture is made of PVC, you know how dirty it can get. So clean it regularly with one-quarter cup of bleach in one quart of water. Put the solution in a spray bottle, label it, and keep it out of the reach of children. To clean your PVC furniture, spray it on and let it soak in for about 10 minutes. Then wipe it off with paper towels.

Do-it-yourself tips for
decorating

Think 'out of the box' when decorating. Who says a piece of furniture must be used only in the room it was designed for? Move a mirrored dresser into the dining room and use it as a sideboard. Or maybe a small chest of drawers, painted to match your decor, is just what you need in the bathroom for your towels and personal items.

Plump up pillows with pantyhose. Old, tattered pantyhose won't make your legs look any better. But they can do wonders for sagging cushions and pillows. Just save your old pantyhose and use them as stuffing.

Update your throw pillows. A quick way to give a throw pillow a new look is to wrap it in a terry cloth bath towel. Just fold the towel around the pillow as if you were wrapping a present and stitch the edges.

Be bold with accessories. When decorating on a budget, choose neutral colors and avoid dramatic patterns for sofas and chairs. Enjoy bright colors or bold prints in accessories, like throw pillows or tablecloths. After a while, when you grow tired of these designs, you can replace them at little expense compared with the cost of new furniture.

Look for a lasting weave. Consider choosing a tight, flat weave for your chair or sofa upholstery. It won't wear down as quickly as material with a loose texture. On the other hand, a moderate texture will be better at hiding dirt and wrinkles.

> ### Weigh differences before buying wood stains
>
> Before you buy a stain for your wood, learn the facts. Water-based stain is easy to clean up and isn't toxic, but it absorbs unevenly into the wood and might streak. Oil-based stain is easier to apply and will give you a smooth finish. Unfortunately, its fumes are toxic, and it's hard to clean up.

Stencil with stain for antique look. You may want to spruce up some old furniture with a decorative stencil but are worried the new paint will clash with the worn patina of the wood. To maintain an antique look, use water-based stain instead of paint and apply it with a sponge instead of a brush. The transparent stain will look like it has been there since the furniture was made.

Salvage your old serving cart. A rolling stone gathers no moss – but an old, rolling serving cart gathers plenty of dust. Drag that metal relic out of storage and put it back to work. You can spruce it up by draping some pretty fabric over it. Then use the cart as a display area for pictures or knickknacks. You can also use it to serve coffee and tea to your guests.

Toss a rug on a distressed table. Hide your worn, scratched coffee table by topping it with a colorful throw rug. If you have trouble finding one you like, why not weave, knit, or crochet one yourself? Painting on canvas is another option for a creative cover.

Cozy up to a colorful couch. You still love your old couch, even though it's seen better days. To give it new life, drape a warm, colorful blanket or afghan over the worn places. It will add some pizzazz without taking away any of the comfort.

Throw new life over an old sofa. When your sofa has reached that worn and bedraggled stage, but your budget isn't ready for new furniture, pull out an extra bedspread or quilt. Use it as a loose "throw." Or, if it's big enough, tuck and pin it snugly, like new upholstery.

Top your tables tastefully. It's nice to display books, vases, and other knickknacks on your tables. But it's also nice to be able to see the table tops. Don't go overboard – your house isn't a museum. For best results, vary the sizes and shapes of the items. The display will be more pleasing to the eye.

Give an old lampshade a new life. Brighten up a tired lampshade with pretty ribbon in a contrasting color. Use a leather punch to make holes, evenly spaced, around the bottom and top of the lampshade. Run the ribbon through the holes, back and forth from bottom to top, making a crisscross pattern.

Add cozy warmth to any room. To add a warm glow to a room, spray paint the outside of a lampshade black and the inside gold.

Lighten up with clean lampshades. If your room seems a little dreary lately, maybe your lampshades are dirty, or they've darkened with age, reducing the amount of light that gets through. Clean or replace them for a brighter look.

Spruce up a lampshade with stencils. Even cavemen jazzed up their caves with original paintings. So why should you put up with a plain lampshade? Buy some fabric paint and sponge or stencil some designs on it. The effect will be marvelous – especially when you turn on the lamp. Just think of it as Stone Age style.

Steam your way out of sticky situation. A picture is worth a thousand words – and most of them are probably unprintable if you're struggling to pry a picture out of its frame. Next time one of your pictures is stuck to the glass of its frame, don't get steamed. Reach for your steam iron instead. Set it to the highest setting and hold it close to the top of the glass. It will loosen the picture, and you'll be able to remove it with ease.

Hang pictures with fishing line. You might not have any pictures of yourself proudly displaying a prize fish. But you can use fishing line to hang the pictures you do have. This strong, durable substance makes a sturdy substitute for a hanging wire.

Position pictures perfectly with putty. Tired of straightening and restraightening your pictures? Next time you hang a picture, stick a small bit of mounting putty behind one corner of the picture frame. It should keep the picture from tilting. You can find mounting putty in hardware stores.

Hang pictures without ugly nail holes. You want to hang a few pictures, but your landlord doesn't allow nail holes in the walls. Or perhaps you don't want nail holes in your own walls. No problem. Use sewing needles instead. They're surprisingly strong. In fact, they can support up to 30 pounds.

Borrow art to brighten your walls. You love art, but you only have so much money to spend on it – and only so many walls to hang it on. An easy solution might lie in your public library. Many libraries let you sign out framed art prints for two or three months at a time – free of charge. You'll have hundreds of prints to choose from so you'll always find something you like. And you'll be able to sample a new print in a few months before you have time to grow tired of the old one. It's a wonderful, inexpensive way to add variety and excitement to your decor.

Keep artwork dry. Never spray water or a liquid cleanser directly on the glass that protects framed photographs, paintings, or prints. Instead, lightly dampen a clean cloth and rub it over the glass. This will prevent any moisture seeping under the glass and ruining your artwork.

Display photos in jars. Apothecary jars and other clear glass containers make decorative picture frames. Just roll the picture slightly to get a curve and put it inside. Fill the jar with marbles, glass beads, shells, or other items that will hold the picture against the glass without damaging it.

Center your picture with toothpaste. When hanging a picture, use this tip to avoid making a hole in the wrong spot. Put a blob of white toothpaste on the hook on the back of the picture or on the place where the center of the wire will be when the picture is suspended on a nail. Hold the picture almost, but not quite, touching the wall until you know right where you want it to hang. Then press it against the wall. It will leave a small toothpaste mark, showing you where to put the nail. The toothpaste can easily be wiped off the picture and the wall.

Devise a decorating plan

Before going into battle, generals will draw up a plan of attack. Take the same approach to decorating your empty room. Arm yourself with color samples, wallpaper samples, and examples of different styles. You can usually find samples at paint and wallpaper stores. Use them to help you plan. Mix and match the colors and styles and test them at different times of day to make sure they're right for the room. Once you have everything figured out, charge into action.

Decorate your home with a dropcloth. Painter's dropcloths are great for decorating. You can sew on braids and trim and use them as slipcovers for folding chairs, cushions, and pillows. A paint-splattered dropcloth makes a unique tablecloth. Dropcloths come in a variety of colors, such as natural, rose, gray, and blue. One is sure to match your home décor.

Tie your rooms together with color. It would be boring if every room in your house looked exactly the same. But you do need some continuity between rooms to tie everything together. You can come up with a consistent color pattern by opening all the doors and walking from room to room. In each room, peek into the next room to determine how much of it you can see from there. Plan your color scheme accordingly.

Set your table for less. Your family probably doesn't care much for presentation when it comes to dinner time. Instead of buying fancy place mats, use dish towels. They work great because they absorb spills and last a long time.

File away chipped goblets. Nothing ruins a toast like a chip on the rim of your glass. To smooth out rough edges on your crystal goblets, gently rub the edges with an emery board.

Brighten your kitchen with a birdhouse. "Tweet" yourself to a unique kitchen accessory. Buy an unfinished wooden birdhouse from a craft store, and cut out part of its roof. Paint the birdhouse to match your kitchen, and turn it into a charming holder for your kitchen utensils.

Bring the country garden look indoors. Frame and hang some empty seed packets in your kitchen. It's an inexpensive way to add a country touch.

Design a pretty caddy for silverware. Instead of hiding your knives, forks, and spoons in a kitchen drawer, display them in an attractive countertop container. Just tuck a floral-print cloth napkin or embroidered tea towel inside a new flower pot, planter, or vase and fill it with your eating utensils.

Find inspiration in a fish tank. Still fishing for new decorating ideas? Try lining the bottoms of your vases with fish tank gravel. It makes a fine substitute for marbles or glass chips. Plus, it comes in a wide range of colors. Find the perfect one or use a combination to match your room's color scheme.

Substitute a bottle for a costly vase. You don't need to spend a fortune on a fancy vase to display your flowers. Empty wine and olive oil bottles make wonderful – and inexpensive – vases. Save them, clean them out, and fill them with pretty flowers.

Shake mineral deposits with salt. Scrub away those ugly hard water stains in your clear vase with salt and a wet cloth. Finish the job by washing with soap and warm water.

Branch out to brighten your home. Sticks and stones may break your bones, but they can also help spruce up a room. Pick some branches from a tree, spray paint them any color you like, and display them in a large vase on the floor. It will add a touch of outdoor charm to the inside of your home.

Top vase with tape for better arranging. For an attractive bouquet in a wide-mouth vase, place strips of green florist tape across the top, forming a grid. Insert stems of flowers in the openings. Flowers will stand up straight with balanced spacing, and the tape will blend with leaves and stems.

Seal a crack with paraffin. Don't throw out your favorite vase just because it has a crack and is leaking. Melt some paraffin and coat the inside of the vase. Let it cool and fill with water. If it holds, just turn the crack away from view and put in some pretty flowers.

Discover the secret to drying flowers. You can dry flowers like a pro. The trick is to use borax and cornmeal. Make a mixture that's one part borax to two parts cornmeal and put some in an airtight container. Lay the flower on top of this layer and sprinkle more of the mixture over the flower. Do this gently so you don't crush or bend the flower. Close the container and let it sit at room temperature for a week to 10 days. Take out the flower and brush off the powder with a makeup brush or soft paintbrush.

Fill your room with foliage. Christmas isn't the only time you can bring a tree into your home. A tree or a large plant fills up space, looks great, and costs relatively little. You can find real or artificial trees and plants for less than $30. That's a cheaper way to fill a room than buying another sofa or chair.

Cheer up your shower curtain. Your shower might be hot, but your feelings for your shower curtain are probably lukewarm, at best. Warm up to it by adding a little more flair. Replace the rings that hold the shower curtain to the rod with pieces of bright ribbon. Then tie your shower curtain to the rod with big, bright bows. The new, cheerful look will let you shower in style.

Enlarge your bedroom by making the bed. Create the illusion of a larger bedroom. Just match the color of the bedspread with the color of the walls. Your small bedroom will appear quite spacious.

Decorate a bedroom fit for a king. For a dramatic look in a bedroom, use a section of tall, wrought iron fencing for a headboard. Use individual bars of wrought iron for curtain rods, and look in thrift stores for wall sconces that complement the look. Add several candles and some rich, floor-length curtains, and your room will take on the feeling of a stately castle.

Plant the seeds for a unique bedroom. Transplant a touch of your garden into your bedroom. Take a length of picket fence, paint it white, and attach it to the wall above your bed. This makeshift headboard will stand out against a sky-blue wall. Complete the effect by decorating the room with birdhouses, watering cans, flower boxes, and other garden accessories.

Make headway without headboards. The twin beds in your guest room don't have headboards. But you can overcome that minor obstacle with some creative decorating. Find large pictures that match the color scheme of the room and hang them at eye level over each of the beds. Then fill the space between the bottom of each picture and the bed with a tasteful arrangement of decorative pillows. No headboard? No problem.

Jazz up a dull dresser. Does your dresser put you in a gloomy mood? Add some cheer to your dark, boring dresser. Start by laying a bright table runner across the top. You could also set colorful vases, picture frames, candles, or other knickknacks on top. Soon, your old dresser will be filled with new life.

Set a place for lace in your bedroom. Capture the elegant look of a cutwork or lace bed coverlet – for a fraction of the usual cost. Simply cover your bed with a lace tablecloth instead. For a full-size bed, use a 70-by-90-inch oblong tablecloth. You'll find it makes a charming substitute for the real thing.

Choose a clean look in carpet

For a floor that doesn't show dirt, bypass carpet in light or dark solid colors. The dark ones show dust and lint, while the light ones show dirt and grime. Perhaps a tweed pattern in a mid-range color would be a better choice.

Get the dirt on carpet samples. When choosing new carpeting, use carpet samples for more than just color preferences. Take pieces home and rub in some soil from your yard. Choose from those that hide the dirt best.

Consult color charts before shopping. Going on a quest for the perfect rug? It might be tough to find the exact color you need in your living room. Before you start on your shopping trip, get some color sample charts from your local paint store. Match the colors you're seeking, write down the dimensions you need, and put the information in a plastic sandwich bag to make your shopping easier.

Raise the ceiling. To make a low ceiling seem higher, use tall lamps that have the shade below the light bulb, sending the light upward. Your eye will follow so be sure the ceiling is in good repair.

Age artwork instantly. To give a new poster or print an antique look, rub a damp tea bag over it.

Stretch a room. Hang a large mirror on a prominent wall to make a small room look bigger.

Perk up dark paneling. Contrary to popular belief, your dark wooden paneling doesn't come with a life sentence. You can brighten your gloomy room with a simple paint job. Lightly sand the paneling and coat it with a primer before you paint the final layer. Choose soft colors, like beige or sand tones. You'll be surprised how much different – and how much friendlier – your room looks.

Frame doors and windows with books. You need a full wall of bookshelves, but you just don't have the space. Consider creating a border of books around doorways and windows instead.

Stencil temporary designs. If you live in an apartment and aren't allowed to repaint the walls, spruce them up with chalk. Start by crushing the chalk into a powder and mixing it with a small amount of water. Then use this "paint" to stencil designs on your walls. You can wipe them off when it's time to get your deposit back.

Cover your wall with a blanket. Who needs expensive artwork? Just hang one of your colorful blankets or throws. A blanket with a pretty pattern or a neat picture will brighten up a large, bare wall.

Convert old ads into antique art. To give a room a vintage look, rip out advertisements from old magazines you've saved or picked up at a flea market. Mount them on white cardboard with rubber cement, and then frame and hang. For a room of memories, do the same with a collage of photos, roadmaps, brochures, theater stubs, and other souvenirs from vacations.

Brighten a room for a few bucks

If your decorating budget is small, a fresh coat of paint may be the best way to achieve a dramatic new look. And you may not even need to paint the whole room. Sometimes just giving one wall a new color will make the whole space look more alive.

Keep tabs on your curtain budget. Give your windows a stylish, modern look with tab curtains. Just don't give up your good, old-fashioned financial sense. Instead of buying an expensive wooden curtain rod, make your own. Buy long, 1 1/2 to 2-inch wooden dowels from your hardware store. Cut them to fit your windows, screw a drawer knob into each end, stain or paint the dowel, and hang your new curtains.

Make new drapes using old shapes. When you want new draperies, don't bother getting out the measuring tape. Just take down your old drapes and bring them to the drapery shop or seamstress. You know they're just the right size.

Get stained glass effect without the expense. Do you like the look of stained glass but can't afford an expensive panel? Get a similar effect by placing a variety of colored bottles in a sunny window. If you only have clear bottles, fill them with water tinted with a few drops of food coloring.

Rejuvenate your curtains with odd rods. It's curtains for run-of-the-mill drapery rods. Try hanging your curtains from a copper pipe or a thick tree branch instead. Just set your makeshift curtain rod on brackets. This unique approach will give your room a fresh, new look.

Weigh curtains down with keys. Slip old keys into the hems of your curtains and the weight will help them hang straight. If the keys tend to slide around, stitch through the hole in the top to keep them in place.

Change the scenery by moving your sofa. Maybe you don't need a new house. You just need a new outlook. Rearrange your furniture so you face the windows with the best view. Try this in the spring to bring you out of the winter doldrums.

Lighten up with lighter curtains. Do your heavy drapes make your room seem dark and gloomy? Escape from the drapes with a simple trick. Just take down the heavy drapes and leave the sheers up. Your windows and the rest of your room will seem lighter, brighter, and more cheerful.

Table tired window treatments. For a fresh look to replace old curtains or draperies, experiment using table linens. Drape a tablecloth, for example, over a curtain rod and secure it with a large, decorative pin. Or hang overlapping cloth napkins diagonally on a rod. With all the creative possibilities, you can change your windows with the season – or your mood.

Remove old wallpaper with new trick. Your old wallpaper certainly doesn't have feelings – but it has become quite attached to the wall. Pry it loose with a simple, homemade mixture. Just fill a spray bottle with twice as much hot water as liquid fabric softener, and spray the wallpaper thoroughly. Focus on the top and along the seams. In about 20 minutes, the wallpaper should peel right off. If not, just keep spraying and try again.

Remove old wallpaper with a paint roller. Old wallpaper loosens up and peels off in seconds – almost effortlessly – with this amazing white vinegar tonic. Just mix equal parts white vinegar and hot water. Pour the solution into a wide pan. Apply with a paint roller, and the wallpaper should peel right off.

Soak wallpaper in a cooler. Hanging wallpaper is no picnic, but you can still pack a cooler. Use a large cooler to soak your prepasted wallpaper. It's portable, and the handles make it easy to move without sloshing water all over your carpet.

Save wet wallpaper when interrupted. You have dampened a strip of wallpaper and are ready to hang it when an emergency calls you away for an hour or so. No need to worry. Just fold the wet paper neatly with glue side sticking to glue side. Slip it into a plastic bag and close it with a twist tie. When you return, it will still be moist and ready to hang.

Stretch your ceiling with stripes. Feeling cramped? Replace your current wallpaper with striped wallpaper. It will make your ceiling seem higher.

Color your way to a roomier home. Use the power of color to transform a small room into a big one. Choose mint green or pale blue wallpaper or paint to "enlarge" your room. Shades of white and beige also work well.

Meddle with metal at your own risk. Metallic wallpaper can give your room added texture and pizzazz – but it might also give you quite a shock. Because metallic wallpaper conducts electricity, you should not use it around sockets and switches.

Save wallpapering for a sunny day. Even if you're normally a night owl, you should become an early bird when you wallpaper. That way, you can take advantage of the daylight. The more light you have, the more mistakes you'll spot right away. You'll be able to fix each problem almost immediately, instead of dealing with a bunch of problems later.

Sidestep slants with plumb line. Did you ever end up with wallpaper that was slightly slanted – or just plumb crooked? Make sure that doesn't happen next time by using a plumb line. This tells you whether your wallpaper is on a perfectly vertical line or not. Do it early on, so you can catch and fix any mistakes before your slight slant turns into a major disaster.

Flatten wallpaper bulges with easy trick. Next time you put up wallpaper, win the Battle of the Bulge. If an annoying bulge appears, slit it with a razor blade. With a knife, lift up the wallpaper to let the air out. Then smooth the wallpaper back down with a wet sponge.

Rip wallpaper to make a patch. You don't need to re-wallpaper your entire wall, but one spot looks pretty ragged. If you plan to slap a patch of wallpaper over it, don't reach for the scissors. Instead of cutting a small square off the roll of wallpaper, just tear off a piece. The rougher edges will help the patch blend in better with the rest of the wall.

Pay less when buying wallpaper. To save money on wallpaper, choose a pattern that repeats every 6 to 8 inches. You won't waste as much when matching the pattern as you would with a paper that repeats every foot or so.

Be prepared with extra paper. If this is your first experience with wallpapering, buy one roll more than you think you'll use. You are likely to underestimate what you'll need and make mistakes in measuring and cutting. If you run short, you may not be able to find the exact match when you return to the store to buy more.

Decorate your kitchen with scraps. Make creative use of wallpaper scraps to tie your kitchen decor together. Glue them to cabinet doors, backs of chairs, and table tops. Seal them with a layer of clear polyurethane for long-lasting protection.

Keep tools at your fingertips. When removing or hanging wallpaper, you'll save yourself lots of trips up and down the ladder if you wear a carpenter's apron. The pockets will hold a scraper, measuring tape, seam roller, and other small tools you'll need.

Hide your errors among the vines. If you're ready to try wallpapering for the first time, select paper with an irregular pattern – perhaps one with rambling roses or berries. It will be hard to spot wrinkles and other imperfections hidden among the tangle of flowers, leaves, and vines.

Shed the right light on wallpaper samples. Wallpaper looks different under different kinds of light. If the store has fluorescent light but yours is incandescent, ask for a sample to take home. If you can't do that, take the sample book or roll of paper to a window or doorway to look at it under natural light.

Take the curl out of wallpaper. A couple of days before you plan to hang wallpaper, unroll it and reroll it the opposite way. This will make it straighter and easier to hang. You can quickly remove the curve of vinyl paper with your hair dryer. Use the warm setting and blow air back and forth over the paper from about 6 to 8 inches away.

Design your own conversation pieces. You don't have to pay a fortune to decorate your home with unique accent pieces. Go to yard sales, salvage yards, and thrift stores and use your imagination. An old stool would make a lovely plant stand. And a weathered, wooden gate could be painted and turned into a beautiful headboard for a child's bed. Treasure hunting can save you a bundle on decorating, and your home will be like no other.

Gather decorating ideas from a garden. If you are going for the country cottage look, why not bring a few of your garden accessories indoors. An old birdbath, for example, makes a pretty table when fitted with a round glass or acrylic top. Put your wooden kitchen utensils in terra cotta pots, and use a cast-iron frog or bunny as a doorstop.

Create your own potpourri. Sweeten the air in your home with homemade potpourri. Just gather your favorite herbs and spices and put them in a jar or basket. Or divide your potpourri into small bags, called sachets, and place them throughout your house.

Design centerpieces with a theme. It's your turn to host the book club meeting. Make the most of it by decorating for the occasion. For a centerpiece, place some old, leather-bound books on the table next to a pair of antique reading glasses. When your old friends from high school visit, arrange old textbooks, a few fountain pens, and your class yearbook as a centerpiece that doubles as a trip down memory lane.

Play interior decorator with old toys. Don't throw out old toys. Use them around the house in unusual ways to store, display, and decorate. From wooden blocks to stuffed animals to wagons or cars, you don't need expensive antiques, just a childlike imagination. Spell out "WELCOME" or "MERRY CHRISTMAS" with blocks. Set dolls or teddy bears on a shelf or a chair. Place bath accessories in a dump truck. Play around – you're sure to find other great uses for toys.

Liven up a dull room with shoe boxes. Add pizzazz to your room decor by creating customized storage boxes. It's easy. Using coordinating or contrasting fabric, cover shoe boxes left over from your last shopping spree. Now you not only have new room accents, you have more closet space.

Turn a tin into a timepiece. It's about time you did something with that old metal tin. Transform it into a unique and charming clock. Buy a clock mechanism from your hardware store and attach it to the top of the tin. Then put a hook on the back and hang it on the wall.

Hats off to hatboxes. Beautify a shelf or table with an unusual and charming design. Simply stack some hatboxes on top. You can find them in all sorts of pretty colors and patterns. Pick out a few different sizes for the best effect. Your guests will tip their hats to your creativity and good taste.

Prop your door for pennies. Open the door to sensible decorating ideas – and keep it open. Instead of paying top dollar for a fancy doorstop, make your own. Just fill a sturdy, metal, cookie tin with dry beans, put the lid on, and use it to hold your door open. It's cheap and practical, but you don't have to sacrifice style. That's because you can find tins in all kinds of sizes, colors, and patterns to fit your home decor.

Defeat dripping candles with salt. Avoid the annoyance of cleaning up runaway candle wax. Stop your candles from dripping by soaking them in a very salty solution for a few hours. Dry them thoroughly, then light your amazing drip-free candles.

Chill your candles to prevent dripping. Forget the junk drawer. Store candles in your refrigerator instead. That way, they won't drip when they burn. Pretty cool, huh?

Get more candle with less wick. Extend the life of your candle by shortening the length of its wick. Just snip the wick close to the candle, and your candle will last longer.

Reflect on a cozy winter. Are you reluctant to give up winter fires when spring temperatures begin to rise? Use candles to get the same effect without the heat. Stand a brass platter on its edge in the fireplace and group candles of different heights in front of it. The warm golden glow will recreate the romantic mood you miss.

Give your mirror a new image. Add some frills to your full-length mirror. Carefully pry the glass out of the frame. Then wrap wide ribbon or light fabric around the frame, attaching it with a hot glue gun. Use colors that match the rest of your room. Put the glass back in the frame, and you have a new, fancier mirror.

Rub off scratches with toothpaste. A broken mirror means seven years of bad luck. A scratched mirror is just annoying. Get rid of the tiny scratches in your mirror or glassware with toothpaste. Rub a small amount of nongel toothpaste into the scratch and polish with a soft cloth.

Don't throw out old mirror. Even though it has a worn spot, hold onto that antique mirror your grandmother gave you. For just a few pennies, you can get that looking glass back to looking new. Just tape aluminum foil to its back.

Add a window without a carpenter. Want to make a room seem bigger with a unique decoration? Find an old, interesting window in a salvage yard or from someone remodeling. Remove the old glass, have mirrors cut to fit as panes, and glaze the mirrors into place just like you would a pane of glass. Paint the window an interesting color. Add a small flower box to the sill and fill it with silk flowers. Hang your creation on a bare-looking wall. The effect will be dramatic, and the mirrors will make your room appear more spacious.

Maximize your hallway with mirrors. Mirror, mirror, on the wall, who has the most attractive hallway of them all? You can – with this simple decorating trick. Hang an assortment of mirrors in pretty frames along the walls of your hallway. It will make your dark, narrow corridor seem brighter, wider, and more lively.

Practical problem solvers for
the home office

Store pens the 'write' way. The pen may be mightier than the sword – but it's even mightier if you store it with the tip down. Pens and markers last longer that way, plus they're always ready to write.

Stack cereal boxes to stay organized. Boxes of breakfast cereal often come with neat prizes inside – but an ordinary, empty cereal box also makes quite a prize. Just cut off the top and side flaps and use the cereal box as a filing tray on your desk. You can even stack empty cereal boxes to store incoming mail, bills that need to be paid, or other papers that require action.

Organize essentials using cans. Looking for a neat and inexpensive way to organize your office supplies? Save and clean a few tin cans of varying sizes – such as a tuna can, soup can, and large juice can. Either wrap them in felt or spray paint them. Then glue the cans together with a hot glue gun to make a nifty office supplies holder for your desk. Use it to hold pens, pencils, rulers, paper clips, staples, push pins, and the like.

Bust stress with a balloon. Make a nifty stress buster for your desk. Using a funnel, fill a heavy-duty balloon with sand. Dampen the sand with some water. Make sure the sand can't move freely around the balloon, yet it should have some "give." Then knot the balloon tightly and keep it handy for times when you need to relieve some stress.

Let kitchen helpers keep you organized. A dish rack makes a handy organizer for bills and other incoming mail. Just slide the envelopes between the slats. You can even label the slats by date, so you know when you have to deal with each piece of mail. You can also keep a dishpan in your cupboard or closet to act as a catchall for miscellaneous items.

Simplify your writing projects. Keep paper projects, like Christmas cards, all in one place. Put everything you need in a plastic envelope and slip the envelope between books on your bookshelf. When you need to work on the project again, just pull out the envelope and get busy.

Nail down important papers. Take a stab at organizing your receipts and other loose papers. Make your own receipt spear, the kind you see in restaurants and other stores. Just drive a heavy-duty nail through a block of dense wood. Use it to hold your receipts and other important papers until you're ready to file them in the appropriate spot. When you're not using your homemade receipt spear, stick a wine cork on the tip of the sharp nail.

Wipe away desk clutter. Your hands are clean – now it's time to make your desk the same way. An empty, hand-wipe container can help. Those upright, cylindrical containers are perfect for holding pens, pencils, or markers.

Turn inner tube into rubber bands. Don't pedal over to the scrap heap to get rid of your old bicycle inner tube. Make better use of it by cutting it into homemade rubber bands.

Hatch a money-saving packing plan. Clean out your empty egg cartons and save them. When you need to mail something fragile, cut them up and use them as packing material.

Lick your envelope problem. Your bill is ready to be mailed. You've made sure the company's address is peeking through the window, you've slapped a stamp in the upper right corner, and you've sealed the envelope – but you forgot to include the check. No problem. Just put the sealed envelope in the freezer for a few hours, then slide a knife under the flap. You can put your check in and reseal the envelope.

Let mail labels work for you. Make things easier for the companies sending you merchandise. Look through your mail for envelopes that have labels with your name, address, and ZIP code. Save those labels. Then when you order something from a catalog, include a label with the order. Your package will definitely find you.

Return to 'sendee.' Your Aunt Ethel is in the hospital, and you want to send her a get-well card. However, you're not sure how long she'll be there. To make sure she gets your card, write her home address on the envelope where you'd normally put the return address. That way, even if she's already back home, she'll still get a card to brighten her day.

Clear paper clutter with one-touch method. That mound of mail and other paper on your desk just keeps growing and growing. When you finally realize that it's not going to go away by itself, you need a plan for tackling the paper stack. Here are some guidelines for swiftly dealing with your mail. Toss out advertisements you're not interested in. If the piece of mail requires a response, either respond at once if it won't take too long or put it in a pile for later if it will take more time. Put receipts and other items that don't require a response in their appropriate places. Glance through catalogs, mark what you want on the order form, tear out the order form and store it in the "later" pile, then throw away or recycle the catalog. When you're done, you should have one small pile of things to deal with – and a whole lot more desk space.

Safeguard your photos with cereal boxes. Make sure your pictures and other documents don't snap, crackle, or pop in the mail. Protect them by sliding the front or back panel of a cereal box into a large envelope. The panel adds some stiffness to the envelope so your photos won't bend.

Try this mailing tip – no strings attached. Brown paper packages tied up with string might be a few of your favorite things – but it's no way to treat a package. If you want your gifts to arrive undamaged, don't tie string around the package. Otherwise, post office workers will grab your package by the string and toss it onto the mail truck. Regular packing tape is a safer bet – it just doesn't make as good a song lyric.

Settle your small accounts. Sometimes it just doesn't pay to have a savings account. Review any account under $500. If your bank charges you a maintenance fee or the account doesn't earn any interest, you should close the account.

Put the squeeze on clutter. Bills and other dated material that require action on your part can really pile up if you don't have a system for handling them. Avoid the clutter by buying an accordion file. Label the dividers with the days of the month. When you get a bill in the mail, slip it into the divider dated a week before the due date. That way, you have plenty of time to write your check and get it in the mail. Simply check the appropriate divider each day to keep up with what needs to be done.

Develop a less-taxing storage system. You should keep personal tax information for six years. But that doesn't mean it has to take up precious space in your filing cabinet. Since you don't need to refer to it often, you can store it on a shelf in your basement or attic. When you finish filling out your tax forms, put that year's documents all together in a large envelope or box and store it on an out-of-the-way shelf. Then throw out another year of old tax information, so you only have exactly six years' worth.

Fight identity theft with a shredder. One of the most common crimes of recent times is identity theft. Thieves can use your personal information to steal from your bank account, run up your credit card bill, ruin your credit, and generally make your life miserable. Protect yourself by guarding your garbage, where thieves rummage for personal information. Invest in a small, cheap paper shredder from an office supply store. Use it to shred bills, advertisements, and credit card offers that include your personal information. You can even use the shredded mail for packing boxes or mulching your lawn.

Hide your PIN within a phone number. It's tough to remember all your PIN numbers for bank cards, phone cards, and whatnot. Of course, it's not a good idea to write the PIN on the card itself. And it's not practical to carry small slips of paper with the PINs written on it everywhere you go. But you can use a simple trick to keep track of all your PIN numbers. Enter fake names in your address book and list what appear to be phone numbers – but are actually PIN numbers – beside it.

Tear out ads to really enjoy magazines. Before you browse through your subscription magazines, tear out all the advertisements. When you read them, they'll be more enjoyable – and less distracting. Plus, you'll be able to store your magazines easier since they're much less bulky without all the ads. If any of the images in the ads catch your eye, save them and use them for decoupage to decorate boxes, filing cabinets, or any other part of your home office.

Store magazines in a cereal box. Looking for a neat way to store your magazines? Look no further than your breakfast cereal. Simply cut off a corner of the cereal box, and slide your magazines inside. It also works as a storage box for random papers or a holding tank for coupons that need to be clipped. Spruce up the cereal box with wrapping paper, newspaper, or drawings by your grandkids.

Label your personal library. Turn the page on lost books. Cut out address labels from mass mailings and glue them to the inside cover of your books. That way, if you ever lend out your books to friends, they'll know where to return them.

Edit musty odor out of books. You love to curl up with a good book – unless it smells. To remove mildew and musty smells from old books, sprinkle the pages with talcum powder or cornstarch. Wait a few hours, then gently brush it out.

Shelve damp books in the freezer. Just when you were really getting into your book, you spilled your glass of water all over it. Next time some spilled water dampens your day of reading, pop the wet book in a frost-free freezer. It will clear up the moisture before mildew sets in.

File away your home office. Don't despair if your house doesn't have a den or office. You can turn any room into a temporary office with ease. Just keep a rolling file cabinet in a closet. That way, you can roll it out when you need it, and it stays out of your way the rest of the time.

Capitalize on your closet space. Turn your closet into a secret home office. Just put in a desk and some shelves. Then install electricity, phone, and cable for a computer modem. While you're at it, you can mount cork tiles on the back wall to serve as a bulletin board or nail little cans or boxes to the wall to store stationery and other writing supplies. Your closet office can feature a computer, a printer, a phone, a fax machine, and more. And it doesn't take up any precious floor space. When you're not using it, all you have to do is shut the door.

Install an economical workstation. Set up a snazzy shelving unit in your home using standards and brackets. Use long brackets for a wide bottom shelf, which you can use as a desk. For a more stable desk, remember to put in an extra standard and bracket to support the center of the shelf. Then use an adjustable angle bracket to put a reading shelf at eye level. Top it off with a bookshelf above that. The whole thing makes a great workstation. You can even install it between two large bookshelves for a continuous library look.

Rest your feet on a phone book. Place a call to comfort. Slip an old phone book under your desk to use as a footstool. You'll be able to raise your feet and reduce the stress on your lower back.

Cook up a new workstation. If you've just remodeled your kitchen, you can also remodel your den or home office. Just lay a countertop across two kitchen cabinets to make a nifty desk.

Cut office costs with carpet scraps. Instead of buying a pricey bulletin board for your home office space, consider this inexpensive – and more colorful – alternative. Just mount a scrap piece of carpet to the wall. You can even put it in an old frame if you want. Then use push pins to stick things to your homemade bulletin board.

Build a desk using milk crates. When setting up a home office, you can really milk milk crates for all they're worth. For example, use them as makeshift filing cabinets. Or slap a board across two stacks of milk crates to form a cheap but efficient desk.

Construct a unique desk with coffee cans. Take a coffee break without leaving your desk. Just build your desk out of coffee cans. It's not as crazy as it sounds. You can stack coffee cans and Krazy Glue them together to form four legs. Spray paint them black, then lay a coffee table top across them to complete the desk.

Go back to school for great deals. "Back-to-School" sales aren't just for kids. You can take advantage of these seasonal low prices to load up on office supplies for the whole year. Notebooks, loose-leaf paper, pens, pencils, sticky notes, and even computers can be found for a fraction of their usual cost. After snapping up all those bargains, you'll feel like the smartest kid in class.

Accept a handout for your home office. Why pay for office supplies when so many companies are eager to give them away for free? Just keep your eyes open. Businesses often give away notepads and pens with their corporate logo, and you can pick up all kinds of things at your doctor's office. Expos and conventions are great places to find free notepads, pens, pencils, highlighters, clipboards, refrigerator magnets, and more.

Hang a homemade bulletin board. Give your home office a chic – and cheap – bulletin board. Just cover a ceiling tile with wallpaper. Glue two eye-loop screws to the back and hang it on the wall.

Protect your computer with pantyhose. Give your computer a feminine touch. Slip some old pantyhose over the back of the hard drive to prevent dust from getting in it.

Clear crumbs from your keyboard. Sometimes it's hard to tear yourself away from the Internet – even for lunch. But eating at your computer can lead to crumbs in your keyboard. Here's how you can get rid of them. Unplug your keyboard, turn it upside down, and smack the back of it with the palm of your hand to dislodge the crumbs. You should also buy a can of compressed air to blow dust and other buildup from between the keys.

Control your computer mouse. Like a real mouse, sometimes your computer mouse becomes a pest. If you move your mouse one way but the cursor on your computer screen jumps all over the place, you might need to clean your mouse. Turn off your computer and turn your mouse over. Remove the ring on the bottom to get at the little ball inside. With a piece of adhesive tape, remove the lint and dust on the ball. Also wipe out the lint and dust inside the mouse and on the rollers. Some gunk might be stuck on the rollers. Get rid of it with a cotton swab and some isopropyl alcohol. Let everything dry, then reassemble your mouse. It should behave better.

Color code your computer cables. Once you unplug the cables on your computer so you can move it, you're faced with a tangled mess. Eliminate the confusion of hooking everything back up. Put a piece of colored electrical tape on each cable. Use a different color for each one. Then make dots with different colored permanent markers on the back of the computer where each cable fits. When you go to hook everything back up, just match the color on the cable with the color on the back of the computer. You'll be up and running in no time.

Team up with a tutor to master your computer. A computer can be a great tool for learning, shopping, and keeping in touch with friends and family. But learning how to use one can sometimes be intimidating or confusing. Instead of enrolling in a computer class, consider hiring a tutor to teach you right in your own home. You'll get plenty of one-on-one attention, and you'll learn on the computer that you'll actually be using. Look in the newspaper or ask at your local school districts or vocational schools. A student or teacher might be willing to make some extra money as a computer tutor.

Spot serial numbers with ease. Imagine if people at a convention wore name tags on their backs or the soles of their shoes. It would be almost impossible to figure out who you were talking to. And about as frustrating as trying to find the serial number on your computer, scanner, or printer. Make things easier for yourself. Print the serial number onto a label and stick it on the front of your computer or other electronic products. It will save you much time if you ever need to call for technical support.

Tint your specs to keep glare in check. Computers are great, but beware of the glare. Shield your eyes from the glare of your computer screen with tinted lenses in your eyeglasses. You can even use different tints to deal with different colored text. For example, brown helps reduce the glare of green text and blue helps with amber text. If you don't wear glasses, a pair of tinted sunglasses might help.

Screen out computer confusion. If your new computer seems too confusing, the solution might be as simple as simplifying your computer screen. Ask one of your children or grandchildren to help set up your screen so it's easier to find things. Instead of searching through all sorts of folders for programs you use, you can just click on an icon to get to your e-mail, Internet, word processing application, or family tree main page. Make sure the icons have different graphics, so you can easily tell them apart and find the one you're seeking. On some computers, you can use the F keys in the same manner. Lastly, bookmark the service numbers for your frequently used programs. Or just write them down and keep them in a handy spot in case you need to call for help. Your computer time will be a breeze – with everything just a click away.

Get your Internet search off to a good start. The Internet can seem like a vast, intimidating wasteland if you don't know where to begin. A good starting point for looking up anything is to go to a general search engine. Some good, basic search engines include the following: <www.dogpile.com> <www.google.com> <www.lycos.com> <www.overture.com> <www.yahoo.com> <www.invisible-web.net> <www.askjeeves.com>

Prop up your papers as you type. Cook up a new strategy for typing on your computer. Use a cookbook stand to prop up papers by your screen. That way, you can keep your head movements to a minimum and avoid eyestrain or a strained neck. You also won't waste time searching for your place in the text. If you don't have a cookbook stand, you can make a handy paper holder by gluing a clothespin to the cardboard backing from an old picture frame.

Reformat disks to save money. Don't buy new disks for your computer. Instead, reformat old computer disks or those freebies you get in the mail. The reformatted disks are as good as new. Just make sure you don't erase anything important on the old disks.

Proven home remedies for
health & beauty

Perk up your bath with a homemade pillow. The holiday season can be very hectic. Take a relaxing break from shopping, wrapping, cooking, and mailing. Scoop up about three cups of those foam packing peanuts you might use to protect a breakable present. Dump them into a large, plastic freezer bag, and squeeze some of the air out of it before sealing. Then slip the peanut-filled bag under your neck while you enjoy a nice, hot bath. Consider your homemade bath pillow a gift from you to you.

Enjoy a scented bath without spending a cent. Want to feel pampered? Splash a little perfume or cologne into your next bath. It will smell great. You don't have to buy expensive products, either – just save bottles of the scents you no longer wear. It's a luxurious alternative to tossing them in the garbage.

Shave shower time to save money

If you're looking for ways to save money, you don't have to look too far. Just try lowering your water bill. You can start by taking a shower instead of a bath, but make sure you keep the shower short. A family of four, with each person taking a daily five-minute shower, uses 28,000 gallons of water a year.

Pamper yourself with bath crystals. Lose yourself in luxury with homemade bath crystals. Just mix two cups of Epsom salt and a drop or two of your favorite scent, like vanilla or lavender. You can also add a few drops of food coloring and a half teaspoon of glycerin for moisturizing. Keep the crystals in a resealable container, and simply toss some in your tub for a luxurious bath.

Give wild hair the brushoff. You enjoyed the Little Rascals, but that doesn't mean you want to look like Alfalfa. If your hair stands on end, dampen your hairbrush with cold water before brushing. This will get rid of the static and put you back in control of your hair.

Give your hair pizzazz with a pen. Use a highlight pen – the kind students use to mark important passages in their textbooks – to give your hair some festive highlights. If your hair is blonde, use a yellow pen. Brunettes should use an orange one.

Cleanse your hair with baking soda. Your hair has become a gathering place for old hair spray, gel, and other residue. Strip away the film in your hair with baking soda. Just blend a little baking soda with your regular shampoo. You can also try mixing baking soda with water and massaging it into your hair before you shampoo. Just be careful not to get any baking soda in your eyes.

Conquer oily hair with aloe. Greasy hair? Get rid of some of that oil by adding a half teaspoon of aloe vera gel and one tablespoon of lemon juice to one-quarter cup of your regular shampoo. Then wash your hair and rinse well.

Get a handle on dirty brushes. You just stepped out of the shower, and your hair is squeaky clean. Why run a dirty brush through it? To clean your hairbrushes and combs, soak them for several minutes in a quart of hot water and two tablespoons of baking soda. Then rinse and pat dry.

Banish buildup with vinegar. Hair spray, gel, and other styling products leave their mark on your hair – in more ways than one. Get rid of the gunk that builds up by rinsing your hair with vinegar. Mix a half cup of apple cider vinegar with two cups of warm water, and pour over your freshly washed hair.

Go bananas to fix dry hair. Sick of monkeying around with dry hair? Mash a banana with a teaspoon of almond oil, and rub the mixture into your hair. Leave it there for 20 minutes, then rinse.

Ditch dry hair with safflower oil. If your hair isn't producing enough natural oil, give it some help. A drop or two of safflower oil works wonders for dry hair. Rub a tiny amount into the palms of your hands, and work it into your hair from the ends toward the scalp. Then leave the oil there to do its job. You won't even realize it's there – but you will notice the difference in your hair.

Tame your hair with fruity spray. Need to keep your hair – and your budget – in place? Try this simple homemade hair spray. All you need is a piece of citrus fruit and some water. If you have dry hair, use an orange. Otherwise, use a lemon. Chop up the fruit and boil it in two cups of water. Let the mixture boil until only half of it remains, then cool and strain. Pour the mixture into a spray bottle and store it in the refrigerator. Add water if you find it's too sticky. You can also throw in an ounce of rubbing alcohol. This allows you to keep the hair spray unrefrigerated for two weeks.

Shine your hair with an avocado. Follow this recipe for shiny hair. Mash an avocado with a tablespoon of olive oil and a teaspoon of baking powder. Massage the mixture into your hair and let it sit for 15 minutes. Then wash your hair and watch it shine.

Eliminate dull hair with vitamin E. Add shine to your hair by adding vitamin E to your diet. Brown rice, nuts, seeds, wheat germ, vegetable oils, and green leafy vegetables give you plenty of this key nutrient. So eat up – and give your hair a treat.

Try a honey of a conditioner. Protect your hair during the harsh winter months with a thorough conditioning each week. Just massage four tablespoons of honey into your scalp and cover your hair with a plastic bag for at least 15 minutes. Then rinse with hot water.

Shake dandruff with salt. If you're worried about your blood pressure, go easy on the salt. If you're worried about dandruff, reach for that saltshaker. To get rid of those unwanted flakes, just rub some salt into your scalp before shampooing.

Now's the 'thyme' to fight dandruff. Has dandruff taken some of the spice out of your life? Try spicing up your scalp to stop the flaking. Boil two tablespoons of dried thyme in one cup of water for five minutes. Let the mixture cool, strain it, and massage the liquid into your hair and scalp. Don't rinse – just let this simple do-it-yourself remedy do its job.

Revive your hair with beer. Your limp hair could use a lift, but who wants to spend money on expensive hair products? Flat beer strips away soapy film and brings new life and bounce to your hair. Just mix three tablespoons of flat beer in half a cup of warm water and pour it over your head during your shower. Finish your shower and rinse. The beer gets rid of the residue from commercial hair products that can leave your hair feeling heavy and lifeless.

Set your sights on great-looking hair. Style your hair with a gorgeous, expensive salon look. It's easier than you think. Just dissolve a teaspoon of unflavored gelatin in a cup of warm water. You'll create an instant setting lotion for your hair.

Revive blah hair. Does your hair need a pick-me-up? Add body to your hair by adding three tablespoons of Epsom salt to three tablespoons of deep conditioner. Pop the mixture in the microwave for 20 seconds, then massage it into your scalp and hair. Leave it on for about 20 minutes before rinsing. Your hair should bounce back to life.

Take charge of oily hair. You use a shampoo made especially for oily hair, but sometimes it could use a little help. Try this simple procedure to rid your hair of oil. First, add nine tablespoons of Epsom salt to a half cup of your shampoo. Then measure out a tablespoon of the mixture, rub it into your dry hair, and rinse. Squeeze the juice from a lemon into a cup of lukewarm water, and pour it over your head. Leave it there for about 10 minutes, then rinse thoroughly with cool water.

Keep hair spray buildup in check. Rid your hair of the buildup from hair spray and gels with a simple homemade solution. Add a cup of lemon juice and a cup of Epsom salt to a gallon of distilled water. Cover the mixture, and let it sit for 24 hours. Pour the mixture over your dry hair and leave it on for about 20 minutes before shampooing.

Amaze your face with baking soda. Why waste money on expensive facial scrubs when you can whip one up in no time with items from your own kitchen? Just toss some baking soda and oatmeal in your blender, then scrub away. Or you can throw some baking soda in with your regular facial cleanser for a gentle scrub.

Erase brown spots with lemons. Feeling blue over the brown spots on your face? You might need some lemon aid. Just cut a lemon in half and squeeze the juice into a bowl. With a cotton ball, swab some lemon juice onto your brown spots for 15 to 20 minutes three times a day. Rinse your face after each session. Stick to this routine, and you should notice your brown spots fading within a month.

Make tweezing more pleasing. Sometimes it hurts to be beautiful. Tweezing unwanted hair, for example, makes you yelp. Numb the pain with a toothache reliever, like Anbesol. Just apply it where needed and pluck away.

Brighten your complexion with salt. Rejuvenate your face with this combination of cupboard ingredients. Mix equal parts salt and olive oil and gently massage your face and throat for five minutes. Then wash your face with your favorite cleanser, and your skin will have a radiant, golden glow.

Refresh your skin with essential oils. To make a refreshing facial toner, add two drops of an essential oil, such as lavender or peppermint, to 8 ounces of mineral water. Refrigerate the mixture and use it whenever your face needs a "lift."

Enhance your skin with fruit. You don't need to spend a fortune on fancy facials. A quick trip to the grocery store will do. Make your own facial treatment with a mashed banana, a tablespoon of honey, and a splash of orange juice. Apply the mixture to clean skin and relax for 15 minutes. Rinse off with warm water, and your face will glow with gratitude.

Discover a sweet facial scrub. If someone told you a sweet, golden mixture is the secret to smoother skin, you might search the ends of the earth for this magical nectar. But the answer lies right in your kitchen. For a gentle facial scrub, combine a tablespoon of sugar with six drops of olive oil. Carefully massage the mixture over damp skin and rinse with warm water.

Follow this recipe for a radiant face. Want to give your face a golden glow? Try this inexpensive mix of honey and cucumber. Put half a teaspoon of honey and half a cup of sliced cucumber in the blender and puree until you get a fine mixture. Spread the mixture on your face and leave it there for about half an hour before rinsing. Your skin will look great.

KO dry skin with mayo. No more dry, flaky skin! Reach into your refrigerator for a peerless "smoothing cream" – mayonnaise. Spread some whole-egg mayonnaise on your face, and leave it there for 20 minutes. Then wipe it off and rinse with cool water. You'll never waste money on expensive facial creams again.

Beat puffy eyes with egg whites. With a makeup brush, apply a beaten egg white to your face. As the egg white dries, your skin will tighten – especially that saggy area under your eyes. You can also add a few drops of witch hazel, which reduces swelling and keeps the egg white from drying too quickly.

Treat baggy eyes to spuds. You're not going anywhere, but your eyes look as if they've packed for a long vacation. Get rid of those unsightly bags by placing a slice of raw potato over each eye. Then relax for 15 minutes.

Halt puffy eyes with salt. It's easy to remove the puffiness from around your eyes. Just stir a teaspoon of salt into a pint of hot water. Soak some pads in the solution and place them over the puffy areas. The salt water will wash away the swelling.

Chill out to relieve puffy eyes. Make a splash in your battle against puffy eyes. Soak your face in a bowl of cold water. The cold water causes your blood vessels to constrict and the swelling to go down. Drinking water also helps because it wards off dehydration. When you're dehydrated, you retain fluids and look puffier.

Tame wild eyebrows with petroleum jelly. Do your eyebrows seem to have a mind of their own? Put them in their place with some petroleum jelly. Just scoop some onto your pinky and run your finger over your eyebrows. It will keep them under control.

Find a perfect match for your makeup. Do you have trouble spotting your favorite shade of makeup amid the dozens and dozens of varieties in the store? Make things easier on yourself. Before you run out of lipstick or nail polish, smear some on a piece of paper. Then, when you need to buy more, bring the paper with you. You'll be able to match the color in no time.

Keep fragrances from fading. Does your favorite fragrance fizzle out too soon? Before you splash on perfume or cologne, rub some petroleum jelly on your skin first. It will make your scent last longer.

Get the most from your lipstick. Why pay for a whole tube of lipstick if you're not going to use it all? Here's a creative way to save that last half inch of lipstick. Buy one of those medication containers with a compartment for each day of the week, then scrape out the last bit of lipstick into one of the compartments. You can do the same with other shades of lipstick so you have a variety to choose from in the same portable container. Then, simply apply the lipstick with a lipstick brush.

Put a dent in a powerful scent. You can have too much of a good thing. For example, your perfume might smell great – but you went overboard with it. Instead of overpowering the entire room with your scent, just douse a cotton ball with rubbing alcohol and rub it wherever you sprayed the perfume. You'll keep the great scent, but it won't be as strong.

Cut the cost of storing cosmetics. Be more businesslike – or more artistic – when you organize your cosmetics. Instead of paying more for a cosmetics case, buy an acrylic desk organizer from an office supply store or an art shop. It has compartments for your cosmetics, brushes, and nail polish – and it's much cheaper than a regular cosmetics case. Now that's a beautiful deal.

Rub out dry skin with salty rubdown. Trying to shake dry, flaky skin? Shake some salt on your body after you get out of the bath or shower. Do it before you towel off, so you're still wet. Then massage your skin with the salt. It will get rid of dead skin and give your circulation a boost.

Smooth your skin with yogurt. Wake up to smoother skin when you use this homemade night cream. Simply squeeze half a lemon into a cup of plain yogurt and stir. Then raid the refrigerator each night for a dollop of this mixture. Rub it onto your face before bed, just like you would use your regular night cream. After three or four weeks, you'll notice healthier-looking skin.

Exfoliate dry skin for pennies. To get rid of dry, flaky skin, combine one-quarter teaspoon of salt and one teaspoon of petroleum jelly. Gently rub the mixture onto your face using a circular motion. Then, wash your face with your favorite cleanser and warm water.

Soothe your skin with oatmeal. Your skin is irritated – but, thanks to this common breakfast food, you don't have to be. Soothe itchy skin rashes, sunburn, poison ivy, and even chicken pox with oatmeal. Cut the foot off a pantyhose leg and fill it with rolled oats. Then, tie the end and hold it under the faucet as you run a bath. The soothing oatmeal bath will ease your discomfort. Plus, you can save the homemade oatmeal bag for next time.

Soften and exfoliate your skin. Revitalize your skin with Epsom salt. Just rub handfuls of it onto your wet skin, from your feet to your face. You can also pour two cups into a warm bath and soak. It will smooth and soften your skin.

Soothe sunburn's sting. You'll be sure to remember your day at the beach – not because of the great time you had, but because of the awful sunburn. Ease your pain with vinegar. Soak a towel with a 50-50 mixture of water and vinegar and place it over your sunburn while you sleep. Or put some vinegar in a spray bottle and spray it on your sunburn for relief.

Eclipse sunburn with green tea. You remembered to wear sunscreen during your day in the sun, but you forgot to wear a hat. Now it feels like the blazing sun has lowered itself directly onto your head. To find soothing relief, brew a pot of green tea, let it cool, and rinse your hair with it after you shampoo.

Cool sunburn with cornstarch. Suffering with a sunburn? Here's a nifty way cornstarch can help. Mix cornstarch and water to form a soothing paste. It's an inexpensive and effective form of relief.

Synthetic detergent on a rope?

Here's a surprising thought – the soap you use might not be soap at all. Real soap is made from fats and an alkali, such as lithium, sodium, or potassium. Most body cleansers are actually synthetic detergents. Some benefits of these fake soaps are that they make suds easily and don't form soap scum. Unlike regular soap, these products are regulated by the Food and Drug Administration. That's because the manufacturers make cosmetic claims about their product's moisturizing or deodorizing ability or drug claims about its antibacterial or antiperspirant powers.

Unwrap the power of soap. Put a new bar of soap to work right away. As soon as you get home from the store, unwrap the bar of soap and put it in your linen closet. Your soap will do double duty. First, it will give your closet a pleasant scent. At the same time, it will harden, making it last longer when you move it into the bathroom.

Save your soap from a watery grave. You want to shower with soap – not soup. So why leave your bar of soap in a puddle on your shower shelf? To keep your soap dry and make it last longer, hang a net produce bag over your faucet and store your soap in it between showers.

Rinse away diaper rash. Cloth diapers save you money and are environmentally friendly – but they might give your baby a rash. Protect your precious little one by throwing a cup of vinegar into the washing machine during the rinse cycle. The vinegar equalizes the cloth's pH balance, so the diaper won't irritate your baby's skin.

Try a salty antidote for poison ivy. You don't seek out poison ivy, but it always seems to find you. To relieve the itching and irritation that come with poison ivy, soak the affected area in hot salt water.

Rub out mosquito bites. Next time you get bitten by a mosquito, rub some rubbing alcohol on the bite. It will stop the itching and virtually make the bite disappear. If you want to be even more prepared, splash some rubbing alcohol on yourself and let it dry before you go outside. This will stop mosquitoes from biting you in the first place.

Stop itching with a dab of soap. To wash away the itch of mosquito bites, simply apply soap to the stung area. You'll experience instant relief and feel cleaner, too.

Slay chiggers with hot water. Like creatures from a science-fiction movie, chiggers attack in bunches and attach larvae to the folds of your skin. The result is much itching and a rash, similar to – but more intense than – poison ivy. Luckily, you don't need a laser gun or any other high-tech gizmos to combat chiggers. Your best defense is a hot bath. If you soak in hot water within hours of being exposed to chiggers, the larvae will be less likely to stick to your skin. Add some Epsom salt to your bath to soothe your skin if it's already starting to itch.

Zap sap with butter. You love walking in the woods and getting closer to nature – until you end up with a hand covered in sticky tree sap. Sometimes it seems that stuff will stay on your hands forever. Don't give up. Rub butter or margarine on your hand, and the black gunk comes right off with soap and water.

Pamper your cuticles for pennies. You want to do something about your rough cuticles, but who can afford a fancy manicure? Try this instead. Mix one cup of baby oil with a half cup of lemon juice. Heat the mixture slightly, and soak your fingers for about 5 minutes. You'll feel like you came right from the salon.

Mellow yellow nails with denture cleaner. Wearing too much dark nail polish may have turned your fingernails yellow, but that doesn't mean you're a coward. Be brave and attack the problem. Drop a denture-cleaning tablet into a bowl of water and dunk your fingernails for a few seconds. It should get rid of the stains.

Shake rough hands overnight. It's not hard to soften your hands. Just rub some petroleum jelly onto your hangnails and cracked cuticles. Slip on some cotton gloves and slip into bed. In the morning, pull off the gloves to reveal your surprisingly soft hands.

Soften your cuticles with shaving cream. You want to paint your fingernails and make your hands look pretty, but that's hard to do when your cuticles are in rough shape. Fortunately, you can soften your cuticles with just a smidgen of shaving cream.

Everyday activity helps your heart

You don't have to run a marathon – or even join a gym – to get the benefits of heart-healthy exercise. Almost anything you do can help lower your risk of heart disease. Go for a walk, climb some stairs, work in your yard, or dance. Even housework can be helpful. Just make sure you do some activity each day.

Sock pain with warm rice. Behold the amazing microwavable heat pad – its actually just a bag filled with uncooked rice. Make your own by filling a soft, cotton sock or a small pillowcase with rice and sewing it closed. Just pop it in the microwave for a minute or two. This warm pouch is perfect for soothing sore muscles at the end of the day or warming cold feet at night.

Try this simple solution to backaches. Many men have chronic back pain that requires them to take out their billfold – and not to pay a doctor. If you carry your wallet in your back pocket, it can put too much pressure on nerves and muscles when you sit down. Clean out those business and credit cards you don't use and start carrying your billfold in your front pocket.

Change a diaper into a dandy heating pad. Here's how you can baby your aching joints and muscles. Simply wet the pad of a disposable diaper and pop it in the microwave. You'll have no trouble wrapping this unusual heating pad around your sore spots. Just make sure you don't overheat the diaper. If you do, let it cool a little before putting it against your skin.

Extend your reach with tongs. Oops! You just dropped something on the floor. If you're in a wheelchair or you have back problems, picking it up isn't always easy. Instead of bending over, try using kitchen tongs to snap up your dropped item. You can even keep extra tongs in other rooms – like your bedroom or bathroom – for easy retrieving.

Sink headaches with limes. British sailors once used limes to ward off scurvy. But limes come in handy for more common ailments, too. If you have a throbbing headache, cut a lime in half and rub it on your forehead. You'll be ready to sail the seven seas in no time.

Clip toenail fungus. Not only is toenail fungus ugly – it's also expensive to treat. But you can clean up your feet without cleaning out your pocketbook. Just soak your feet in a vinegar and warm water solution. You can use equal parts vinegar and water or one part vinegar and two parts water. Soak between 15 and 30 minutes a day, and in six weeks, the fungus should go away.

Relieve itchy feet with cinnamon. Spice up your battle against athlete's foot. Brew a batch of cinnamon tea – not to drink, but to soak in. Add about 15 to 20 broken cinnamon sticks to eight cups of boiling water. Remove from heat, and let the mixture steep for an hour. Then, pour it in a bucket and soak your itchy feet for 15 minutes. Rinse off your feet with warm water. They should feel great – and smell much better.

What is Epsom salt?

You've heard of Epsom salt. But did you know it's a white or colorless needle-shaped crystal with a wide variety of uses. The official name of the compound is magnesium sulfate heptahydrate, but it's called Epsom salt because it was first made from mineral water in Epsom, England.

Give stinky shoes the boot. Has your foot odor turned your shoes into stink bombs? Try soaking a tissue in rubbing alcohol and leaving it in your shoes overnight. This will kill the bacteria that cause odor.

Banish foot odor with baking soda. When your feet send your nose an SOS, here's a surefire way to drown the odor. Combine two tablespoons of baking soda and two quarts of water and soak your feet for 30 minutes.

Don't sweat foot odor. Sweaty feet mean smelly feet. That's why you might be able to control foot odor by using an antiperspirant on your feet. If your feet don't sweat so much, maybe they won't smell so bad.

Smart way to polish your toes. Next time you get a package in the mail, save some of those Styrofoam peanuts. You can slip one between each toe to keep them apart while you remove or apply nail polish.

Starch your shoes to fight odor. Sprinkle a little cornstarch into your shoes to combat foot odor. It will absorb moisture and odor and leave your feet feeling freshly showered.

Beat blisters with the right socks. A blister on your foot can ruin your whole day. You can avoid them by buying socks that are cut to fit. Never mind the one-size-fits-all tube socks that are popular. The extra material can bunch up and cause blisters.

Curtail calluses with special care. Follow this simple plan to prevent calluses. First, soak your feet in lukewarm water. For more power, try adding baking soda or herbs, like chamomile. Next, put on some moisturizing cream and rub your feet with a pumice stone. Do this at least once a week, and your feet will stay nice and smooth.

Greatest corn remedy since sliced bread. Here's a simple way to get rid of corns and calluses without spending a lot of bread. In fact, you'll only need one slice. Just tape a piece of stale bread soaked in vinegar over your corn or callus overnight. You could probably substitute a cloth for the bread and get the same amazing results.

Free your toes from friction. The tips of your toes aren't always in tiptop shape. If your toes have blisters or redness, try putting some petroleum jelly on them. It will reduce the friction caused by your foot moving around inside your shoe.

Fascinating way to foil athlete's foot. Crush several garlic cloves and cover them with olive oil. It sounds like the beginning of a delicious recipe – but it's really an unusual remedy for athlete's foot. Let the garlic soak in the oil for a few days, then strain the oil to get rid of the garlic pieces. To soothe the itching and burning of athlete's foot, just rub some of the oil onto your feet.

Smooth cast's path with pantyhose. Nothing is fun about wearing a cast. On top of the heat, itching, and awkwardness, there's the struggle to push the bulky cast through a sleeve or pant leg when you get dressed. Make the task easier by using an old pair of pantyhose. Just snip off one leg, cut off the foot, and slip the whole thing over your cast. It will slide right into your clothes.

Treat feet to a briny bath. Muzzle those barking dogs after a hard day. Throw a handful of salt into a bucket of warm water and soak your sore feet. Rinse them off in cool water. Then fetch your slippers.

Lick ticks with petroleum jelly. Ticked off because you can't get a tick off? Remove a tick from your body with petroleum jelly. Just put a big dollop of petroleum jelly on the tick and leave it there for about half an hour. You should be able to wipe the tick off with ease.

Find first aid in your freezer. Ouch! You just banged your head on a cupboard door. Instead of an ice pack, grab a can of frozen juice from the freezer. It's quicker than fumbling around with ice cubes and baggies, and it fits easily into your hand.

Pack a lunch box with first aid supplies. Your children – or grandchildren – might not think it's too cool to carry a lunch box anymore. But you can turn those old lunch boxes into cool first aid kits. Throw in some bandages, scissors, antibiotic ointment, aspirin, anti-itch cream, nail clippers, sunscreen, and lip balm. Label it "First Aid Kit" on the top and bottom. If you have more than one lunch box, keep one in the house and one in the trunk of your car for emergencies.

Pop a homemade ice pack in your freezer. You never know when an emergency might pop up. That's why you should always be ready with an ice pack. Luckily, you can make one easily. Just put unpopped popcorn kernels in a zip-lock bag and freeze.

Soothe scrapes, stings, and sore muscles. Consider adding some Epsom salt to your first-aid kit. It comes in handy for a variety of ailments. For example, you can reduce the swelling of scrapes and insect bites with a warm Epsom salt compress. Or use a cold compress to soothe an insect bite's sting. A warm Epsom salt bath also helps relieve muscle aches and pains.

Overcome the 'ouch' of wasp stings. Have you heard the buzz about vinegar? It can help soothe wasp or yellow jacket stings. Just soak a cotton ball in cider vinegar and hold it on the sore spot. The pain goes away in a few minutes.

Shake the ache of bee stings. Rubbing salt in a wound adds to your agony. Yet, putting salt on a bee sting actually helps relieve the pain. Just wet the spot where you've been stung and pour some salt on it.

Take the zing out of stings with onions. Bee stings can be an awful experience. But you can banish the pain simply by applying an onion to the wound. Cut an onion in half and hold it on the bee sting for a few minutes to ease the pain.

Hang up on germs. Because so many hands touch your phone, it might be connecting you to germs as well as the party on the other end. Remember to include the telephone – and other commonly handled items, like doorknobs, light switches, and the remote control – when you're cleaning. A quick wipe with some rubbing alcohol should do the trick.

Beware of grungy towels. You wouldn't wipe germs all over yourself after a shower, would you? Well, that might be exactly what you're doing when you dry yourself with your favorite fluffy towel. Dampness and dead skin help make towels inviting to bacteria. But it's not hard to keep bacteria at bay – just wash your towels at least once a week.

Flush germs from your toilet handle. When you think about protecting your health, you probably don't think about your toilet. But maybe you should. Because bathroom guests flush the toilet before washing their hands, the toilet handle can be a prime spot for germs. Avoid the problem by keeping your toilet handle clean. Rubbing alcohol works just as well as disinfectants you find in stores.

Reorganize to remember refills. Don't be left without a refill when your prescription medicine runs out. Keep your refill labels in the medicine cabinet, right near your medication. When you have about a two-week supply left, take a refill label with you. Put it in your wallet or purse and stop at the pharmacy when you have a chance.

Jog your memory with a simple trick. Can't remember if you took your pill last night? Here's an easy way to ease your mind. After you take your pill at night, turn the bottle upside down. The next morning, check the bottle. If it's upside down, you know you took your pill. Then turn the bottle right side up again. Repeat this routine every day.

Relieve nausea with lemons. Lemons may make you pucker up, but they're also an astonishing remedy for motion sickness. If you feel queasy while riding in a car or boat, try sucking on a lemon wedge. It should help relieve the nausea. Another natural remedy for queasiness is ginger. You can buy ginger supplements at health food stores. Powdered, grated, and whole ginger are also widely available. One cup of boiling water poured over two teaspoons of powdered ginger and steeped for 10 minutes makes a soothing tea.

Treat a tummy ache. Next time you have an upset stomach, try this old-fashioned remedy. Mix one-third of a glass of milk with some ginger ale and drink. Use enough ginger ale so the milk doesn't curdle.

Soothe stomach ills with baking soda. This quick cure for stomach problems costs just pennies. Reach in your kitchen cabinet for a little baking soda, mix half a teaspoon of it into half a glass of water, and drink. Because it neutralizes stomach acid, the baking soda will provide relief from indigestion and heartburn.

Live longer by flossing

Still need a reason to floss your teeth? Chew on this. Recent studies found that people who floss live longer than people who don't. It could be because people who floss live healthier lifestyles in general. But it can't hurt to give flossing a try. Who knows — it might add a few extra years to your life.

Give cold sores a 'pep' talk. Think pink the next time you get a cold sore. Bismuth subsalicylate (Pepto Bismol), known for coating your stomach to relieve indigestion, works the same way on pesky cold sores. Just apply some to the affected area. It will coat and contain the cold sore virus.

Whiten your teeth with salt. Want to pulverize the plaque that leads to tooth decay? First, pulverize some salt in your blender. Then mix one part salt to two parts baking soda. It makes a wonderful teeth cleaner and whitener – and it's good for your gums.

Two-minute warning for teeth. Think you spend enough time brushing your teeth? Think again. To do a thorough job of cleaning your teeth, you should brush for two minutes. Use a timer along with your toothbrush next time. You'll be amazed at how long two minutes seems – and how clean your teeth will get.

> ### Harder isn't better when it comes to brushing
> You might be gung-ho about brushing your teeth, but there's no need to launch an attack. Brushing your teeth harder doesn't get them any cleaner. And when you brush too hard, you damage your teeth and wear away your gums. Remember, brush smarter – not harder – to combat tooth decay.

Eat cheese to ward off cavities. Cheese for dessert? It sounds bizarre, but it might be a good idea. Sugary foods help bacteria in your mouth produce acid, which causes tooth decay. However, eating yellow cheese after a meal helps neutralize these acids. So if you simply can't resist that piece of cake after dinner, remember to chew on some cheese, too.

Beware of hidden arsenic. Since treated wood contains arsenic, it's always a good idea to keep it away from human and animal food. And don't use it to make cutting boards, countertops, containers for food, mulch, or pet bedding.

Give your old toothbrush new life. Your toothbrush has seen better days. Whether it's caked with old toothpaste or just not smelling very fresh, your toothbrush might need a boost. Dump a teaspoon of bleach in a glass of cold water. Soak your toothbrush in the glass for about 15 minutes, then rinse well. Your toothbrush will be clean enough to clean your teeth again.

Fill the gaps with dental floss

No matter how thoroughly you brush your teeth, you're still missing spots. In fact, you're missing nearly 40 percent of each tooth's surface. The solution is simple — floss. Flossing gives you access to the whole tooth and shields you from gum disease. Why settle for cleaning only 60 percent of your teeth when you can get 100 percent protection?

Curb nicotine cravings with herbs. You're trying to quit smoking, but you feel as if you're fighting a losing battle. Send for some herbal reinforcements. Certain herbs — such as catnip, chamomile, peppermint, and valerian — help you relax and reduce your craving for nicotine. Just brew a pot of herbal tea and sip your way to victory.

Sweeten your breath with eucalyptus. For sweeter breath, rub some eucalyptus oil on your teeth and gums after you brush and floss. The oil helps kill odor-causing germs.

Take two aspirin and gargle in the morning. A sore throat can be a real headache. So why not fight it with aspirin? Dissolve two aspirin tablets in warm water and gargle. You'll feel hours of soothing relief. Just make sure you don't use coated aspirin tablets or acetaminophen.

Sweeten your breath naturally. You can make an effective — and cheap — mouthwash with ingredients from your pantry.

Just combine a half teaspoon salt and a half teaspoon baking soda with a cup of water for a potent weapon against bad breath.

Fight bad breath with good hygiene

Don't drastically change your diet to conquer chronic bad breath. Some foods, like onions and garlic, temporarily affect your breath – but they are not the real culprits. Bacteria break down leftover food particles in your mouth, producing foul-smelling sulfur compounds. That's what gives you bad breath. Brushing, flossing, and scraping your tongue with a tongue cleaner will get rid of these bacteria. So eat up – but practice good dental hygiene afterward.

Splash on amazing deodorant substitute. If you run out of deodorant, don't sweat. Chances are you have an emergency backup in your medicine cabinet. Antiseptic mouthwash can kill the bacteria that cause odors. Just splash some under your arms and go about your business.

Whip up homemade deodorant. Not again! Your deodorant has just run out. If you find yourself in this situation – or if you're just tired of spending money on deodorant – make your own with two everyday household items. Just mix equal parts talcum powder and baking soda.

Rub out body odor with rubbing alcohol. Here's a clear alternative to deodorant – rubbing alcohol. Just spray some under your arms or onto your feet with a spray bottle or apply it with a cotton ball. Rubbing alcohol works because it kills the bacteria that cause odors. It also dries quickly and leaves no odor of its own.

Mash acne with potatoes. Use potato power to fight your next acne breakout. Rub half a raw potato over your face, leave the juice on for 20 to 30 minutes, and rinse with cold water. Sound strange? Then consider this – when was the last time Mr. Potato Head had a pimple?

Keep an eye on your complexion. Pimples are a sight for sore eyes. But you can get rid of them with eye drops that relieve redness. Just squeeze a few drops onto a cotton swab and hold it against your pimple for about 30 seconds. You'll see a clear improvement.

Tame pimples with oats. For clearer skin, combine two tablespoons of oatmeal and enough olive oil to make a paste. Massage the paste into the affected area, and leave it there for about five minutes. Then rinse with warm water.

Use yogurt and yeast to thwart pimples. Do you feel trouble brewing on your face? At the first sign of pimples, smear a mixture of brewer's yeast and plain yogurt on your face. Leave it there for a few minutes before wiping it off.

Heal pimples while you sleep. Who needs expensive acne medications? Just dab a bit of toothpaste on your pimple at night. The next morning, wipe off the dried toothpaste with a warm washcloth, and the redness will be gone.

Spray your way to a sneezeless night. It's hard to get a good night's sleep when you spend more time sneezing than snoring. If you're bothered by nighttime allergies, squirt on some hair spray before hitting the sack. The hair spray will help catch some of those pesky pollen particles before they drift into your nose.

Ease asthma attacks. Don't waste money on costly spacer devices for your asthma inhaler. An empty cardboard toilet paper tube works just as well. Just hold the inhaler in one end of the tube, and place the other end against your mouth. This trick comes in handy in a pinch because even if you don't have a spacer, chances are you have some toilet paper.

Clean up carpet pollution. Dust, mites, mold – these things pile up on your carpet, get kicked into the air by your feet, and end up in your lungs. Put your foot down on this cycle of pollution by vacuuming your carpets often. For best results, make sure the bag is airtight and changed regularly.

Don't get your dander up. If you have animal allergies and pets, you know how important it is to keep your home clean. Have a professional clean your air ducts and heating and cooling system at least once each year and install high-energy particle arresting (HEPA) filters. Ask a nonallergic person to vacuum your house every week using HEPA vacuum cleaner bags. Choose washable rugs and slipcovers for furniture, whenever possible, and wash them often.

Tame the savage yeast. It's alive! Alive! Although baker's yeast isn't as frightening as Frankenstein's monster, it is a live organism. Make sure you wash your hands after baking bread or else you could be at risk for a yeast infection.

Face it – hemorrhoid cream works. You know certain creams can help relieve the itching, burning, and swelling of hemorrhoids. But hemorrhoid cream can also be used on your face to fight wrinkles, puffy eyes, and a saggy jaw line. Give this unusual treatment a try. Just be careful not to get any in your eyes.

Cool hemorrhoids with vinegar. If your hemorrhoids flare up, you might not have time to drive to the store for some special ointment. Soothe the itching and burning with something out of your kitchen – apple cider vinegar. Just soak a cotton ball with apple cider vinegar and dab it where you need relief. If the vinegar stings, use a half-vinegar, half-water mixture instead.

Focus on bifocals' beginning

How's this for foresight? Way back in 1784, Ben Franklin invented the first pair of bifocals. He combined the glass for nearsightedness with the glass for farsightedness and cut the glass to fit in one frame.

Guard your glasses with nail polish. Nobody wants to go around with a screw loose – especially when it's holding the lens of your eyeglasses in place. After you tighten a loose screw on your spectacles, dab some clear nail polish on it. It will stay tight longer.

Clean your glasses the scratch-free way. Without your eyeglasses, you probably wouldn't get very far. Don't you think you should treat them a little kinder? If you just wipe your lenses with a tissue, they're likely to get scratched by dust, grit, or the tissue fibers. Instead, always wet your lenses before you clean them. Use warm, soapy water and wipe them with a clean, cotton cloth.

Stop spectacle streaks with alcohol. It's not exactly magic, but it's close. Next time you need to clean your eyeglasses, try using some rubbing alcohol and a soft, cotton cloth. Presto! The rubbing alcohol will dry almost instantly – and make any streaks and fog disappear.

Rx for scratched glasses. Seeing the world through rose-colored glasses might be fun, but looking through scratched glasses is anything but. If your plastic lenses are scratched, make them like new again with Pledge furniture polish. Just spray the furniture polish on both sides of the lenses, gently rub it in, and wipe with a soft cloth.

Save money and clean your glasses. Here's a tip that's right on the money. Use a dollar bill – or a $5, $10, or $20 bill – to clean your eyeglasses or sunglasses. It will pay off in the form of clear, streak-free lenses.

Find lost contacts easily. It's a contact wearer's worst nightmare – one of your contact lenses falls out of your eye and onto the floor. Instead of groping blindly for it, take a piece of bread and dab it on the floor. The lens will stick to the bread, and it won't get scratched.

Vacuum to find lost contact. Your contact lens could be anywhere on the rug. Hunt it down with a vacuum cleaner and some old stockings. Just securely fasten a piece of the stocking over the vacuum cleaner hose, and run the vacuum over the rug. Your contact lens – or any other small, missing objects – will be caught by the fabric on the end of the hose.

Dry up swimmer's ear with vinegar. When you have "swimmer's ear," water is trapped in your ear canal. Often, water brings with it bacteria or fungi, which grow and infect your ear. The next time you get water in your ear, let vinegar come to the rescue. Mix one part vinegar to five parts lukewarm water, and put several drops of the mixture in your ear three times a day. This will kill the bacteria and fungi and rinse out your ear before it has a chance to become infected.

Quick tips for beautiful hair

Dry shampoo	Corn starch or baby powder sprinkled in and brushed out
Hair conditioner	1/4 cup mayonnaise and half an avocado for 5-10 minutes
Hair conditioner	Warm olive oil massaged in, wrapped in warm towel for 20 minutes
Hair highlights	Paste of alum and honey in sun for 45 minutes
Hair rinse	1 tablespoon lemon juice and 1 gallon water
Hair rinse	1/2 cup apple cider vinegar and 2 cups warm water
Hair rinse	Cold, black coffee
Hair rinse for chlorine	6-8 aspirin in 1 glass warm water for 10 minutes
Hair rinse for chlorine	Tomato juice for 2 minutes

Clever cost cutters for
clothing care

Shop 90210 for used treasure. To find the best brands and latest styles at consignment shops, head for the wealthier zip codes. People with high incomes upgrade their wardrobes more often and will trade in many gently-worn, designer labels for you to choose from.

Turn one dress into four. If you can only buy one or two good dresses, choose a classic style in a dark color. A brightly colored outfit will be remembered, but a dark one can be jazzed up with accessories to look special each time. Add a bright silk scarf, a belt, unique jewelry, or a jacket, and you'll look well dressed on every occasion.

Maximize your wardrobe. You can appear to have a much larger wardrobe if you build it around one or two darker, neutral colors. Black, gray, navy, or brown make good choices. Put together an outfit of similar hues – such as all grays and blacks – for a super-sophisticated look. But don't think you can't have variety. Liven up your neutral tones with splashes of color in scarves, blouses, and accessories.

The magic of nylon

Nylon was unknown until World War II when it was developed for use in parachutes, flak vests, and other military equipment. But because supplies were limited, the public had to wait until after the war to get their hands on this magical material. Stronger yet lighter than natural fibers, nylon opened up a whole new world of possibilities. These days, nylon is everywhere – in clothing, stockings, tents, kites, luggage, carpeting, and a host of other products.

Buy dress shirts that fit well. To look good under a suit, you need to buy men's dress shirts according to neck and sleeve measurements. But don't assume you know your husband's shirt size. Although his sleeve length is unlikely to change, his neck size will. Men can bulk up their necks quickly with certain exercises, and a weight loss or gain will also alter those measurements. So measure first, or take him along to try before buying.

Know an oxford from a pinpoint

Oxford, broadcloth, pinpoint. What does it all mean? When you're a man shopping for a dress shirt, these terms can be confusing. Here's the scoop. An oxford is made out of heavy, textured material, and it will stand up to a lot of use. It goes well with casual, textured sports coats, but because of its weight, it doesn't work well with suits made of fine fabrics. Broadcloth is a smooth, lightweight fabric that looks sharp under any suit or sports coat. A pinpoint's weight and texture are somewhere in between.

Be wary of fads. Those outfits you bought in the latest colors and styles last year seemed like a great idea, but now they look silly. Buy classic styles instead of fads, and you'll be a hit on the runway season after season for a lot less money.

Balance your clothing budget. Spend the bulk of your wardrobe budget on items you'll use frequently, like a well-made coat, and scrimp on those that will only get occasional use, like a fancy dress.

Latch onto a lined jacket. To top off a great outfit with a great jacket, choose one with a lining over one without. A lining will make a jacket hang smartly and wear better in the long run. You might have to pay a bit more for it, but you'll be paid back in compliments.

Save a fortune on your wedding dress. Take a chunk out of the cost of your wedding by buying a "pre-owned" or antique wedding dress. After all, you're supposed to wear something old, new, borrowed, and blue. Look in upscale thrift shops and watch for ads in newspapers. When you find a beauty in your size, buy matching shoes and borrow some elegant jewelry. You're on your own for something blue.

Tuck a tuxedo into your closet. Have you always thought only rich people owned tuxedos? Think again. Good businessmen know they'll save money by buying fancy duds, even if they wear them only once a year. To really save money, look for a tux in a consignment shop. Chances are good you'll pay less than the cost of renting a tuxedo. Or ask about buying a slightly used one from a tuxedo rental store. While you're at it, ask about a shirt, a bow tie, and a cummerbund, too.

Measure a shirt with a jacket. Your husband is in the market for new dress shirts, but he's not sure how long the sleeves should be. Tell him to bring along a suit jacket that fits well and to try on shirts with the jacket. The right fit should extend about a half inch past the jacket sleeve.

Buying a belt that fits. Your husband's waist measures 34 inches, so that must be his belt size, right? Wrong. His belt must go around both his shirt and pants, and allow for a little breathing room. Always buy the next size offered. Since belts come in even sizes only, he'll need a 36-inch belt.

Clean your jewelry for pennies. Why spend a lot of money on jewelry cleaner when you can make your own for pennies? Mix half a cup of ammonia with a cup of warm water and let your jewelry soak in it for about 15 minutes. Rub the jewelry with a soft cloth, then rinse with warm water. Dry on a clean linen towel or pillowcase. Pearls are too delicate for this cleaner. You can clean them gently with mild soap and water. Rinse and let dry.

Turn back time on an old watch. You can make an old, scratched watch look new again by getting rid of the scratches. Using a cotton swab, gently spread a little nail polish remover on the face of the watch. Keep rubbing, and the scratches will disappear in no time.

Polish silver jewelry with toothpaste. Don't bother with expensive cleaners for your silver jewelry. You have something at home that will work just as well – white toothpaste. Just dab a little on your silver, rub, and rinse with warm water. If that doesn't make your jewelry sparkle, try some baking soda made into a paste with a bit of water. Rub the mixture on your jewelry with a soft cloth, rinse, and pat dry.

Make gold jewelry glow. Make your real gold jewelry shine like new by washing it in warm, sudsy water. Gently nudge dirt from ridges and grooves with a soft toothbrush. Rinse with cool water, then rub dry with a soft cloth.

Shine silver with care. Be careful cleaning your silver jewelry. Don't try polishing it with tissues or cleaners containing chlorine. Use only felt or special cloths made for cleaning silver. Some day, your children will be glad you took such good care of it.

Keep your diamonds clean and safe. The next time you scrub your bathroom, don't wear your diamond ring. Chlorine-based cleaners can damage your beautiful gem, and it could get dirty and grimy. So leave it in your jewelry box when you're doing housework. If you need to clean it, use a bit of ammonia in water to make it sparkle again.

Treat your pearls like treasure. If you're lucky enough to own cultured pearls – the real thing – take good care of them. These natural treasures can be easily scratched by other jewelry, such as diamonds. Store pearls in velvet or silk, and clean them occasionally with gentle soap and water. Experts recommend you have your pearls restrung every year by a jeweler.

Keep gold jewelry out of the pool. That gold chain looks great on your tanned skin, but for heaven's sake, don't wear it into the pool. Even though you won't notice it right away, in time, chlorine can damage the precious metal.

Remove jewelry before bed. No matter how tired you are after a party, don't go to sleep wearing your jewelry. Not only can you break an expensive chain or twist an earring out of shape, you can also injure yourself by getting poked with metal or choked on a necklace.

Listen to your pearls. Wondering if your pearls are coming loose? Gently tap them one at a time, while holding the string up to your ear. If you hear one that sounds different from the others, it may be time to see a jeweler.

Watch the battery on your watch. It's great not having to wind watches anymore, since the typical quartz watch battery will run for about two years. But when batteries run out, they sometimes leak acid and ruin the watch. Your best bet is to have a jeweler replace the battery before it dies. If you have a watch with several functions, like games and a calculator, your battery might wear out much sooner. Have it replaced every six months to be safe.

Fasten a bracelet with ease. Do you feel like a dog chasing its tail when you try to fasten a bracelet? Save time and avoid frustration by anchoring one end of the bracelet to your wrist with a piece of tape. Then you can calmly and leisurely find and fasten the clasp.

Protect costume jewelry from tarnish. You could probably keep your costume jewelry from tarnishing if you kept it in an airtight vault and only wore it on rare occasions. But that might be a little extreme for inexpensive baubles. Try this instead. Add a piece of white chalk to your jewelry box. It should keep tarnishing to a minimum.

Say goodbye to drab white shoes

Warm weather is coming, and you're itching to wear your white shoes again. To get them ready, rub your shoes with a raw potato or rubbing alcohol before you attack them with white shoe polish. Then crumple a piece of wax paper and buff them. Once the polish dries, spray them with a touch of hair spray. No one's shoes will look quite as dazzling as yours.

Slip on whiter sneakers. New, white, canvas shoes sure look spiffy – for the first day or two. To keep that new look, spray them with plenty of starch.

Baby your white tennis shoes. If your white canvas shoes look a little tired between washings, sprinkle some baby powder on them. They'll look whiter and smell good, too.

Perk up tired white sneakers. Whitewall tires get spattered with dirt every day, but whitewall cleaner makes them look good as new. Why not try some whitewall cleaner on your white sneakers? Spray a bit on your shoes and rub it in with a small brush. Repeat if necessary. Now you and your tires can look sharp.

Restore scuffed shoes. Do your light-colored, patent leather pumps have scuff marks that make them look old? You can restore them to their former glory with a bit of baking soda. Just rub a little onto the marks and watch scuffs disappear.

Don't scuffle with scuff marks. Don't let scuff marks ruin the look of your white leather shoes or ice skates. Dab a little nail polish remover on a clean, soft cloth, and rub off the scuff marks.

Give painful blisters the boot. Ouch. New shoes and boots never feel as good as old ones. If you have a new pair that are giving you blisters, try stuffing the toes with crumpled newspaper. Pack it in as tightly as possible, and your foot won't move enough to cause a blister.

Untying is 'knot' complicated. Are you tied up in knots over a tangled shoelace? To help untie a stubborn knot, sprinkle it with cornstarch. You should be able to loosen it easily.

Hold up your boots with a bottle. No need to keep tripping on those tall boots slumped over in your closet. Just place an empty, one or two-liter, plastic soda bottle in each boot. They will stand at attention without the cost of expensive wooden inserts to keep them upright.

Log miles on all your shoes. Keep your shoes looking good by giving them equal time. A favorite pair will wear out quickly if you don them every day. But if you wear several pairs each week, they'll all last longer.

Boot road salt from shoes. Don't wander around all winter with those white rings of road salt stuck to your leather boots and shoes. Mix a small batch of equal parts water and vinegar and wipe the salt away with a cloth.

Put your best foot forward. Go ahead and buy good shoes – the ones that cost more, look great, and fit best. They'll make everything you wear look a little better, and you'll feel more confident.

Restore rope-trimmed shoes. Have you stopped wearing your rope-trimmed dress shoes because the rope is yellowed or dirty? You can restore your shoes to their former glory by cleaning the rope with a toothbrush dipped in carpet shampoo.

Keep a spare pair at your office. If you wear sneakers to and from work because you have to walk several blocks, leave a pair of versatile dress shoes at your office. Why chance forgetting to bring your shoes on a day you really need to look great?

Tame untied shoelaces. If your shoelaces untie themselves no matter what you do, there's an easy solution. Spray a bit of water on them and tie them while they're still wet. The bow will dry in that position and stay put.

Help sneakers resist soiling. Your freshly washed sneakers will stay white longer if you coat them with spray starch before you wear them.

Make shoe odor yesterday's news. Extra! Extra! Read all about it! Newspapers can help get rid of unpleasant odors in shoes and boots. Just crumple up newspapers, shove them in the offending footwear, and let the newspaper absorb the odors. When you put shoes away for the winter, stuff the toes with newspaper so they'll smell fresher when spring comes around.

Rebuff scuffs with olive oil. Never mind that you're out of shoe polish. Don't run out the door with those scuffed, leather shoes. Just pour some olive oil on a soft cloth and buff. You'll be on your way in no time with great-looking shoes.

Sneak cat litter into your sneakers. When you take off your sneakers, do people rush to open windows? You can combat stinky tennis shoes with cat litter and knee-highs. Pour some cat litter into knee-high stockings, add a bit of scented powder, and leave them in your shoes overnight. Better still, place these in your sneakers whenever you're not wearing them, and the odor will soon disappear.

Treat your feet to shoes that fit

Walking is a great way to get out of the house and get some exercise. Unfortunately, a short trek can seem like a marathon if your shoes aren't comfortable. Experts offer three keys to finding the perfect pair. The first is flexibility. You should be able to bend and twist them with your hands. The second is flatness. That means no high heels, ladies. Last, but not least, is size. Your walking shoes should be one-and-a-half sizes bigger than your dress shoes, since your feet will swell after you've walked for a while.

Take a shine to new shoes. Want your new shoes to keep looking new long after you take them out of the box? Wipe them off, then coat them with a clear, cream polish before you wear them. You'll add an extra barrier against scuff marks, while moisturizing the leather.

Prolong the life of old leather. You can make old, scratched-up leather belts, shoes, and purses look great again with a permanent marker. Find a matching color and simply mark over the worn spots.

Clean patent leather with milk. To get rid of fingerprints on patent leather purses or shoes, dab on a little milk. When it dries, buff with a soft cloth. Your shoes and purse will look new again.

Clean satin with bread. Did you get a bit of dirt on your light-colored satin dress shoes last night? Don't despair. Use a piece of day-old white bread to gently coax the smudge mark off the shoe. This trick will work on your matching satin purse, too.

Scavenge clothes before discarding. Before you toss that old dress that's falling apart, give it a good look. Does it have pretty buttons you could use to spruce up another outfit? Save anything of value, including the cloth, which might look nice in your next quilt.

Exchange discards for treasures. Want to know your neighbors better and get rid of clothes and accessories you don't want? Plan a neighborhood exchange. Everybody drags outside all the stuff they no longer wear. As neighbors wander around socializing and looking for treasures, the discards disappear from yards like magic. To make the most of the day, donate the leftovers to charity.

Dress down for the hairdresser. Wear an old shirt when you have your hair permed or colored so the dyes and chemicals won't ruin your good clothes. Even the fumes from some of these products can damage your clothing.

Make worn-out shirts wearable. Does your husband always wear out the cuffs on his good shirts, making them unfit for the office? Don't throw them out. Recycle them for summer. Cut the sleeves off just above the elbows and hem them.

Get the shine out of worn pants. Are your pants getting a little shiny in the knees? You can get some extra wear out of them with a mixture of one teaspoon of ammonia in a cup of cold water. Sponge it on the knee area of the pants, then press with a steam iron.

Make play clothes work harder. Do your kids wear out their play clothes before they outgrow them? To make them last longer, iron patches on the inside of their pants at knee level. If you put the patches on before the pants are even worn, they'll last a lot longer.

Air your dirty laundry. For longer-lasting clothes, turn them inside out and let them air for a while before you throw them in a hamper. If you don't, perspiration could cause mildew, which can stain your clothes.

Sponge away lint. Have you ever been on your way to a meeting when you noticed your wool suit was covered with lint? You can avoid looking scruffy by keeping a small cellulose sponge in your purse or briefcase. Gently brush your suit with the dry sponge, and the lint will leap off the wool and onto the cellulose.

The story of pant cuffs

The cuffs on your pants have a rather humble beginning. Many working class men in England turned up their pant legs to keep them out of the mud. Tennis players also did this for practical reasons. But in the late 1800s, men from the English royal family started turning up their trousers, too, and the general public decided to get in on the act. Soon tailors began to add them to pants, and they are still popular today.

Fashion your own skirt hangers. Make your own skirt hangers with clothespins and wire coat hangers. You'll save a small fortune and keep your skirts neatly stored.

Keep dresses from slip-sliding away. Stop your dresses from sliding off their hangers and landing in a heap in your closet. Wrap rubber bands around each arm of the hanger, and your dress straps will have something to hang onto.

Make long dresses fit in your closet. Do your full-length dresses tend to lounge all over the floor of your closet? Don't leave them there to be stepped on. Sew small loops of fabric into the inside waist area.

Now you can turn the dress inside out, flip the top part into the skirt, and hang the dress neatly from the loops.

Make your own pants hangers.
Here's yet another ingenious use for a cardboard paper towel tube. If you don't have fancy hangers for your slacks, cut lengthwise down the cardboard tube and slip it over a regular hanger. Your slacks will rest nicely on the tube instead of wrinkling or having a crease at the knees.

Chase mildew from your closet. If you live in a humid climate, or have a closet connected to your bathroom, the constant moisture could cause your clothes to mildew. But that's an easy problem. Install a light fixture in your closet, screw in a 40- or 60-watt bulb, and turn it on for a short time each day. Don't leave it on all the time, or your clothes might start to fade.

'Can' moisture in closets. Don't let your closets become damp or moldy. Put charcoal in coffee cans, punch some holes in the plastic lids, and put one in each closet. The charcoal will absorb moisture, keeping your clothes and possessions dry.

Repel moths, not friends. Moths hate mothballs, but so do people. So why not protect your clothes with something that smells good to people, but bad to moths – cloves. Put this spicy sweet alternative in the pockets of wool coats while storing them. You can also make a moth repellent for your closet by putting some cloves in cheesecloth. Sew it up and hang it with your clothes. Your closet will have a pleasant scent, but moths won't bother to visit.

Don't hang an innocent sweater. Avoid hanging your sweaters in the closet. The sweater's own weight will stretch it out of shape. Instead, lay white tissue paper between folds and keep them in a sweater box. If sweaters are stacked, put the heaviest ones on the bottom of the pile and lightweight ones on top.

Protect your clothes from cedar chips. If you scare moths away from your closet with cedar chips, be sure the chips don't come in contact with your clothes. Cedar chips can cause clothing to yellow.

Secure slippery slip straps. To keep your silky slip straps from slipping off your shoulders, use a paper clip. Just anchor the slip strap to your bra strap on each side.

Lift blood stains from leather. To remove fresh blood stains from leather, pour a bit of 3 percent hydrogen peroxide on a cotton ball and gently apply it to the stain. The peroxide will bubble, helping to lift the blood from the leather, and you'll be able to wipe it off easily.

Restore worn velvet. Rich velvet looks fabulous until it starts to wear. Shiny patches on elbows and collars can make a beautiful outfit look like a hand-me-down. You can restore velvet by spraying the shiny spots with a mist of water, then brushing against the pile with a clean nail brush.

Make bird droppings take wing. Your last outing in the park with the pigeons turned out like a scene from "The Birds." Now you're left with horrifying stains on your leather coat. Don't scream. Just rub a bit of petroleum jelly on the spot and wipe it off with a soft cloth.

Keep leather and suede out of plastic. Plastic bags are no place for leather, suede, or fine material. Because air can't get through the plastic, leather and suede will dry out, and fabric will begin to yellow and fall apart.

Clean suede with pantyhose. Be careful when brushing suede. If you brush it too vigorously, the suede can become shiny and look worn. Instead, use an old piece of pantyhose to rub the material. The nylon will clean off lint and loose dirt without wearing out the suede.

Unwrap clothes from the cleaners. Don't think you're doing your light-colored clothes a favor by keeping them in the dry cleaner's plastic bag. Over time, moisture in the air can turn the bag – and your shirt – a yellowish color. So remove the plastic as soon as you get your clothes home. If you know you won't be wearing the clothes for some time, cover them with an old pillowcase. Just poke a hole in the top for the hanger.

Air 'clean' between dry clean. If you're like most people, you only wear your church clothes for a few hours. That's why there's no need to spend money on dry cleaning every time you put them on. Just keep them fresh by letting them air out before returning them to your closet.

Recycle dry-cleaning bags. Remove your freshly dry-cleaned dress from the plastic bag and let it air out to remove the chemical smell. But don't throw away the bag. Recycle it by returning it to the cleaners.

Warn dry cleaner about spills. If you spilled a clear beverage on your clothes – even if you can't see a spot – tell the dry cleaner where it is. If it's not removed, it may show up later, especially when heat is applied, and it will be harder to get out.

Save money on clothes and cleaning. Stretch the time between trips to the dry cleaner, and your clothes will last longer. Help them stay fresher looking by brushing often to remove lint and dust. Go over heavier fabrics with a handheld vacuum cleaner.

Steam the wrinkles out of wool. Even no-iron wool slacks occasionally need a touchup, but don't just attack them with your iron. Wool needs moist heat to shed its wrinkles. Use a steam iron on the "wool" setting. In a pinch, you can iron using a damp, clean cloth placed over the wool to create moisture. Choose a cloth in the same color family as the wool so you don't have to deal with lint. Move the cloth as you iron, being careful to lift it as you go.

Freeze creases to make them disappear. If you come across a particularly stubborn crease, wet the fabric, put it in a plastic bag – making sure it's lying flat – and freeze it overnight. The next day, carefully iron the crease and leave it alone for a few hours on your ironing board.

Give static cling the slip. Is static cling making you feel like a giant roll of plastic wrap? Give it the slip by rubbing some hand lotion into your palms, then smoothing it over your pantyhose or under your trouser legs. If you don't like the feeling of lotion on your clothes, try carrying several fabric-softener sheets with you. Rub the sheet under the creeping, clinging material, and watch it settle down.

Strike out pantyhose runs. If you can't wear pantyhose without getting a run, try washing them with a few drops of fabric softener added to the final rinse. The softener strengthens the fibers and keeps them run free longer. Or try soaking them in a bucket or sink of salty water before washing. Add a half cup of salt for each quart of water you use, and let them soak for about 30 minutes.

Walk tall and carry a glue stick. Putting nail polish on pantyhose runs is so "old school." Try the latest brainstorm – a glue stick. Rub the stick over the beginning of a run. It'll stop the run in its tracks and is less sticky than nail polish.

Make your outfit 'scentsational.' Your perfume will make a lasting impression if you dab some on your ironing board before pressing your outfit. As you iron, the perfume will be steamed into your clothing for a mysteriously pleasant scent that lasts all day.

The history of zippers

You probably can't picture life without zippers, but the world got along without them until 1891. And even then, they weren't used for clothes but for things like sleeping bags and luggage. Zippers weren't used in pants until the 1930s when male British royalty made the switch from buttons.

Say 'sew what' to lost buttons. Make an emergency sewing kit for your purse out of an empty dental floss container. Stock it with a few needles, each wrapped with several feet of basic thread colors, and a few average-size buttons. If a button falls off, or a hem unravels, you'll have the situation all sewn up.

Make designer accessories from scraps. Your clothes will look like designer outfits if you save the fabric from shortened skirts and dresses. Fashion the scraps of material into headbands, scarves, and sashes to match or contrast with your outfits.

Put the zip back in your zipper. Don't throw out that jacket or sweater with the broken zipper. You might get a lot more wear out of it. Check to see if the zipper teeth are broken at the bottom only – a common problem. If so, simply stitch a block of thread over the few broken teeth, matching the thread color to the zipper. Your zipper will work just fine, and no one will be the wiser.

Snag a sweater snag. Yikes! Your beautiful new sweater has a loose yarn that is threatening to unravel. Don't sweat it. Use a crochet hook or a bent paper clip to pull the yarn inside the sweater. Once you have it there, secure it to another piece of yarn with a knot.

Anchor a button in seconds. You're on your way out the door when one of the buttons on your shirt falls off. If you don't have time to grab your sewing kit, grab a twist tie instead. Pull the paper coating off, and push each side of the wire through your button and your shirt. Then twist the wires together and flatten them against the inside material. This works best on loosely woven material. Don't forget to replace the wire with thread before you wash the shirt.

Give your zipper a manicure. When frayed threads keep catching in a zipper, you can correct the problem easily. Cut the threads as close as possible without causing the fabric to unravel, and paint over them with clear nail polish. When it dries, your zipper should be back on track.

Keep down jackets fluffed up. You're not doing your down winter jacket any good by cramming it into a box for the off season. Down, pile, and fiberfill must be fluffed to give you the most protection from the cold. Once you crush them, they'll lose some of their ability to keep you warm.

Keep old coats looking new. When storing coats for the winter, be sure to empty all pockets. If a pocket is bulging out with items, storing it that way could cause the fabric to stretch and the coat to look old and worn.

Freshen winter sweaters in minutes. You clean your sweaters before you store them, but by the time winter rolls around again, the smell of mothballs is enough to knock you down. Must you wash them again? The answer is no. Just pop them in the dryer on the fluff cycle for about 20 minutes. Throw in several scented dryer sheets, and you'll replace that awful smell with a pleasant one.

Store seasonal clothes in cedar. Use a well-made cedar trunk to store off-season clothing, especially if you plan to keep the clothes in an attic. A strong cedar trunk will keep away nearly every kind of animal or insect that might have designs on your clothes.

Style yourself tall and thin. Want to look taller and slimmer? You can create that illusion by using darker colors rather than bold ones and matching your stockings to your skirts and shoes. Focus attention on your face by choosing interesting jewelry, scarves, and V-neck tops. And when wearing a jacket, leave it unbuttoned for a loose-fitting look. Before you know it, your friends will be asking if you've lost weight.

Slim your legs with tapered pants. For a casual, slimming look, choose dark, tapered pants and tuck them into the same color ankle boots. You'll look lean and stylish, to boot.

Look taller with fashion sense. To appear taller, don't wear horizontal stripes, wide belts, or chokers. Choose V-neck tops, pendant necklaces, and vertical lines that draw the eye up and down.

Plant pants on your waist. Don't take your fashion cues from Fred Mertz on the old "I Love Lucy" show. He looks like he is being swallowed by his pants because he wears them several inches above his waist. Equally bad is the guy who lets his beer belly hang over his waistband. This actually makes you look heavier and draws attention to your stomach. Wear your pants even with your navel to look your best. You may have to switch pants sizes, but your wife will thank you.

Find the right pleated pants. Pleated pants can make you look thinner if you buy the right size. Find pants that fit without pulling or straining any seams, and choose the type of pleats with the folds facing away from the fly.

Look dashing in everyday clothes. A sharp dresser will line up the right edge of his belt buckle with the outer edge of his fly and his shirt. This creates a strong, solid, vertical line that makes you look tall and dapper.

Suit yourself for swimming. You could just grab the first bathing suit you find in your size. Then again, you might want to try on several styles to find one that flatters your figure and fits well. And make sure it stands up to sitting, squatting, bending, and twisting without riding up.

Save your swimsuit from chlorine. You know how fast bathing suits wear out and lose their color when you swim in chlorinated water. And the manufacturer's instructions to rinse the suit in cool water doesn't address the chlorine problem. But it's easy to remove the nasty chemical from your swimsuit. Many pet stores carry bottles of chlorine remover for use in fish tanks. Use a few drops of the stuff in a clean pail of water and throw your suit in. Then rinse it in the sink with cool water. Your suit will smell fresh and the color will last longer.

Clean your caps and saucers. Good news! Your husband no longer has to walk through a car wash to clean his baseball caps. Just put them in your dishwasher and wash as you would a load of dishes. Unlike the washing machine, which is too rough on a cap, the dishwasher will clean but not change the shape of your husband's favorite head wear.

Hats off to hair combs. Do you have a beautiful hat that looks great when it's not slipping off your head? You can keep your hat right where you want it by sewing a small hair comb to the inside. Get the kind used in wedding veils, and simply attach it to your hair.

Turn office outfit into evening elegant. If you're pressed for time between work and a fancy function, you can go from business dress to evening glamour without running home to change. Go to work wearing a classically simple black dress with matching shoes, and bring a bag of accessories to add when the clock strikes five. Pack an elegant scarf, a fancy pin, a string of pearls, and matching earrings. Touch up your makeup and hair, and you're ready to go.

Tie the perfect tie. Ever wonder how some men get their ties catalog perfect? The trick is to form a hollow just under the knot. Create the space by holding your finger under the knot while tightening it.

Choose a 'smart' tie. If you're a man, put some thought into choosing your tie each day. Pair bold designs and stripes with plainer shirts and suits, and match a solid or patterned tie to a striped shirt. But never, never wear a striped shirt with a striped tie.

Save silk scarves from wrinkles. If you've ever ironed a long, silk scarf, you know it can take a long time. You can avoid this chore by keeping scarves out of drawers where they get crushed. How? Gently attach them to clothes hangers with clothespins. Your scarves will be ready to wear whenever you want one.

Keep your socks inseparable. If you have trouble finding a pair of matching socks every morning, try using the plastic clip from bread bags to link them. Simply clip the cuffs together, and your socks will no longer be lonely for their mates.

Handy hints for
home improvement

Organize projects with an egg carton. It doesn't do any good to take something apart and fix it if you can't put it back together. An empty egg carton provides an egg-cellent solution to this problem. Just number each of the 12 compartments. When you take something apart piece by piece, put each screw, bolt, or part in the matching egg compartment. Place the first set of screws in compartment one, the next group in compartment two, and so on. When you want to put everything back together, start with the compartment you filled last and work your way back to number one.

Mend rug's braids with hot trick. Your braided rug might be falling apart, but that doesn't mean it's ready for the junkyard. Use your hot glue gun to repair it. Seal the gaps by putting hot glue on the edges of the braids and pushing them together. It's a quick and easy way to save money and extend the life of your rug. Be sure to put some wax paper down to protect your floor while you make your repairs.

Repair carpet damage quickly and easily. You need three things to repair burn holes and stains in your carpet – a circular carpet cutter, a can of seam sealer, and double-faced carpet tape. All three are available wherever carpet is sold. To remove the damaged area, twist the cutter back and forth over the stain. Just make sure you don't cut the padding below the carpet. Next, cut a piece of carpet tape to fit the hole and press it down. Using the carpet cutter, cut a piece of carpet from a remnant or out-of-sight section of your carpet, such as a closet, matching the size of the piece you removed. Squeeze a thin line of seam sealer around the hole, insert the remnant, and press down firmly.

Stop a squeak with a candle. Tired of sliding doors that squeak or drawers that don't budge? Rub the runners with a candle for a smooth and silent solution. The same trick works for stubborn windows with aluminum casings. As an added bonus, you can still use the candle when you're done.

Heat your drawer to help it slide. A dresser drawer usually sticks because the wood has gotten wet and expanded. To fix it, you need to dry the wood. Empty the drawer and place a safety light containing a 60-watt incandescent bulb inside. Turn on the light and leave it in the drawer for about 20 minutes. The heat from the bulb will help it slide easily again.

Camouflage floor flaws with a crayon. Fixing a scratch on a wood or vinyl floor is as easy as coloring between the lines. First, match the floor's color with a crayon from your child's collection and melt it in the microwave. Next, pour the liquid wax into the scratch until it blends in smoothly. When the crayon hardens, wax the floor. Nobody will ever know the difference.

Silence squeaky floors like the pros. You can eliminate squeaky floors forever in two easy steps. Start by locating the floor joists. They are usually 16 inches apart and go lengthwise from the back to the front of your house. Next, drill a 1 1/4-inch long number 8 wood screw through the carpeting into the floor joist nearest the squeak. This should fix your squeak, since most of them are caused by the sub-flooring boards rubbing on dried-out joists that have shrunk.

Plan ahead when installing floor. Save leftover material when you install a new floor. It will come in handy when you're confronted with unavoidable repairs. Several yards of flooring or 12 extra tiles should be enough.

Repair vinyl floor with a food grater. To repair a gash in your vinyl floor, find an old scrap piece. Rub it against a food grater until you have a pile of fine dust. Stir this into clear nail polish and use it to fill the hole. You'll be surprised how well it blends in when it dries.

Stop skid marks in their tracks. If you have a pet dish, a table, or anything else that slides around your hardwood floor, make it slide proof with a glue gun. Simply apply the glue all over the bottom of the object and let it dry before turning it upright.

Drill a hole-in-one. Next time you're drilling into sheet metal, make sure to hit your mark. Press on a strip of masking tape where you plan to put the hole. The tape will keep the drill bit from slipping and damaging the metal.

Help your drill see in the dark. Strap a penlight onto your drill using rubber bands or tape. Wherever you drill, you'll be able to see exactly what you're doing.

Depend on your vise for advice. To match a drill bit with a particular bolt shaft or screw, grip the bolt or the screw in a vise. Tighten it carefully but firmly so it stays put. Next, try to fit different size drill bits between the vise jaws. When a bit can't quite fit between the vise, you know you have the right one.

Take the mess out of drilling. Drilling in drywall or plaster can be messy. To catch the dust before it gets all over, tape an empty, plastic bag where you plan to make the hole, and drill into the tape. Chunks of wall and dust will fall into the bag instead of onto your floor.

Tighten knobs with nail polish. Loose knob on your dresser or cabinet? Take the knob off and dip the screws in nail polish. After you screw the knob back on, the nail polish will dry, and the knob won't be loose anymore.

Repair screw holes with tees. If you have screw holes that are too large to hold screws, dip wooden golf tees into carpenter's glue and bang them into the holes. After the glue dries, saw off the part of the tee that's sticking out of the wall.

Tighten a screw with steel wool. If you have holes that are too worn out to hold a screw, add a dab of wood glue to a small piece of steel wool and stuff it in the hole. Let it dry and secure the screw.

Loosen a rusty screw with vinegar. If you have a rusty screw or nut that needs loosening, call on one of these household super heroes – vinegar or hydrogen peroxide. A shot of either one will get the job done.

Pop open a lock with Coke. If you're having a hard time opening a rusty lock, don't throw away hundreds of dollars calling a locksmith. Fix it yourself with a Coca-Cola bubble bath. Just pour Coke or any carbonated drink on the lock, screw, or bolt, and the carbonation will loosen it for you.

Dull your nails to protect wood. When you're hammering nails into molding or other thin piece of wood, you need to be careful you don't split the wood. Just tap the point of the nail a few times with the hammer before you put it into the wood. This will blunt the nail and help it push through the wood, preventing splitting.

Shield wood when pulling nails. To yank out bent nails without worrying about damaging your woodwork, place the brim of an old baseball cap underneath the head of your hammer. The cap will protect the wood.

Keep plywood from splitting. Attach a piece of masking tape to the spot where you plan to saw through plywood. Believe it or not, the tape will keep the wood from splitting when you start cutting.

Give yourself a hand while hammering. If your aim with a hammer is a little rusty, find a fork, a comb, a bobby pin, or a paper clip. They can hold the nail in place instead of your fingers.

Personalize your putty. For your next woodworking project, make wood putty that will match the particular wood you're using. Take a spare piece of wood and sand off a pile of the finest sawdust you can manage. Then whip the sawdust into clear epoxy. You'll have personal putty that could make any carpenter envious.

Scoop up extra glue with a straw. When you're building or repairing a wooden box or drawer, don't let glue pile up in the corners and around the edges. Fold the end of a drinking straw lengthwise and run its V-shaped edge along the seams of the wood. The straw will scoop up the excess glue.

Wipe out old glue with vinegar. To remove old glue without a fight, wet a rag with vinegar and let it sit on the sticky spot overnight. In the morning, the glue will wipe right off.

Keep your caulk handy. If you're in the midst of a multi-day caulking project, you don't need to recap the tube after each use. Just leave a small dab of excess caulk at the tip of the tube. It will harden and seal the tube shut. The next time you need it, just flick off the hardened caulk. If you plan to store the caulk for longer than several days, it's best to use the cap.

Grab a straw to help you caulk. A bendable straw can help you caulk hard-to-reach spots. Tape the straw to the tip of your caulking gun, aim it where you want it to go, and give it a good squeeze.

Smooth your caulk with ice. Instead of getting excess caulk all over a rag or your hands, use an ice cube to wipe it away. The ice will also make your caulk lines look neat.

Squeeze out every drop of caulk. Your caulk gun can't get out all of the caulk because the plunger doesn't extend far enough. Save this caulk from being wasted by building a super plunger. First, cut a section of dowel that's 1 1/4 inches in diameter and 3 inches long. Take the caulk tube off the gun, slip the dowel into the tube, and put the tube back on the gun. Now when you pull the plunger, the dowel will push out the rest of the caulk.

Reach new heights in 'elevator' shoes. To give your back and neck a break when you're fixing the ceiling, make yourself a pair of sturdy stilts. First, take two buckets and remove the handles. Turn the buckets over and put old work shoes on the bottom. Drive screws into the soles, through the buckets, and into wood blocks on the insides of the buckets. Now you're ready to get to work.

Pour your own steppingstones. If you have some extra concrete mix and a 5-gallon bucket lying around, you can make your own steppingstones. First, cut off the top of the bucket above the handle. Place the bucket top on plywood and fill it with concrete mix. You can even get creative and set decorative objects in your steppingstones as they dry.

Say 'adios' to concrete stains. Mix one cup of ammonia with one gallon of water and you'll be able to deal with any concrete stain. Just scrub the solution into the stain and rinse off with a hose.

Drive away oil spills with cat litter. To make grease spots disappear from your driveway, cover them with cat litter. If the spots are fresh, the cat litter will soak up most of the oil right away. If the stains are old, pour some paint thinner on the stain and toss on the cat litter. Wait 12 hours then sweep your driveway clean.

Shed light on your electric bill

Save money and electricity by following this simple rule – always turn off lights when they're not in use. You might have heard that turning lights on and off is less cost effective than leaving them on. But it only takes 1/20,000 of a second to turn on a bulb. That barely registers on your meter. So enlighten yourself and stay in the dark.

Choose the right fuse. Replacing a fuse? Before you do, make sure you know the current strength, or amperage, of the old fuse. If you put in a new fuse with amperage that's too low, it will blow out quickly. If you put in one with amperage that's too high, it can't offer the protection it's supposed to provide.

Save yourself from a deadly shock. Before you do electrical work, save yourself a shocking surprise by cutting off the power. If you're not sure which switch to flip in your fuse box, leave a radio on in that room. Turn the volume up so you can hear it from the fuse box. Then turn the fuses off one at a time. When you hear the radio go silent, you'll know you've got the right one.

Make peace with your extension cords. Here's how to connect two extension cords so they can't pull apart by accident. Start by tying them together as if you were making a knot, but don't yank them tight. Just plug them together.

Shed a little light on your project. Make your own movable safety light. Just plug a small, hooded night light into an indoor extension cord.

Change a light bulb with a broomstick. Use your broomstick to help change the bulbs in those hard-to-reach light fixtures. Just take a bulb clip – the kind found in some lampshades – wrap it in electrical tape and tape it to the end of your broomstick.

Follow these 6 top tips for roof replacement. When you're replacing your roof, follow these six top tips to keep dry and secure for many years to come. Always check out your roofing materials to make sure they're dry. Since wet shingles can warp and blister, always return them to the store for dry ones. Make sure your roof is dry before you begin working. Clean off algae from your old roof before you put down new shingles. Use bleach, zinc strips, or an environmentally safe cleanser to do the job. Remove any curled shingle tabs from your old roof with a flat-nosed shovel. This will help your new shingles lie flat. To set up a new drip edge, cut the old shingles so they're about an inch away from the edge of the roof. Always hammer four nails in each shingle – six if you live in a windy area.

Spot roof damage without a ladder. The next time you use your binoculars to bird watch, take a peek at your roof. At least once a year, stand in front of your house with your binoculars and look for damaged, moldy, or missing shingles or tiles. If you see a problem, call a repairman right away.

Rub small jobs the right way. Sandpaper can be too clumsy when you need to work on something small or hard to reach. Try using an emery board to get the job done.

Turn sandpaper into an eraser. Use sandpaper with the pinpoint accuracy of a pencil eraser. Cut out a piece of sandpaper with a hole-puncher and glue it onto the end of a pencil eraser. This will make it easier to sand tight spots.

Mold your sandpaper to fit. Sanding curved molding is tricky work – unless you take advantage of a professional's secret. First, find a deep socket in your toolbox that fits the molding's curves. Wrap your sandpaper around it and sand away. Or try this. Using a hand-saw, saber saw, or band saw, cut a hand-size portion of PVC piping. On both sides of the piping, attach sandpaper with adhesive backing or glue. This will make your sanding job a lot easier.

Grab some sandpaper for perfect spackling. It's important to sand spackle after it dries to make sure it's flat and smooth, like the rest of the wall. That's because spackle shrinks when it dries. Your best bet is to use 150- to 220-grade sandpaper. And don't hesitate to spackle and sand the area again if you're not happy with the results.

Reach new heights with sandpaper. Make a long-handled sander for those high, hard-to-reach places by covering the pad on a sponge mop with sandpaper.

Rejuvenate a sluggish slide. If your kids' slide has lost its zip, try this. Give your children a sheet of wax paper and have them sit on it on their way down the slide. They'll get a fun ride and a faster slide all in one.

Glue wood projects like a professional. When gluing something together, don't make the embarrassing mistake of gluing your project to your workbench. Instead, before you start gluing, slip sheets of wax paper between the project and your bench.

Unstick stubborn doors. Doors that stick can sometimes be fixed by adjusting the hinges. If that doesn't work, stack newspapers on the floor under the edge of the door. The door should just be able to slide over them. On top of the papers, tape a piece of coarse sandpaper. Then move the door back and forth over the sandpaper. Keep sanding the bottom of the door until it can slide smoothly over the floor.

Focus on safety when removing glass. To safely remove a broken window, grab your hammer and roll out the masking tape. With strips of tape, crisscross the window on both sides of the glass. Then gently tap the inner edges of the pane with your hammer. When the pane comes free, peel off the tape and any shards will peel off with it.

Locate wall studs with electric razor. You need to know where the studs are if you're going to hang something on your wall. If you don't have a stud finder, turn on your electric razor and run it over the wall. When it passes over a stud, its tone will change.

Rescue a lazy tape measure. Just like a car, a retractable tape measure needs a lube job every once in a while to keep it running smoothly. But instead of engine oil, rub on a light coat of paste wax or car polish with a soft cloth. That'll get your tape measure back in tiptop shape and protect it from dirt and grease.

Turn your hammer into a handy ruler. To hammer in nails exactly where you need them, make your hammer a handy ruler. Measure 12 inches from the head of the hammer to the handle and mark the spot with colored electrical tape. Then measure a mark 6 to 8 inches from the head. If your handle is long enough, make a 16-inch mark.

Soften your hammer's blow. Hitting a piece of wood with a standard metal hammer can seriously damage the wood. Here's a great solution. Cut an "X" into a tennis ball and slip it on your hammer. If you're not a fan of racquet sports, use a rubber tip for furniture legs. Either way, you'll instantly have a softer and safer hammer.

Wax screws for easier woodworking. Make it easier to put screws into wood by rubbing them across a block of paraffin. And, unlike soap, paraffin doesn't attract moisture so your screws won't rust.

Bench your old hacksaw. An old hacksaw, attached to your workbench with its teeth up and slightly above the edge of the bench, could come in handy for tasks like cutting sandpaper down to size. All you have to do is place the paper on the teeth and pull down.

Change blade angle to battle knots. Wood knots can make sawing a chore. When you hit one, make it easier on yourself by tilting your saw up and down to change the angle of your slice.

Keep your footing when climbing a ladder. Feel safe the next time you climb up your ladder. Attach burlap to the bottom rung and wipe your feet on the way up. You'll be much less likely to slip.

Save steps with an apron. Save yourself trips up and down the ladder by keeping all of your tools in a carpenter's apron that you've tacked or tied to the rung above you.

Figure out ladder safety. Remember this formula if you want to be safe next time you're up on a ladder. Divide the ladder's height by four to figure the farthest distance you can stand your ladder from a wall. So, for instance, you would need to place a 12-foot ladder 3 feet or closer to the wall.

Protect ears from ear protectors. When you're in the middle of a tough sawing project, you don't need hot, sweaty ears bothering you. Unfortunately, that's what happens when you wear hearing protectors for too long. To make the headset cool and comfortable, buy a pair of athletic tube socks. Cut off the feet and slip them over the plastic ear pads. Your ears will love the feel of the cotton, and you will love being able to wash them when they get dirty.

Protect your ears with a baseball cap. Earplugs are a must when you work with blaring power tools. To keep them as close to your ears as possible, attach them to your favorite baseball cap. First, cut a pair of attached earplugs in half and thread the ends of each half through the vent holes in the top of the cap. Hang the earplugs so they're a couple of inches lower than your ears. Fasten the plugs in place with a simple knot. If baseball caps aren't your thing, attach the earplugs to a pair of safety goggles. Just drill holes in the earpieces and slide the earplug string through the hole in each side. Tie a knot in the string so the earplugs hang about 2 inches lower than glasses.

Sharpen your pencil with a chisel. Get a point on your carpenter's pencil using a sharp chisel. Carve four edges into the pencil for the perfect wedge.

Wear your carpenter's pencil. Take away half of a spring-loaded clothespin and attach your carpenter's pencil in its place. Now you can clip your new contraption to your shirt pocket, your sleeve, or your belt. Wherever you put it, your pencil will always be there for you.

Uncover the secret to cleaner hands. Before you start your next project, apply a light coating of shaving cream to your hands. When it's time to clean up, dirt and grime will slide right off.

Beware of treated wood. Wear gloves whenever you are working with treated wood. After following that safety precaution, it's still important to wash up with soap and water before eating and drinking and after you are finished for the day. Your work clothes also need to be washed before you wear them again. To be on the safe side, wash them separately from other clothes.

Banish damp smells with cat litter. Next to a haunted basement, a dank, smelly cellar can be a homeowner's biggest nightmare. To scare away moisture and odor, mix 10 pounds of cat litter with 5 pounds of baking soda. Every week, put about 2 inches of litter in shallow pans and place them around your basement.

Make your workshop seem bigger. If you want an extra countertop in your workshop but don't think you have enough space, think again. Just attach a fold-down table to the wall. When not in use, you won't even notice it. But in a jiffy, it becomes an additional workspace.

Throw your tools in the gutter. Cheap rain gutters make surprising storage bins for strips of molding, lightweight lumber, pipes, and other spare parts lying around your garage or workshop. Cut the gutters the length you need, screw the brackets into the studs, and attach the gutters.

Substitute a ladder for a sawhorse. For a convenient, dependable sawhorse, open a ladder and lay it on its side.

Keep your shop vac in one piece. There's no need to hunt for your shop vacuum cleaner attachments anymore. Apply a piece of Velcro to the attachment and a piece to the vacuum. Put the two together, and they'll always be there when you need them.

Hide your home's imperfections. White liquid correction fluid, the stuff that's helped hide typos for years, can also make your house free of blemishes. Dab a little on white tiles or appliances that are dinged up. Or touch up your white molding. Follow with a coat of clear nail polish if you want a shiny finish.

Shelter your phone from messy hands. Put your cordless phone in a plastic, zip-lock, sandwich bag when you start a messy project. If the phone rings, you won't have to wash your hands before answering it. And don't worry – you'll be able to talk and hear through the plastic.

Do away with indoor pollution. Put a damper on pollution by cutting back on things in your home made of polyester, rubber, vinyl, and plastic. These materials can give off harmful gases, especially when they are in sunlight. Wool carpet and wood mini-blinds, instead of synthetic carpet and plastic blinds, could be a healthy investment.

Defeat dust in your ducts. To keep the air in your house clean, have your air ducts checked for leaks. They should be airtight. If they aren't, they could release dust into the air, even if you clean them often. This is especially important if you live in an older house.

Give treated wood special treatment. Throw out treated wood like you would any other piece of garbage. Just don't burn it, since the heat could release toxic chemicals into the air.

Save yourself from sawdust. Always saw, sand, and drill treated wood outside. That way, you'll inhale as little of the potentially harmful sawdust as possible, and none of it will build up in your house. If you can't avoid working indoors, at least wear a dust mask.

Demolish corrosion with club soda. Fizzle away corrosion with club soda or scour it away with baking soda and water.

Tried & true tricks to
care for tools

Cook up a rust buster. Protect your metal tools, furniture, and other valuables from rust with this simple recipe. In a double boiler, mix one-quarter cup of lanolin with one cup of petroleum jelly and stir over low heat until combined. Cool slightly and pour the mixture into a clean, glass jar. While it's still warm, pour it over the metal and let the mixture dry. Don't wipe it off. Store the left-over mixture in the jar and reheat it when you need it again.

Don't toss a rusty tool. Before you decide to throw away that rusty trowel or other gardening tool, try soaking it overnight in cider vinegar. Wipe away the residue with a cloth, and you may find it's as good as new.

Lengthen the life of your sandpaper. Changes in humidity can damage sandpaper and sanding belts. Protect this equipment by storing it in sealed, plastic bags and containers.

Salvage old sandpaper. Make sure your old sandpaper is really worn out before you throw it out. It might just be clogged, which happens more often than you would think. Try cleaning the sandpaper with a vacuum or rubbing it across the grain with a fine brush.

Store sandpaper in used envelopes. Overnight delivery envelopes can keep your sandpaper safe and flat. Also, many of them have clear plastic pockets on the outside where you can put a sample piece of sandpaper. That way, you'll always know which type of sandpaper you have without digging through the envelope.

Extend the life of your drill bits. Make your drill bits last longer. Use vinegar as the cutting agent when you drill holes in metal.

Hammer together a hammer holder. Make yourself the handiest hammer storage rack on the block. Hammer 2-inch drywall nails into a board and hang it on your shop wall. Use as many nails as you have hammers. Then rest the claw of each hammer on a nail as if you were going to try and pull the nail out. This V-notch will fit onto the nail snugly so you won't have to worry about falling hammers. Plus, your hammers will stick out at easy-to-grab angles.

Rough up your hammer. Don't let wood and metal residue build up on the head of your hammer. Every once in a while, rub it with fine sandpaper. Now your hammer will hit nails head-on, instead of slipping and hurting the wood or the nail.

Wax your saw's teeth. Paste wax can make a handsaw easier to use. Just rub on a light coat before using your saw, and it will slide right through wood. On top of that, the wax will protect your saw's teeth.

Dip ropes to halt raveling. If you're at the end of your rope with ropes that keep unraveling, dip the ends in shellac.

Store tape for easy unrolling. For a convenient place to store rolls of tape, attach a toilet paper holder onto a wall or bench in your workshop. If you have lots of tape, use a paper towel holder.

Hook your wrenches together. Keep track of all your wrenches – both box and combination – with the rings that hold carpet samples together. Unscrew the rings from the samples and slide the wrenches on in size order. They'll be organized, easy to carry, and easy to find.

Cover sharp edges with tennis balls. When it comes to spades, pitchforks, and other sharp tools, play it safe. Cover the sharp edges with old tennis balls.

Give your tools a home. Keep track of your hand tools by storing them on a pegboard on the wall. Around each one, draw an outline with chalk or a marker. That way, you'll know where each tool goes and which ones are missing.

Store tools in a recycled can. A can makes a convenient spot to hang your hand tools. Cut the top and bottom off a can and nail the remaining piece to the wall vertically. Place the handles through the opening of the can.

Take a bite out of tool grime. Toothpaste makes a great cleaner for hand tools. Just rub on the paste with a damp rag. It won't damage cutting edges or leave deposits on the tools. For really heavy grime, like caked-on gels and grease, wear a pair of gloves and use a spray-on cleaner.

Revitalize aging hand tools. To keep your hand tools looking new, wipe their wooden handles with linseed oil. It will keep unvarnished and unpainted handles looking as good as the day you bought them. If the handle is loose, linseed oil can fix that, too. Soaking the handle in the oil will cause it to swell and fit better.

Zap sap from your shears. After trimming trees and bushes all day, it's no wonder your pruning shears are covered with sap. To clean them, dip an old toothbrush in vinegar and scrub the sap away.

Extend the life of your vacuum. Keep your workshop vacuum running smoothly by keeping the filter clean with the help of an old pair of pantyhose. All you need to do is cut off one leg of the pantyhose, wrap the open end over the filter, and secure it with a large rubber band. Then trim off the extra fabric and tie the end closed. Save the other leg as a replacement for the first one when it gets dirty.

Protect your tools from damage. It sounds like something you'd read in *Poor Richard's Almanac*. You store your tools carefully so they'll be in tiptop shape when you need them. Then just when you least expect it, you damage a tool as you're using it. To prevent this from happening, lay a foam mat or a carpet remnant on your workbench for added protection.

Stop looking for a yardstick. To measure your projects easily, attach a yardstick to your workbench. And if you attach the yardstick with keyhole slots, you'll be able to move it where you need it.

See past foggy safety glasses. Safety glasses aren't so safe if they're all fogged up. You can banish the fog by rubbing a thin, even coating of dishwashing soap on the inside of the lenses.

Wipe away hand strain. Some tools, like files and screwdrivers, can be tough on your hands. Protect them by putting an old kitchen sponge between your palms and the handle. It will provide comfortable padding and help you keep your grip if your hands start to sweat.

Get a grip on slippery tools. To give your hand tools a more comfortable grip, wrap flat weatherstripping around their handles.

Helpful hints for
home heating & cooling

> ### Heat up for summer savings
> Want to save up to 25 percent on your next cooling bill? Set your thermostat at 78 degrees instead of 72 degrees in the summer.

Plant trees to chop down utility bills. Take advantage of the natural cycles of trees to lower your utility bills. Plant trees around the south and west sides of your house. In the summer, the shady boughs will keep your house cool. In the winter, the sun will peek through the bare branches and warm up your house.

Give cooler a spot in the shade. You may remember the days when parasols were used to ward off the sun's rays. These popular lacy contraptions kept the ladies beneath them cool and efficient. Do the same favor for the compressor unit on your air conditioner. Rig up a lacy lattice or feathery tree to give it some shade, and it will thank you by working harder for your money.

Draw the curtain on blinds. Layering is the key to conserving energy. Whether you are braving the snow, trekking through the desert, or sitting in your own living room, more is better. Take your windows, for instance. Hanging blinds behind your drapes will increase your protection from heat in the summer and cold in the winter.

Cool your house with a new coat. If you love the winter because your utility bills drop, it's time to improve your cooling system. Paint your house a light color, which will deflect hot sun rays, instead of a dark shade, which will absorb heat. You might also want to put lighter shingles on your roof. Lighten up, and those summer heat waves will roll right over you.

Flip the switch for cool savings. Any light source produces heat. That's why leaving an extra light on puts an extra strain on your air conditioner – and your electric bill. To keep your electric bill under control, turn off any lights you don't need.

Slip between cool sheets. Sometimes the old ways are the best ways. If your cooling system is on the fritz, spray your sheets lightly with water before getting in. Open the windows and let the breezes cool you off. You can always re-mist if you wake up, hot again, in the middle of the night.

Pull the plug on heat loss. Finish sealing your house by insulating your outlets. Turn off all the electricity, remove the face plate, and fill the hole around the socket with fireproof insulation. You may discover, with a shock, that you've just saved a bundle on your heating bills.

Buffer your bed from cold air. Cold air is sneaky. It doesn't just attack from above – it can also creep in from below and the sides. So when you prepare for bed on a chilly night, make sure you put some extra blankets between the bottom sheet and the mattress, as well as on top of you. One surprisingly effective trick is to use a big sheet of Bubble Wrap under your bedspread or quilt to keep warm air in and cold air out.

Put a damper on heat loss. Santa Claus may come in through your chimney, but heat can exit the same way. Keep your damper closed when it's not in use to keep hot air from heading up the chimney. If possible, cover your grate with glass doors to further insulate your house.

Show your thermostat you mean business. If your thermostat seems to have a mind of its own, its connections may be clogged with dust or dirt. To clean it, remove the cover and run a business card through the connectors. With no dirty little excuse, your thermostat should quit its crazy behavior.

Steam away winter's chill. Turn up the heat without touching the thermostat. Just set a pot of water on the stove to simmer. Throw in some cinnamon sticks for a cozy, homey feeling.

> ### Go with the flow when decorating
> Make sure your heating vents are clear. Blocking floor or wall vents with carpets and furniture can leave you with cold corners.

Boot out cold air. Don't tiptoe around drafty doors. Sock it to them. Fill an old tube sock or stocking with sand, rice, or beans, and tie up the loose end. Lay it against a leaky door or window to stop drafts dead in their tracks.

Dodge drafts with wall quilts. Cover drafty windows with a favorite quilt or blanket. Simply tack the blanket to the wall around a window, and stuff a rolled up towel in the window cracks behind it. The quilt will keep you warm and add a soft touch to otherwise stark walls.

Arrange furniture for a lower heating bill. If you're trying to cut costs on your heating bill, check to see if any of your furniture is blocking a heating vent. If a couch or chair is pushed up against a vent, the furnace will keep running as it tries to regulate the room temperature. Arrange furniture away from vents to keep the air circulating and your heating bills low.

Filter out dust. Remove the front panel of your air conditioning unit and take out the filter. Hold it up to the light. If you can't see through it, vacuum it with a brush attachment or replace it with another filter.

Cool down your upstairs. Hot air in your attic will heat up the ceilings of the rooms below and jack up the temperature. To keep your cool, open all the vents in your attic. The hot air trapped under the heated roof tiles will cool, relieving your overworked air conditioning unit. Or install a reversible fan to suck hot air out during the day and blow cool air in at night.

Ban dust from your fan. Dust that collects on the blades of your fan can blow through your house and aggravate your allergies. Be sure to clean the blades once a year with a mixture of one-quarter cup of ammonia and a few drops of liquid dishwashing soap in a bucket of water.

Let in a breath of fresh air. Choose a balmy day to replace the stale air in your house. Open all the windows and doors, turn on the fans, and enjoy the fresh breeze for five to 10 minutes. Remember, it's more energy efficient to change all the air at once than to do it bit by bit.

Outwit air conditioner mold. If your window air conditioner is putting out a moldy odor, its drain hole could be clogged. Unplug it, take off the front panel, and look for the hole underneath the evaporator area. Then poke it clear with a wire hanger or a long bottlebrush.

Uncommon fixes for
plumbing problems

Tie down annoying drips. It's 2 a.m. and you can't sleep because a water drip in the sink is driving you crazy. To keep your sanity until the plumber comes in the morning, tie a 2-foot length of string to the end of your faucet. The drops will run down the thread and silently disappear down the drain.

> ### Don't throw money down the drain
>
> Dripping pipes are not just a nuisance — they are hazardous to your pocketbook. You could be watching 5,000 gallons go down the tubes every year with just one leaky faucet. A running toilet can waste up to 50 gallons of water a day.

Hush dripping faucets. Emergency! Your faucet is dripping and you can't sleep. Try this tip and snooze all you want. Just tie an old washcloth or hand towel around the spout, and go back to bed. You can call the plumber in the morning.

Protect your pipes. Wrap any pipes running through unheated areas of your home with insulating tape. The extra layer will keep them from freezing in the winter. It will also prevent pipe sweats in the summer.

Tape tools to sidestep scratches. Bathroom fittings cost a fortune, but they look great while they stay shiny. To protect the finish on your chrome tap, wrap the tips of pliers and wrenches with electrical tape before taking your faucet apart.

Clamp down on heat loss. Pipe insulation comes in various sizes. Figure out what width you need. Screw an adjustable wrench down until it lightly grips the pipe. Then take it off and measure the distance between the jaws.

Silence squeaky faucets. Does your faucet screech in protest every time you turn the handle? Unscrew the handle from its base and smear petroleum jelly on both threaded sides. The extra lubrication should soothe your grumpy faucet and your aching ears.

Test valve to prevent disaster

The last thing you need when your bathroom is flooding is a rusty shut-off valve that won't budge. To keep the valve in working order, turn your water off and on again once every six months.

Caulk your tub with confidence. Before applying new caulk between your bathtub and the wall, fill the tub with water. The extra weight will expand the sides, giving you a tighter seal and protecting the new caulk from cracking under pressure.

Unclog drains with thrifty threesome. Don't waste money on expensive drain cleaners when this pantry trio clears clogs just as well. Mix a cup of baking soda, a cup of salt, and three-quarters of a cup of white vinegar, and pour the mixture into your congested drain. Let it soak in for about 20 minutes, and rinse with a gallon of boiling water.

Keep your drains spick-and-span. Spic and Span is not just a floor powder – it's also a powerful ally in the war against lingering drain clogs. To conquer your drain, fill it with Spic and Span and pour in a quart of boiling water. Let the powder work for a few minutes, then wash it down the drain with running water.

Release the grease in your drain. Use heat to beat the grease clogging your drain. Boil some water in a large saucepan on the stove. Hold the pot under the drain trap under your sink. Turn on the hot water and keep it running. The greasy goop inside the trap will soften and wash away.

Catch your leak in the act

If you suspect a leak, write down the reading on your water meter before you and your family leave the house for a while. On your way back in the door, check the meter again. If the numbers match up, your pipes are sound. If the numbers differ, you've sprung a leak somewhere.

Unclog drain without toxic chemicals. Clogged drain becoming a pain? Here's the safest solution around. Simply boil a gallon of water, and pour half of it down the drain. Wait five minutes, and pour in the rest. Pour directly into the drain so you don't crack the porcelain basin. Do this once a week. It's the simplest method to keep drains running clean – and it requires no harsh chemicals or hard work.

Sink a brush in your drain. Running a brush through your hair caused the problem. So use a brush to solve it – a bottle brush, that is. Remove matted hair from your drain with this handy bristle wire. Simply plunge and twist to clear the way.

Break up hair clogs with bleach. Dissolve hairy gunk in your drains with a monthly dose of bleach. Carefully pour a cup of bleach down the drain. Five minutes later, rinse with cold water. This treatment will stop clogs before they start. Better yet, pry the cover off your drain and remove most of the hair by hand. Then let the bleach finish the job for you.

Wash without waste. An average 10-minute shower uses 25 gallons of water. To cut down on water use, fit your shower head with a flow restrictor. Most have several different settings, allowing you to enjoy a pounding stream or a gentle spray.

Fix leaks to conquer mildew

Fix plumbing leaks as soon as they happen if you want to keep bacteria, mold, and mildew out of your home. These organisms thrive on moisture.

Camouflage toilet bolts. With the ugly bolts popping out of its base, your toilet looks like Frankenstein's monster. To hide these hideous eyesores, cover them with the rounded caps of roll-on deodorants. You can even look for caps that match the color of your bathroom.

Clear clogs with a coat hanger. Make your own plumber's snake out of a simple coat hanger. Unbend a wire hanger, and sharply fold one end to make a small hook. Lower the hooked end into the drain and poke around until you find the clog. Push and prod until the clump loosens. Then flush the toilet to clear it completely.

Spy on sneaky toilet leaks. You suspect your toilet is leaking, but have no proof. Pour a few drops of red food coloring into the tank, and don't flush the toilet for a few hours. Inspect the bowl for traces of red dye. If telltale evidence appears, "Operation Code Red" was successful. You can now call the plumber to fix the leak.

Break down toilet bowl buildup. Soften your approach to toilet buildup. After flushing, lightly sprinkle half a cup of water softener around the inside rim of your toilet. The softener will eat through the calcium deposits but stop short of the porcelain. For a really stubborn ring, scrub with a pumice stone. Just be careful not to scratch the finish on your toilet.

Bust the rust ring. If your sink seems permanently stained from a dripping faucet, wet a washcloth in a bath of water, dishwashing soap, and ammonia. Lay the cloth on the stain and let it soak in for a few hours. Wipe the stain away to reveal a sparkling sink.

Crisis reminders for flooded bathrooms

When your toilet overflows, don't just reach for the plunger. Turn the shut-off valve on the water pipe clockwise to stop the flow of water into the tank. Next, reach into the holding tank and make sure the rubber seal on the flush valve is closed properly. When the water stops running, use your plunger to unclog the drain.

Super secrets for
car care & repair

Repel rain from your windshield. Rain, rain, go away. Dump some baking soda on a damp rag and wipe your windshield. It will keep rain from collecting on it.

Fight windshield grime with homemade fluid. Keep your windshield clean with a simple, homemade washer fluid. Just add two tablespoons of liquid detergent, three cups of rubbing alcohol, and enough water to fill a clean gallon milk jug.

Pull the plug on windshield bugs. Splat! Your windshield is starting to look like a graveyard for bugs. Get rid of them with some common kitchen items. Squirt a little bit of dish detergent and water on your windshield and scrub it with a mesh onion bag. The mesh won't harm your windshield, but it will scrape off the bugs. When you're done, wipe the windshield with a clean rag.

'Club' grease from your windshield. The trunk of your car probably contains several handy items. Here's one more – a bottle of club soda. You can use it to get grease off your windshield.

Shield your wipers from ice. When your windshield wiper blades get grungy, clean them with rubbing alcohol. You'll get more than just clean wipers – you'll also prevent ice from forming on the blades.

Ward off ice with vinegar. Keep ice off your car during those cold winter months. Before you go to bed, spray a mixture of three parts white vinegar and one part water on your car's windshield and windows. The next morning, your car should be in the clear.

Stamp out icy windshields. If you hate to see your car's windshield covered with ice in the morning, cover it with rubber mats before you go to bed. You'll wake up to an ice-free car.

Patch holes with nail polish. Pebbles and other flying debris can make things rough on your car. You won't believe what you can use to fix a crack in your windshield or window – and you can find it right in your cosmetic bag. To fill small holes in your windshield, simply apply some clear nail polish. It also works for holes in your car's paint job.

Stamp out fog with shampoo. Your windshield keeps fogging up, and you haven't the foggiest idea how to fix it. Just keep a bottle of shampoo and a rag in your car. When your windshield fogs up, squirt a few drops of shampoo onto the rag and wipe the inside of your windshield. The fog will roll away.

Wipe out streaks with ammonia. Smears and streaks on your windshield can hamper your ability to see while you drive. Avoid them by keeping your windshield wipers clean. Get rid of the dirt, sap, and grime by rubbing both sides of each wiper with a rag soaked in ammonia.

Steer clear of streaks. Are your windshield wipers doing more harm than good? If your wipers cause streaks, wash them with a solution of baking soda and water. You'll clearly see the difference.

Erase steamy windows. Go back to school to solve a common car problem. If your windows get steamed up, clear them with a chalkboard eraser. You'll be able to see all the way to the head of the class.

Clear condensation with simple trick. Feeling frustration over condensation? In the winter when condensation forms on the inside of your car windows, turn on the air conditioning along with the heat. Your windows should clear up in no time.

Prevent slams with a tennis ball. Loading up the car for a family trip can be hectic, especially with little children around. Protect little fingers by wedging a tennis ball between the car door and the car. The door will stay open, even if the wind blows or somebody bumps it.

Ace parking with simple trick. You're slowly inching your car into the garage. You pull in a little further ... a little further ... a little further ... and BANG. Your car hits the back wall of the garage. Again. You can stop this from happening. First, park your car exactly where you want it. Then hang a tennis ball from the garage ceiling so it gently rests on your windshield. From now on, when you pull into the garage, you'll know to stop when the tennis ball touches your windshield.

Make use of old oven mitts. Your ratty, old oven mitts might clash with your nice, clean kitchen, but they're perfect for your car. In fact, you can keep them in your trunk. Slip on some oven mitts when you wash your car or fiddle with hot engine parts under the hood.

Reflect on defective headlight. A burned-out headlight can mean more than a ticket from the police. It can also spell danger. Make sure you're visible to other drivers by covering your headlight with reflector tape until you make it to a service station or auto parts store.

Safeguard yourself during nighttime repairs. It's tough enough doing roadside repairs at night without cars whizzing by at top speeds. Help other drivers see you by taking a simple precaution. Wrap some old coffee cans with bright reflector tape and put them in your trunk. When you're stuck alongside the road, set them up like flares.

Address your forgetfulness with labels. You've often been told you'd lose your head if it wasn't screwed on. Imagine what might happen to your car's gas cap. Consider taping an address label to your gas cap in case you accidentally leave it at the gas station. That way, someone can return it to you.

Keep instant rain gear in your car. Don't get caught in a downpour when you're away from home and your raincoat. Keep several 30-gallon plastic trash bags in your car to use as instant rain ponchos. You can customize them easily by tearing a hole in the top for your head, and one on each side for your arms.

Cover all your bases with a cap. Keep a baseball cap in your car. Not only does it advertise for your favorite team, it also keeps rain out of your face and sun off your head. And in a winter emergency, it can help you preserve your body heat.

Smother fires with baking soda. Keep a box of baking soda in your car at all times for emergencies, like a small engine fire. You might want to keep some baking soda in your garage, too.

Turn your hubcap into a hero. When is a hubcap not a hubcap? When you need to dig your car out of sand, mud, or snow, a hubcap makes a pretty good shovel. Or if your radiator needs water and you don't have a bucket, a hubcap will do the trick.

Sock it to hard-working hands. When it comes to your car, your hands often have to perform heroic feats. Whether it's changing a tire or brushing snow off the windows, the task can be rough on exposed hands. Keep a pair of old socks in your trunk, and slip them onto your hands during roadside repairs. Your hands will stay clean and dry.

Take the ordeal out of getting stranded. When cold weather hits, always store the following items in your car trunk or back seat in case of emergency – an extra blanket, gloves, a heavy coat, boots, motor oil, antifreeze, a cell phone, water, and food. And make sure you have enough for everyone who rides with you.

Take action after an accident. Nobody wants to be in an automobile accident. But everybody should know what to do in case you are. Here's a quick rundown of steps to take. First, do not leave the scene. Call for medical help if there are injuries. When a police officer arrives at the scene, get his name and precinct address and ask how to get a copy of the accident report. Keep a notebook in your car to jot down the details of the accident – the date, time, street, city, weather, road conditions, and a description of what happened. Include the speed you were going and the direction you were traveling. Also, make sure to get the names, license plate numbers, and insurance information of the other drivers involved.

Snap photos to recall accident. Picture this – you're involved in a minor traffic accident. Amid all the confusion, you have to sort out the details and remember them. That's why you should keep a disposable camera in your glove compartment. It comes in handy in case you have a fender bender. You can take pictures of the accident scene and the damage to your car. If a picture is worth a thousand words, you'll have plenty to say to the insurance company.

Keep bulging trunk closed with pantyhose. Every once in a while, you need to transport something just a little too big for your trunk. Keep an old pair of pantyhose in your trunk for just such an occasion. You can use them to tie down your trunk during your journey.

Handle car needs with a handbag. Does your trunk seem like one big car-care grab bag? Organize your car stuff in a large handbag or tote. With all the pockets and zippers, it makes a handy, portable storage system. Use it to hold things like jumper cables, flashlights, maps, and scrapers.

Create a new use for an old briefcase. Put your old briefcase back to work. Fill it with tools and store it in the trunk of your car in case of an emergency.

Find a helper on your car's floor. Your floor mats have it easy. They just lie on the floor of your car all day. Next time you get stuck on a patch of ice, put them to work. To get the traction you need, lay a floor mat under your tire. You'll be able to drive off the slippery area, and your floor mat will be able to return to the car floor for a well-earned rest.

Help yourself out of snow. Make use of those old carpet scraps sitting in your basement. Cut them into strips measuring 1 by 4 feet and keep them in your car's trunk. If you get stuck in the snow, just put a strip under each tire.

Slash scraping time with an onion. Avoid the dreaded winter task of scraping by rubbing half an onion all over your windshield. It will help stop ice from forming.

Battle winter elements with sand. Fill plastic milk jugs with dry sand and keep them in your trunk for weight. They're much easier to move than sandbags, and they won't break open and spill. Plus, if you need help getting past a slippery area, you can just sprinkle some of the sand under your tires.

Shake a leg for nifty storage. Can't bear to part with your favorite pair of worn-out blue jeans? You don't have to. Turn one of the denim legs into a sturdy storage bag for those bulky chains you keep in your car's trunk.

Dig yourself out of a snow jam. Think of all the times you wish you had a shovel when your car got stuck in snow. If you don't have room in your trunk for a big snow shovel, buy a child's shovel. It will get your car moving just as well.

Put a bag on frosty mirrors. No garage? No problem. Put plastic bags around your car's side mirrors at night during cold weather. You can hold the bags in place with clothespins. The next day, your mirrors will be clear.

Guard against trouble with monthly checks. You know the basics of car maintenance – change your oil every 3,000 miles and get regular tune-ups, usually every 30,000 miles. But you can do a little bit more to keep your car running smoothly. Stay on top of things by making a few monthly checks. Fill your car's fluids, such as the oil, coolant, brake fluid, windshield washer fluid, transmission fluid, and power-steering fluid. Check the pressure in your tires, including the spare, and look for any leaks on the engine or under the car. With this monthly plan, it will be a lot harder for car trouble to sneak up on you.

Head for the open road. Too much stop-and-go city driving isn't good for your car's electrical system. Treat your car to a weekly 20- or 30-minute jaunt on the highway. That should be enough to give the charging system a boost.

Don't forget the dipstick. Quite simply, your engine needs oil. Check your oil every two weeks or whenever you fill up your car with gas. If you change your own oil, catch it in a clean, plastic milk jug and take it to a local service station or recycling center.

Put a lid on it. Your car needed some oil, but you didn't need to use the whole can. Save the rest by covering the can of motor oil with a one-pound coffee can lid.

Fashion a handy holder for car fluids. Next time your family orders takeout, save the cardboard multiple-drink carrier the restaurant gives you. Reinforce the bottom with some tape. Then use the pockets of the carrier to hold your bottles of oil or transmission fluid. It will keep them from sliding around in your trunk when you make sharp turns.

Use oven cleaner on whitewalls. Put the white back in your whitewall tires. Simply spray them with oven cleaner, hose them off, and admire.

Increase your gas mileage for free. Get 5 to 10 more miles per gallon when you drive. Just check your car's tire pressure frequently. Underinflated tires increase resistance, which causes your tires to wear out quicker and your car to consume more gas. Try to keep your tires filled to the recommended level. It's a cheap and easy way to improve your mileage. While you're at it, make sure you get regular tune-ups for your engine, too. A misfiring spark plug can lower your gas mileage by 30 percent.

Brush up on wheel polishing. This will make you smile. The same stuff you use to brighten your teeth does wonders for your car's chrome or aluminum wheels. Instead of buying expensive wheel polish, just use some plain, white toothpaste. Your wheels will sparkle – and they won't get cavities.

Foil dullness with aluminum foil. Make your chrome hubcaps shine again. Crumple up some aluminum foil and rub it on your hubcaps to polish them. If your hubcaps are rusty, you can get rid of the rust by dipping the aluminum foil in cola first.

Help hubcaps find their way home. If one of your hubcaps flies off, chances are you'll never see it again. But if you take one simple precaution, your odds skyrocket. Inside your hubcaps, write your name, address, and phone number in permanent marker. You also might want to include the word "reward." Someone might find your hubcap and return it to you.

Put the brakes on accidents. You might feel safe because your car features anti-lock brakes. But you're not any safer if you don't use them properly. Instead of pumping the brakes, you should push down on the brake pedal firmly and continuously.

Put the brakes on costly repairs. Make sure you change your brake fluid every two or three years or every 30,000 miles. Otherwise, the combination of age and moisture will turn your brake fluid into a dangerous substance that can damage your car's expensive brake components. It's up to you. You can spend a little money on preventive maintenance – or a lot of money on replacement parts.

Get a jump on corrosion with petroleum jelly. Your car won't start, and you need a jump. But your battery posts are so corroded the jumper cables can't get a good connection. Don't be left stranded with corroded battery posts. Prevent corrosion by rubbing petroleum jelly on them.

Bathe your battery with baking soda. Ever take a look at your car battery? Sometimes it's not a pretty sight. Get rid of the corrosion with a mixture of baking soda and water.

Use common cents for car maintenance. Protect your car's battery for only a penny. Just tape a copper penny to the top of your battery. Corrosion will be drawn to the penny and leave your electrodes clean.

Slow down for a safer charge. Take your time recharging your battery. If you do it wrong, you could not only ruin your battery but also damage expensive electronic features, like your car's digital clock.

Check fuses first. Next time you have a problem with your car's electrical system, don't blow a fuse. Check to see if your car did. Fixing the problem might be as simple as replacing a broken or blackened fuse. You might save a great deal of money by not towing your car to your dealer or a garage for repairs.

Jump at junkyard deals. Your car might need a part – but that doesn't mean you have to pay top dollar for a brand new one. Check around at junkyards or salvage yards. You might find a perfectly usable part for a fraction of the cost. Buy it and bring it to your mechanic to install. It takes a little extra effort, but it might be worth it in savings. Not all garages install junkyard parts, so ask before you buy anything.

Help your antenna slide. The music you listen to when you drive may be smooth – but the way your car's antenna pops up is anything but. To help your antenna slide out easier, rub it with wax paper.

Use a straw to thaw frozen lock. Your car door lock is frozen again. Try shouting, "That's the last straw." Then reach for a plastic drinking straw. Blow warm air through the straw directly onto the lock to heat it. Your door will be ready to open in no time. Keep your "last straw" handy during the winter months.

Heat key to beat frozen lock. Thawing a frozen car door lock is simple. Just heat your car key with a cigarette lighter. It will melt the frozen lock within minutes.

Foil frozen locks with all-purpose oil. You've heard of a lube job for your car – but what about for your car doors? Squirt an all-purpose lubricant, like WD-40, into your car's locks to prevent them from freezing. If the lock is already frozen, spray it with lubricant at room temperature to thaw it. Keep bottles of spray lubricant in your home and office, as well as in your trunk. That way, if your trunk lock is frozen, you still have access to some.

Sidestep frozen locks with magnets. Few things cause more frustration than trying to force your car key into a frozen lock, especially when you're shivering all over. Prevent a frozen keyhole in your car's door next time it dips below freezing with a refrigerator magnet. Just stick the magnet over the keyhole, and your car will be ready to go when you are.

Stash spare key behind license plate. It happened again. You locked your keys in the car. Instead of kicking yourself or searching for a coat hanger, have a simple backup plan. Keep an extra car door key behind your license plate. Just unscrew one of the screws that holds your license plate on, slip your key behind the plate, and put the screw back. Make sure the screw goes through the hole in the key as well as the license plate. Now you have an ideal hiding spot. When you need the spare key, loosen the screw with a coin – and there it is.

Discover the 'key' to avoiding a locksmith. Slam! Is there anything louder than the sound of your car door slamming shut with the keys in the ignition? Perhaps your sigh of relief as you remember your spare key. Keep a copy of your car door key in your wallet for just such an emergency.

Take the plunge and eliminate dents. Your car is a little banged up, and you want it fixed. Yet, body work can be expensive, and you don't want to spend a fortune. No problem. You can suction out small dents using a simple toilet plunger.

Bust rust with a screwdriver. If you want to stop your car from rusting, you should go down under. Not to Australia – just underneath your car. Look for drain holes that allow water to drip out and moisture to evaporate. When these holes get plugged up, rust sets in. Poke them with a small screwdriver or wire hanger to open them up again.

Camouflage car scratches with crayons. The paint scratches on your car need to be fixed, but you're short on cash. No problem. Here's an amazing way to get rid of scratches on your car – without spending a cent. Just reach for a box of crayons. Find a crayon that matches the color of your car and rub it on your car to cover the scratches.

KO tar with mayo. During your travels, your car might pick up an unwanted passenger – road tar. Luckily, a common household condiment can take care of that. Just slather some mayonnaise over the tar. Let it sit a few minutes, then wipe it with a clean rag.

Control tar on your car. Tar can put your car in a sticky situation. Get rid of pesky tar by covering it with linseed oil. You can also mix one cup of kerosene with one gallon of water to form a potent tar-removal mixture.

Stop sticky sap with ice. Transporting your Christmas tree on top of your car is a holiday tradition. Unfortunately, so is trying to scrape the tree sap off your vehicle. Here's an easier way to get rid of that sticky stuff. Hold an ice cube on the sap until it hardens. Then peel it off.

Slide bugs off bumper with cooking oil. Bugs getting caught on your bumper and grill? Get rid of them easily with a little spray of cooking oil. Just spray some onto your car's clean bumper and grill. Your next cleanup job will be a snap.

Drive a cool car. Here's a shady way to keep your car cool. Buy a cardboard sunshade. It's cheap, and it keeps the hot sun out of your car's interior. Put one in your windshield and one in your rear window when you park your car. You can find sunshades in all sorts of designs and colors.

Turn on the AC in winter. It's the middle of December. The last thing on your mind is your car's air conditioner. However, you might want to turn it on for 10 minutes or so, just to keep it in shape. If you leave your air conditioner off for too long a stretch, you risk damaging it. That's because the lubricant won't move through the system. Play it safe – run your AC every few weeks all year long.

Remove stubborn decals the easy way. Nail polish remover can remove more than just nail polish. If you need to get rid of an old decal on your windshield, soak it with nail polish remover for a few minutes. Then gently scrape it off with a razor blade.

Give old bumper stickers the heave-ho. That "My other car is a Mercedes" bumper sticker doesn't seem so funny anymore. But it's stuck to your car, and you're stuck with it. Or are you? Rub some cold cream over the sticker and let it soak in. Once it does, you'll be able to peel the sticker right off.

Make decals disappear like magic. Those decals that stubbornly stick to your windshield seem as if they've been attached by magic. Fortunately, you have something even more magical in your kitchen. Just soak a paper towel with white vinegar and lay it on top of the decal. You'll be able to peel it off before you can say "Abracadabra."

Wash your car with a helping hand. You care enough about your car to wash it by hand. But why not make your job a little easier? Make your own special car-washing mitt. Just take two washcloths, put one on top of the other, and sew them together. Leave enough space on one side to slip your hand in between the washcloths, but make your mitt tight enough so it won't slip off when you dunk it in the suds bucket.

Freshen car with laundry detergent. You carry a spare tire in your trunk – but you might want to carry a spare box of laundry detergent, too. Next time you shop for powdered laundry detergent, buy two boxes and keep one in your trunk. It makes a great air freshener for your car.

Extinguish car odors. Even if you don't smoke, you can still make use of your car's ashtrays. Fill them with baking soda to absorb any stale odors.

Expel cigarette smell with ammonia. Nothing lingers like the smell of cigarette smoke. To rid your car of the odor, fill a shallow pan with ammonia and leave it in your car overnight. The next day, take out the pan, roll down the windows, and let your car air out. It'll be smoke free and ready to drive.

Ditch skunk odors with mustard. You drove a little too close to a skunk, and now your car smells like Pepe Le Pew. Get rid of foul skunk odors by dissolving a cup of dried mustard in a bucket of warm water. Then splash the mixture on your tires, wheels, and underbody.

Filter in freshness. Give your car a fresh, pleasant smell. Just slip a dryer sheet in your air filter.

Shine chrome with vinegar and oil. You don't have to spend a fortune to make your car look good. To make chrome shine, clean it with apple cider vinegar, then polish it with baby oil.

Dismiss wax with ammonia. Your car looks great – except for those unsightly wax marks on the trim. To get rid of them, carefully apply some ammonia with a rag.

Coddle cargo with shower power. It's curtains for clanging cargo – literally. Use a spring-loaded shower curtain rod to keep items in the back of your pickup truck from banging all over the place. You can use one rod to secure large items against the back of the passenger compartment or use several rods as dividers throughout the bed of the pickup.

Oil your hands after an oil change. You've probably heard of the health benefits of olive oil. Well, here's another bonus – it helps clean your hands. Keep some olive oil in your garage. After you're done working on your car, pour some olive oil on your hands and rub them together. This should dislodge the grease. Wipe the gunk off with a paper towel, then wash your hands with soap and water.

Battle greasy hands easily. Your car is fixed, but now your hands are a greasy mess. Before you work on your car again, prepare this economical grease remover. Combine one-half cup of vegetable shortening, one-third cup of cornmeal, and one-quarter cup of powdered soap. Keep the mixture in a covered container, and use it whenever you need to get grease off your hands.

Pop goes the oil stain. Your car has certainly left its mark on your driveway. Get rid of those unsightly oil stains with soda pop. Just pour some soda on the stains, then hose them off with water.

Select a safe color for your car

Red or black cars might look snazzy, but they're actually the most dangerous. According to insurance companies, your safest bet is a greenish-yellow car. Other safe colors include cream, yellow, and white. You might not look as cool, but you're less likely to be hit by another vehicle. Light colors stand out from their surroundings better, so they're easier to see and avoid.

See the light during your test drive. When it comes to a test drive, the nighttime is the right time. Make sure you test drive the car you're thinking of buying at night. That way, you won't be left in the dark about any problems with the headlights, dashboard lights, or other things that should light up at night.

Walk away to drive a bargain. Buying a new or used car off the lot? Salespeople admit this simple but powerful secret gets you the lowest price practically every time – just walk away. Your willingness to walk out the door might be your best bargaining chip. Once salespeople realize you're prepared to leave rather than settle for an unreasonable price, they often sweeten the deal.

Sit up straight with a sunroof. Give yourself some more headroom. Order your new car with a sunroof or have one installed on a used car. With a sunroof, you get an extra inch or two. It could mean the difference between a mashed hairdo and a comfortable ride.

Curb car odors with baking soda. Next time you clean the inside of your car, clean more than meets the eye. Sprinkle some baking soda on the seats and carpet before you vacuum. You'll suck out the smell of cigarette smoke and other odors that have seeped into the upholstery.

Oil leather to keep it together. Sometimes you have to baby your car. If your car has leather seats, cover them with a thin coat of baby oil every once in a while. It will help prevent rips and tears.

Replace mats with carpet samples. Here's a really cheap way to replace the floor mats in your car. Instead of buying expensive floor mats, go to your local carpet store and pick up some carpet samples. You might find samples that are just the right size.

Repair tears for less. Don't let a small tear in your car's upholstery make a big rip in your pocketbook. Instead of taking it to the dealer for an expensive repair job, try mending your seat with iron-on patches. You can find them in discount stores or fabric stores. Just look for patches that match your car's interior.

Dust your dashboard with dryer sheets. Looking for an easy way to clean the inside of your car? Wipe down the dashboard, upholstery, and carpets with sheets of fabric softener. When you're done, you can stash a dryer sheet under one of the seats to keep your car smelling fresh.

Toss floor mats in washing machine. Cleaning your car's floor mats might be as simple as tossing them in your washing machine. Just wash them in warm water with a mild detergent. They should come out looking like new. Let the mats air-dry before putting them back in your car.

Switch shoes before you switch gears. You have shoes to match every outfit – but you probably don't stop to think if they're a good match for your car. Certain types of shoes, like high heels, wear holes in your car's carpet. Consider keeping a pair of shoes suitable for driving in your car. And put carpet scraps under the gas and brake pedals to protect your carpet.

Fix your car for free. Don't just shell out money to get your car fixed. Thanks to secret warranties nobody's telling you about, you might be entitled to free auto repairs. Here's how it works.

Secret warranties are a response to a common problem in particular vehicles. For example, maybe the brakes are shoddy or the paint peels in certain models. The manufacturer agrees to fix the problem for free – but doesn't tell the public. The automakers profit from this strategy, because most times, the consumer gets stuck with the bill. Unless you play detective.

At any time, there are at least 500 secret warranties out there. The tricky part is finding them. Because only four states have laws requiring automakers to tell you about secret warranties, you usually have to uncover them on your own. Your best bet is to look for technical service bulletins (TSBs) that deal with the model and year of your vehicle. These documents from the manufacturer let dealers know about common problems with certain cars – and, sometimes, how to fix them. TSBs are available to the public. Just ask your dealer for copies.

Other good sources of help include the Center for Auto Safety, the National Highway Traffic Safety Administration, and the Federal Trade Commission. Also, keep your eyes open for stories in the media or trade magazines about automobile defects.

Remember, these warranties are secret. So they're not going to be called "secret warranties." They might be called "goodwill adjustments" or something similar. But you can find enough evidence to show your dealer that you know a secret warranty exists. The key is to be well-informed and persistent.

Trusty tips & tricks for
painting

Pour over these do's and don'ts. For a professional-
looking job, wait until your first coat dries before applying a second
one. Otherwise, you could end up with a wall that looks like the
back of an alligator. Always clean a surface before you paint it.
Putting paint over a dirty, wet, or greasy spot can cause the paint to
peel. Don't make your coats too thick or the paint will wrinkle when
it dries. Last but not least, only go over a spot once during each coat.
Doubling back with a brush or roller will only mess up the work
you've already done.

ID that old paint. Before you paint old walls, rely on rubbing
alcohol to determine what kind of paint is on them now. Dab the
alcohol on the paint. If the old paint comes off, it's a latex-based
paint. If it stays on, it's an oil-based paint. That's important because
you don't want to put new latex on old oil paint.

Consider the weather when you paint. Oil-based
paint is harder to smooth on in cold weather. Latex is more difficult
to handle when it's hot.

Watch out for rainy days. Wait at least two days after it
rains before painting your house to be sure it's dry.

Prevent spills with a cereal box. Cut a circle out of an
empty cereal box and use it to hold your open paint can. It will protect the can from tips and your floor from drips.

Nail leaky paint can problem. Use a hammer and a
small nail to make six or more holes in the groove around the rim of
your paint can. Instead of running down the side of your can, the
paint will drip back inside.

Slow down for super spackling. The secret to a professional spackling job is smoothing out the spackle before it dries. If

you spackle slowly, you might find this hard to do. However, if you add a little sugar to the spackle, it will dry slower and give you time to do the job right.

Smooth spackle with a sponge. A sponge works just as well as sandpaper to smooth spackle, and it won't kick up dust. Moisten the stiff sponge and rub it firmly into the spackle. When dust builds up on the sponge, brush it off into a garbage pail.

Prepare your new plaster. Before painting over new plaster, you have to cure it. Mix together one pint of vinegar and one gallon of water and apply it to the plaster. Wait until the plaster hardens and then rinse it with plain water. After it air dries, brush or roll on primer, followed by your top coat.

Sand before painting over glossy finish. Before you paint over a glossy finish, lightly sand the area, then wash off the dust with soapy water. Your new paint will stick much better.

Find wall flaws before you paint. A great paint job starts with a good prep job. That means caulking and sanding every hole and crack in your walls. To find them, dim all the lights in the room and shine a bright light against the wall. The play of shadows will help you find the imperfections you didn't see before.

Warm enamel paint for easier spreading. Sit your can of enamel paint in a pot of hot water before you use it. Just like butter, enamel paint spreads more smoothly when it's warm.

Discover new use for old tablecloth. Your old, plastic tablecloth might be too stained for your dining room table, but it would make a great drop cloth the next time you paint.

Encourage your brush to glide. Interior painting will go more quickly if you stir one quart of semigloss latex paint into a gallon of flat latex paint. The finish won't look any different, but your paintbrush will glide more easily.

Keep track of your paint tab. Don't waste paint next time. While you still remember how much paint it took to cover the room you just finished, write it down where you won't lose it. An ideal location is on the wall itself, hidden under a light switch plate.

Shield your trim from paint. Try something new to keep your trim and molding free of paint. Instead of protecting them with tape, get out an old set of Venetian blinds. Cut a few slats free from the strings and fill in the string holes with tape so paint can't sneak through. Hold the slats against the wall where the trim and the wall meet. When too much paint builds up on the slat, toss it and use a fresh one.

Blow away toxic paint fumes. If you have to paint indoors, keep the area as well-ventilated as possible. Open all the windows and doors and turn on fans, including exhaust fans. Avoid painting in the basement since the toxic paint fumes will seep through the rest of your house. Wherever and whenever you paint, buy paint brands labeled "Low VOC," which means they give off the least pollution. Ventilation is even more important if you're a weekend warrior who enjoys a couple of beers while you're painting. Alcohol can make you more susceptible to the harmful effects of paint fumes. Hold off on the alcohol until you're finished for the day.

Splatter-proof eyeglasses with plastic wrap. Protect your glasses from splatters when painting by covering the lenses with plastic wrap.

Sand door edges before painting. Your door could actually get too big for its frame after you repaint it, making it difficult to open and close. To prevent this and keep your door swinging smoothly, sand the edges of the door before you start painting.

Keep hands clean with petroleum jelly. No matter how careful you are when rolling or brushing, paint somehow finds its way onto your hands. If you rub petroleum jelly on your hands before you start painting, the paint will come right off.

> ### Evaluate sunlight when picking colors
>
> The sun brightens a room facing south far more than a room facing north. The rising sun adds a white glow to a room facing east. A room with windows facing west gets the warm, orange light of the setting sun.

Use this trick to choose paint color. When you find a color you like on a paint chip, grab the next paler shade off the shelf. Then you'll have the color you want. This rule works because colors look brighter on large surfaces, like walls, than they do on small paint chips.

Forget old rule about white ceilings. Ceilings don't have to be white. A splash of color can add a lot to a room. An aqua ceiling, for instance, can give the room a relaxed, breezy feel. A peach ceiling can soften the look of a room.

Jazz up your old paint job. Want a new look for a tired room, but your budget is really tight? Invest in just enough paint for a dramatic redo of the molding and trim around doors and windows. Select a shade that contrasts with the wall color.

Mix putty and paint for perfect match. If you need to reputty around your windowpanes, mix the putty with paint to match the windows so you won't have to paint over it.

Test drive your color choice. Before you start painting, try out the paint color on poster board. After it dries, hang it up and look at it from different angles. See what it looks like in natural light and artificial light. If you still like the color, you'll probably like it on your walls.

Explore the many shades of white. Antique, eggshell, starlight – these shades of white can look the same when you compare paint chips in a store. To help you decide, take the paint chips home with you and put them on a white piece of paper. The choice will be easy.

Enhance bright colors with white. The best way to show off a brightly colored room is to paint the trim white.

Enjoy designer colors for less. You fall in love with a new designer color, but the cost of the paint will put you over budget for your decorating job. Ask the salesperson at the paint store if he can make the same color using a cheaper brand. In most cases, he'll be able to mix up a close match.

Mix custom paints for a perfect match. Before you use custom paints, find two clean 5-gallon buckets. Dump all of the paint into one of the buckets. Then pour them back and forth between the two buckets. If you have any paint left over, pour it back into the cans. It's important to mix custom paints like this since the colors can be different from one can to the next.

Brighten the insides of cupboards. Paint the insides of your cupboards a light color. They will reflect light, and you'll be able to see the contents more easily.

Plan ahead for touchups. As soon as you've finished a painting job, write down the color of paint you just used on a piece of masking tape. Attach the tape to the back of an outlet plate before you screw it back on. You'll always have it there for future reference.

Manipulate color for optical illusion

When painting shutters, remember that a dark color — like navy or black — will make your house look smaller. A color closer to the hue of the house will make your house look larger.

Pick the right roller cover. The secret to painting like a professional is the pile, or thickness, of your roller cover. For smoother surfaces, you want a thinner pile. For rougher surfaces, you want the opposite – a thicker pile. The perfect size pile will hold just the right amount of paint.

Soften an old paintbrush with vinegar. To soften a paintbrush that is stiff with old paint, simmer the bristles in vinegar. Then use a wire comb or brush to scrape away the softened paint. After you've cleaned and rinsed the brush, massage a few drops of oil into the bristles to make that softness last.

Revitalize stiff paintbrushes. Oops! Forget to wash your brushes last week after that paint job? If they're stiff, soften them up by washing them in a capful of fabric softener and water.

Straighten out crooked bristles. It's easy to restore the shape of your paintbrush bristles that were left sitting in paint remover. First, soak the bristles in warm water to make them more flexible. Then sandwich them between two thin pieces of wood and secure with a rubber band. In a few days, you can remove the splint, and your bristles will be straight.

Extend the life of your paintbrushes. Here's how you can get the most out of your paintbrushes. Tape pieces of paper cut from a brown paper bag around the bristle ends of the brushes to protect them from dust. Store them flat or hang by the handles to keep the bristles straight.

Carry touchup paint in a handy container. For those times you're doing detail work with a small brush, put your paint in an old coffee mug or a powdered laundry detergent measuring cup. The handle will make it easy to carry around, and it won't be as heavy or messy as a paint can.

Prepare your brush for battle. Wash a new paintbrush before using it so you don't risk loose hairs messing up your paint job. If a stray bristle does fall out, remove it with tweezers while the paint is still wet.

Do away with lint before you paint. New roller covers can leave more than just paint on your walls. They can drop off lint, too. Even rollers that claim to be "lintless" on their wrappers can leave lint behind. Your best bet is to take the lint off the roller before you start painting. Wrap a strip of masking tape around your hand, sticky side up, and roll the cover over your hand a few times. Or wrap up the roller in the tape like a mummy and pull the tape off – and the lint with it.

Blend lap marks for better painting. When rolling paint on your walls, always keep a spare roller cover handy. Use it to blend lap marks, the raised lines of paint left by the edges of the roller you're using.

Don't skimp on paintbrushes

It pays to buy high-quality paintbrushes. In fact, a good brush gets better with use. Try natural bristles with oil-based paints and synthetic ones with water-based paints. Foam brushes are handy for touchups.

Flag the best brushes. When you're buying a new paintbrush, shop for quality with this simple tip. Look for bristles loaded with split ends. Professionals call these "flags," and they help spread paint evenly. Good brushes have half or more of their bristles flagged.

Save money with homemade paint tray. A shallow cardboard box makes a cheap alternative to a store-bought paint tray. Just cover it with a trash bag or aluminum foil.

Tackle tiny paint jobs with tiny brush. The little brush that comes with eye shadow is great for painting tiny areas on your walls and window frames.

Take a step toward better traction. Give your outside concrete steps traction as well as a new color. Mix a handful of clean sand into your paint before you brush it on the stairs. The sand will give your feet the grip they need to keep from slipping.

Swab away painting imperfections. Even if you've done a great paint job, you're likely to find spots that need touching up. Instead of using your big brush, use a cotton swab. You'll save a bucket load of effort and time on cleanup.

Make a paint holder from a laundry jug. A clean 100-ounce plastic laundry detergent jug can make a great paint holder. Just slice off the top two-thirds of the plastic jug and throw out the bottom part. Screw the cap on tightly, turn the jug upside down, and pour in the paint. The wide top makes it ideal for any size brush, while the handle makes carrying it easy. And when you're finished with the job, hold the spout over your paint can and unscrew the cap to return the paint to the can without a mess.

Band together to prevent drips. It is possible to pour paint out of a can without leaving a trail across your floor. Wrap a wide rubber band around the bottom and top of the paint can. The band should stretch across the middle of the can's opening. Then use a ladle to dish out the paint into your roller pan or paint dispenser. Wipe the paint drips from the dipper on the rubber band.

Paint chairs like a master. Painting a chair can be a time-consuming job as you wait for the legs to dry so you can stand it upright. Here's a tip so you can get the job done quickly. Push thumbtacks into the bottom of each leg before you get started. Next, paint the underside and legs of the chair. Now you can flip the chair onto its legs without having to wait for the paint to dry. Paint the top, and you're done. Leave the thumb tacks in the chair to keep the chair legs from scraping your floors.

Avoid mess when painting small objects. When you're painting something small, fasten the object to a piece of cardboard with double-sided tape. That way, you won't have to hold it, and you won't care when paint gets all over the cardboard.

Let cardboard lend a hand. Find yourself a simple piece of cardboard when it's time to paint the pipes that run along your walls. Slip the cardboard between the pipes and your wall. No matter how sloppy you are, the paint will cover the pipes or the cardboard – not the wall.

Unclog your spray paint can. Remove the clogged nozzle from your can of spray paint and soak it in paint thinner or turpentine for a few minutes. Take a straight pin and clear the softened paint from the spray hole and you are ready to paint again.

Take aim with spray paint. For the neatest spray painting you've ever done, find yourself a big old cardboard box, like one that would come with a television or a stereo system. Lay the box on its side and place the object you're going to spray paint in it. The box will act as a shield as you give the object a thorough blasting.

Work wonders with wood paneling. If your wood-paneled walls look dull, or you want a different look, paint them. It's easy to do if the panels are made from wood. If they are plastic or vinyl, the paint won't stick. Test by sanding a small area in an inconspicuous place. Or paint part of a panel and see if the paint sticks.

Adorn your walls with stripes. Here's an easy way to paint stripes on your walls. First, paint the walls with a base coat and let them dry. For the stripes, take a clean, foam paint roller and wrap masking tape tightly around it at intervals – the distance apart that you want your stripes. This will flatten some areas and leave others raised. Now you're ready to paint the stripes using a second color.

Stencil favorite designs like a pro. When stenciling a pattern on your wall, use only a small amount of paint on your brush and paint from the outside edges toward the center.

Apply varnish perfectly. The key to a great varnish finish is the number three. That's the number of times you need to brush each coat. Brush once going along the grain of the wood. Then brush across the grain. Finish by going along the grain again. It might seem like triple the work, but you'll shine with pride when you see the results.

Keep bugs off wet paint. To keep insects from nose diving into your wet paint, add a few drops of citronella oil to your paint can. The citronella will repel the bugs without hurting the look of the paint.

Screen good paint from bad. If you have a spare piece of window screen, use it to get rid of paint lumps and clumps. Cut a circle out of the screen that's just small enough to fit into the paint can. Lay the screen flat in the paint. It will sink to the bottom and trap the lumps underneath it.

Prevent paint spills with a paper plate. Dab a little paint on the bottom rim of your paint can and stick the can on a paper plate. The plate will stop spills, detain dribbles, and round up paint rings before they touch your floor.

Free your window from paint. If you paint your window shut, free it by sliding a utility knife, a spackling blade, or some other sharp, narrow object along the window frame. If that doesn't work, try a 2-by-4. Lay it flat against the window frame and tap it with a hammer. The vibrations should loosen the paint.

Use a paintbrush like an expert. Here's how you can have a steady hand, like a master painter. When painting edges and corners, remember to go slowly, breathe out, and push the brush away from your body. If you pull the brush toward you, your heartbeat could change the movement of the brush. And if you breathe in while brushing, the muscles in your shoulders and rib cage could also affect the brush's movement.

Calculate paint coverage

The amount of coverage you'll get from a gallon of paint will vary, but in general, count on one gallon of paint for every 450 square feet of wall space.

Store leftover paint in a handy jar. Keep some of your leftover paint in a sealable, glass container, like a mayonnaise jar.

The paint will keep better, and you'll be able to get at it without the mess of opening the can.

Mark paint level on the can. Before you close up that paint can for storage, check to see how much paint is left and mark how high it is on the outside of the can. When you need the paint a few months later, you'll know if you have enough for your new project.

Save leftovers for touchups. Always save paint, wallpaper, and fabric left over from your remodeling projects. When you need to do the unavoidable touchup, you'll be able to do it in a jiff.

Store paint cans upside down. Store your paint so it stays fresh and usable for months. Stretch plastic wrap over the top of the can and tap the lid with a hammer to make sure it won't leak. Once you're sure the lid is secure, turn the can upside down. The paint creates a tight seal and keeps the paint like new.

Dispose of unwanted paint safely. There's a better way to get rid of unwanted paint than just tossing it in the garbage – donate it to a local church, recreation center, or theater group. If the paint isn't worth donating, check to see what type of paint it is before disposing of it. Latex paint should be air-dried by dumping it into a paper bag or box and covering it with absorbent material, like cat litter or shredded newspaper. When it's dry, toss away the paint and clean and recycle the paint can. For oil-based paints – and any paint in some states – check with local recycling centers to see how you should dispose of it properly.

Erase paint goof-ups on glass. Instead of hacking at the dried paint on your windows with a dangerous razor blade, remove it safely with a pen eraser.

Soak up carpet spills. Whenever you spill latex paint on your carpet, blend together one tablespoon of liquid dish detergent, one tablespoon of vinegar, and one quart of warm water. Sponge the spill away with this super paint remover.

Cut paint drips out of your carpet. When only a drop or two of paint hits your carpet, hold off on your first impulse – to wipe it up with a rag. Rubbing the stain only makes it bigger. Instead, wait for the drips to dry and cut them out with scissors.

Stick chair legs in bowls to protect floor. Removing old paint with a liquid stripper can be a messy job, and the drips can ruin your floor. Put plastic bowls under the legs of chairs or tables to catch the excess. What's more, you won't waste any stripper since you can use it again.

Wipe away window paint. It's easy to remove old spatters of paint from windows. Just dab on some nail polish remover, leave for a few minutes, and wash off.

Do away with new paint smell. Onion gases neutralize paint fumes. Chop up an onion and put it in a bowl of water. Leave it in the middle of a freshly painted room overnight to remove the fresh paint smell.

Paint tricky objects with a mitt. If you plan to paint a wrought-iron fence, a fancy stair railing, or some other detailed object, ignore your paintbrush and use a painting mitt. To make one, put your hand inside a plastic bag and wrap an old towel around it.

Try a sponge for decorator look. Any time you want to give a room a snazzy, professional-looking paint job, use a sponge instead of a brush.

Shield your phone from paint. Keep a worn, clean washcloth or hand towel by the telephone when you are painting. If it rings, use the cloth to protect the receiver from sticky hand prints.

Be creative when choosing a 'brush.' Cosmetic sponges make great painting tools for detail work and touchups. You can buy them at your local pharmacy or discount store. Use them by themselves or make a slit in the bottom and insert a popsicle stick as a handle.

Swap your paint scraper for a spatula. A metal spatula is actually a better paint scraper than anything you can buy at a paint store. Store-bought paint scrapers have sharp edges. Even if you are careful, they can damage the wood underneath the paint. You'd have to press really hard to do that with a spatula.

Unstick painted surfaces with powder. If you have two painted surfaces that keep sticking together – like a door and its frame – dust them with talcum powder.

Sponge away wall stains. When you're washing dirt or crayon marks off of your painted walls or woodwork, use a sponge – not a rag or a cloth. Rags or cloths can leave behind shiny spots.

Clean walls before repainting. Before repainting your walls, try cleaning them with one of these powerful cleaning solutions. They work so well you might think twice about repainting. Pick either two tablespoons of ammonia, two tablespoons of laundry detergent, or one tablespoon of tri-sodium phosphate and mix it into one gallon of warm – not hot – water. Be careful not to make these mixtures stronger than recommended or you could damage the paint. Work in small sections using a sponge. Then rinse with clean water and absorb moisture with old towels.

Fast fixes for
pesky pests

Prevent ants with peppermint. Raise a stink to get ants out of your house. To an ant, nothing stinks more than peppermint. Squirt some peppermint flavoring or place some peppermint tea bags inside your home where ants seem to enter. Do the same outside your house. The ants will smell that they're not wanted there.

Corner ants with cloves. Ant-proof your kitchen for a whole year. Just put bay leaves or whole cloves in the corners of your cupboard shelves and windowsills. These long-lasting spices will foil any ant invasions.

Keep ants at bay with bay leaves. Bay leaves are great for cooking. But who ever figured they'd ant-proof your pantry, too? Ants can't stand the smell of bay leaves so they'll avoid them at all costs. Crumble some bay leaves on your windowsills to keep ants out of your kitchen. For extra protection, you can also toss a bay leaf or two into your flour or sugar canisters.

Halt ants with salt. It's easy to stop ants. All it takes is some reasoning – and some seasoning. Figure out where ants are entering your house. Then dump a layer of salt in their path. The invading ants will stop and turn back in defeat.

Surprise ants with spices. Set a spicy trap for those black ants roaming through your home. Shake some ground red pepper or curry powder at their point of entry. Chances are, they won't come back any time soon.

Send ants scurrying with cinnamon. Ants hate the smell of cinnamon. But you will love it – and the way it keeps ants out of your kitchen. Just sprinkle some cinnamon where you see ants, and they will turn the other way.

Curtail ants with catnip. The next time ants come marching in, rain on their parade. Simply sprinkle catnip in their path to stop them.

Chalk up a victory over ants. When it comes to ants, you have to draw the line somewhere. Just make sure you draw it with chalk. Some people say ants will not cross a chalk line. So keep ants at bay by drawing a few chalk lines on your floors or countertops.

Plant plants that stop ants. Use your green thumb to squash ants. Plant mint or onion around the foundation of your house to keep ants away. Other plants that thwart ants include spearmint, southernwood, and tansy.

Kill fire ants with Southern hospitality. Make those pesky fire ants feel at home. Feed them a nice helping of instant grits. Just sprinkle some on the fire ant hills in your yard. The ants will nibble on the grits, then seek out water. When that happens, the grits expand inside the ants and kill them. Seconds anyone?

Dampen ants' enthusiasm for pet food. Make your pet feel like the king of the castle. Give it a moat. Set your pet's food dish inside a bigger, shallow dish containing an inch of water. This makeshift moat will keep ants from crawling into your pet's food.

Hide pet's food dish from ants. Why tempt ants? Pick up the dishes of dog food or cat food between meals. If left on the floor, your pets' food dishes make inviting targets for hungry ants.

Stymie ants with vinegar. Make life a little more sour for ants. Splash vinegar around door and window frames, under appliances, and anywhere else you've noticed ants marching. It should deter them.

Abolish ants with ammonia. Ants invade your home all the time. Why not attack theirs? Pour some ammonia down the ant hole in your yard. You'll kill the ants before they have a chance to mount an assault on your house.

Stop ants with slick trick. Prevent ants from crawling all over your hummingbird feeder. Coat the string of the feeder with petroleum jelly, and the ants should slide right off.

Lube feeder tube to thwart ants. The sweet water you feed to the hummingbirds can attract ants as well. To keep the tiny visitors away, put a little bit of olive oil on the tip of the feeder tube. The ants can't get to the liquid so they'll leave it for the humming-birds. They aren't bothered by the oil.

Give ants the slip with baby oil. Next time ants invade your home, don't let it slide. Let them slide instead. Apply baby oil to areas where the ants tend to march. The little pests will have trouble making their way across the slippery surface. Eventually, after you repeat the baby oil trick a few times, the ants will give up and retreat.

Rattle ants with baby powder. Guard your house the gentle way. Simply sprinkle baby powder wherever ants might enter. The baby powder smells good and won't harm children or pets – but it stops ants, who will not crawl through the powder.

Repel ants with a line of flour. Guard your house from an ant invasion. Just make a line of flour anywhere you think ants might enter. It will keep ants outside looking in because they will not cross the line.

Deter ants with dryer sheets. If you let them, ants will get into anything – including the sugary syrup you put in your hummingbird feeder. Put a stop to those antics with a dryer sheet. Wrap the dryer sheet around the feeder's hanger and fasten the ends with either tape or rubber bands. Ants will stay out of the forbidden territory.

Squeeze lemons to control ants. Who says lemons are only good for cooking? They're also great for ant-proofing your kitchen. No insecticides needed. Just squeeze lemon juice in the holes or cracks where ants are getting in. Scatter small slices of lemon peel around the entrance, too. The ants will catch on that they're not wanted. Lemons also help with roaches and fleas. Squeeze four lemons into a half-gallon of water and toss in the rinds. Then rub the mixture on your floors. The pests can't stand the smell, and they will abandon your house.

Banish ants with an orange smoothie. This powerful recipe will send ants scurrying out of your yard. In your blender, combine orange peels and water until smooth. Then pour this mixture on an anthill early in the morning, before the ants leave their nest. You can also use hot chili peppers instead of orange peels.

Spice up your boat to fight barnacles. If your boat has become a barnacle magnet, try this simple trick. Next time you paint the hull of your boat, mix plenty of cayenne pepper with the paint. Barnacles will find some other boat to cling to.

Open windows to make a bat scat. If you have a bat in your house, don't worry. You should be able to get rid of it fairly easily. Just before dark, open all the windows and any doors that lead outside. Then turn out your lights. The bat should fly outside. As soon as it does, close all the windows and doors.

Bees get quite a buzz from nectar

For bees, nectar provides a great source of energy. How powerful is the stuff? If a single bee could guzzle a whole gallon of nectar, it could travel 4 million miles at a speed of 7 miles per hour.

Drive out bees with darkness. When you want to get rid of a bee in your house, reach for the light switch. If the room is dark, the bee will make its way to the light of an open window and fly outside.

Ban book lice by lowering humidity. In the winter, when the rooms of your house are heated and dry, you don't have to worry about book lice. But in the spring and summer, when it's humid, these pests thrive. Take a few steps to keep them under control. Reducing the humidity in your house will get rid of the mold and mildew that book lice feed on. It will also dry out and kill the book lice themselves. Dry books, papers, and furniture in the sunlight, and air out the room with a dehumidifier or fan. Simply opening the doors of a damp room helps.

Try different tricks to frighten deer

When it comes to driving deer out of your garden, you have plenty of options. Everyday items you can use to deter deer include cayenne pepper, hot-pepper sauce, baby powder, dog hair, deodorant soap, and aluminum pie tins. You can also blare your radio or play a recording of a barking dog to frighten the deer away. The key is to use a variety of these tactics. Switch things around every now and then. Otherwise, the deer will catch on.

Smell swell to repel bugs. Sometimes avoiding bug bites is a matter of common "scents." Apply some lavender oil, just like you would perfume. People will think you smell great, but insects won't agree – and they'll leave you alone.

Gum up the works to control bugs. Keep bothersome insects out of your cabinets with a chewy, mint-flavored repellent. Just leave a few sticks of mint chewing gum where the bugs seem to be entering. It doesn't matter if you unwrap the gum or leave it wrapped. Either way, the bugs will avoid the area.

Raise woodpile out of insects' reach. You spent a lot of time and energy chopping wood. Don't just leave it unprotected. Stack the woodpile on a rack about 3 to 6 inches off the ground. That way, insects won't get into it.

Stick with this pest control strategy. Sure, you could roll up a magazine and swat the bug crawling on your wall. But you might be left with a big, ugly smear. Instead, snag the bug with a piece of tape. It will stick to it, and you can get rid of the bug without making a mess.

Shoo away pests and rust with mothballs. Make use of those old mothballs by scattering them around your garden and flower beds to keep rodents and cats away. On top of that, toss a few in your tool chest to prevent rust on your tools.

Impede centipedes with borax. Get a leg up on centipedes and millipedes. Scatter some borax near doors, windows, or any other places these pests are getting into your house. Just make sure the borax is out of the reach of children and pets.

Chiggers 'mite' get attached to you

The hot summer months bring picnics, Fourth of July festivities ... and chiggers. These annoying pests often attack your ankles, behind your knees, or the areas around your waist and under your arms. If you get bitten by chiggers, you'll be itching for weeks. What, exactly, is a chigger? It's the larva of a harvest mite. During the larval stage, the tiny red chigger moves quickly and survives by attaching itself to other animals and humans. Once it finds a good spot, the chigger pierces your skin and injects a fluid that prevents your blood from clotting. The area around the bite swells, and the chigger remains hidden in the swollen flesh, feasting on your skin's tissues. When it's full, it drops off and burrows into the ground.

Clobber crickets with borax. To get rid of crickets, you have to do more than wish upon a star. You have to take matters into your own hands. Put some borax in a squeeze bottle and sprinkle it along your baseboards and in any cracks crickets might be using as a hiding spot. Just make sure children and pets can't get at it.

Spray to keep strays at bay. Spray your garbage cans with ammonia or a pine-scented cleaner. The scent should keep stray dogs from rummaging through your garbage.

Eliminate earwigs with bay leaves. Put the bite on earwigs before these sinister creatures take a bite out of you. If you suspect earwigs are slithering into your house, crush some bay leaves and scatter them along your windowsills and baseboards. It should keep the earwigs out.

Force fleas to flee. If you've ever had a flea infestation in your house, you know how hard they are to get rid of. They can even multiply in your vacuum cleaner bag. To keep that from happening, place a flea collar in the bottom of the bag.

Pass the salt to defeat fleas. If you're worried about fleas or ticks in your home, give the pests a salty welcome. Pour several boxes of salt in a blender and blend until you get a fine powder. Shake the powder onto your carpet and under your appliances. With a broom, work the powder deep into the carpet, where flea eggs hatch. Let the salt do its job for a few days before you vacuum. The salt should dehydrate the pests and kill them.

Strike back at flies. Use your stiff plastic fly swatter with more precision. Instead of aiming directly at the fly on your table, aim about an inch and a half behind it. That's because flies tend to fly upward and backward when leaving a horizontal surface.

Snag fruit flies with soda bottle trap. Catch those pesky fruit flies with a simple homemade trap. Just put a cup of vinegar, two cups of water, and a tablespoon of honey in a 2-liter soda bottle. Shake well. Poke holes in the side of the bottle above the liquid, and hang the trap about 5 feet above the ground. It should fill up with dead fruit flies in no time. Prevent fruit flies in the first place by letting fruit ripen in a paper bag fastened with a paper clip or clothespin. When it's ripe, put the fruit in the refrigerator. Besides fruit, other things that might lure fruit flies include liquid from the refrigerator or sink drain, spoiled animal food, and damp mops or rags.

Halt fruit flies with household herb. Stop those annoying fruit flies from swarming all over your fruit bowl. Just add some fresh basil to the fruit bowl, and fruit flies will stay away. You can also grow basil in pots outside your door to keep fruit flies from entering your house.

Take hands-on approach to swatting flies. You have two hands – use them. Instead of stalking a fly with only the hand holding the fly swatter, go after it with both hands. Hold them out and wave them back and forth. This will confuse the fly, which will not know which way to go. That hesitation should cost the fly its life.

Blow away backyard bugs. Don't let flies, gnats, or mosquitoes wreck your backyard barbecue. Drive them off, naturally, without smelly bug sprays. Just use a portable electric fan. Aim it at the center of the party to keep your guests cool and the bugs away. For even better results, aim a second fan toward the same area from another direction.

Give gophers bad vibes. Rid your yard of gophers with this unusual tactic. Put a large patio stone, at least a foot in diameter, in the middle of your lawn. Then, using a shovel with a straight wooden handle, pound on the stone two to three minutes a day for two to three days. The vibrations will drive the gophers away. Before you begin, you might want to explain your plan to your neighbors, who might otherwise be concerned about your bizarre behavior.

Cut the grass to cut down on bugs. High grass means a high likelihood of pests. That's because insects hide and breed in tall grass. To protect yourself – and neaten your lawn – keep your grass trimmed to about 3 inches.

Ambush beetles with a vacuum. Your vacuum cleaner can be a valuable tool in ridding your house of ladybugs and beetles. Simply suck up the critters, then dump the bag outside so the bugs end up where they belong. You'll also have to make sure they can't get back in by sealing any holes or cracks in your house.

Enhance your mouse knowledge

A single mouse won't eat you out of house and home. In a typical day, a mouse eats only about 3 grams of food. This adds up to less than 2 1/2 pounds of food in an entire year. However, mice can ruin a lot of food. That's because they often nibble at many different foods, leaving them partially eaten.

Scare off critters with cat litter. Trick mice into smelling danger. Gather some used cat litter from your cat's litter box and put it in several containers around your garage. Mice will smell a cat and run for their lives.

Sack mice with steel wool. The Pittsburgh Steelers football teams of the 1970s featured the outstanding "Steel Curtain" defense. Defend your garage from mice with your own steel curtain – a pad of steel wool. Just shove steel wool pads into any openings you find. Mice, try as they might, won't be able to chew their way into the end zone.

Stop mice with this pleasant aroma. Keep your garage in "mint" condition. Just put peppermint extract on items you want to protect from mice. Mice can't stand the smell of peppermint and won't go near those areas.

Banish mice with baking soda. You've probably heard of several amazing uses for baking soda. Here's one more – it deters mice. Simply sprinkle baking soda around the edge of your basement walls, in dresser drawers, or any other area where you spot evidence of a mouse. An added bonus is the easy cleanup. Just vacuum.

Track down mice with talcum powder. If you're having trouble finding out how mice are getting into your house, let the rodents do the work for you. Just sprinkle some talcum powder along the baseboards. Once the mice scurry through it, their powdery trail will lead you right to the mouse hole.

Mouseproof your house with mothballs. To stop mice from scurrying around your garage or attic, put mothballs along the walls to discourage them. In addition to deterring mice, the mothballs will also keep spiders away.

Slam the door on mice and insects. Most of the time, mice and insects don't bother with secret passageways. They get into your house the same way you do – through the garage door. Before you try any other preventive measures, make sure your garage door closes all the way, with no cracks for critters to slip through.

Spoil the soil for moles. Whip up a concoction to put moles on the move. In a blender, mix 3 ounces of castor oil and three tablespoons of liquid dishwashing detergent until you get a frothy mixture. Throw in eight tablespoons of water and blend until it's frothy again. Put a cup of the potion into a 15-gallon hose-end sprayer. Fill the rest with water and spray the mixture on your yard and garden. Make sure you thoroughly soak the soil. This treatment won't harm the moles, but they'll look somewhere else to tunnel.

Foil mosquitoes with special oil. It's a beautiful, warm, windless night, the perfect night for sitting out on your porch – if it weren't for the mosquitoes buzzing around your head. Reclaim your own territory with products containing oil of citronella. When you light these special candles, torches, or coils, the smoke keeps mosquitoes away.

Bail out standing water. Swamps, ditches, puddles, and other areas containing stagnant water make perfect breeding grounds for mosquitoes. Make sure your backyard is free of standing water. Get rid of any tin cans, tires, buckets, or anything else that holds water. Change the water in your birdbaths and wading pools at least once a week. Fill or drain ditches, puddles, tree holes, or swampy areas. Remove any debris from your rain gutters so water won't accumulate there. Make sure there are no leaks in your air conditioning unit or from your septic tank. And don't let water gather on flowerpots or your pets' food dishes for more than two days.

Banish mosquitoes with plants. Discourage mosquitoes from buzzing near your home. Plant some tansy or basil around your patio and house. The mosquitoes will steer clear of the area.

Mow down mosquitoes

Cutting down weeds and regularly mowing your lawn does more than improve the look of your property. It also lessens your chances of being bitten by mosquitoes. Mosquitoes love to rest atop weeds and in high vegetation. When you trim the weeds and the grass, you eliminate potential shelters for these pests.

Keep moths at bay with bay leaves. Sometimes you wonder which is worse – moths eating your clothes or your clothes smelling like mothballs. But there's another less-offensive smell that moths will avoid – bay leaves. Sprinkle them around your clothes, and moths will leave them alone.

Use 'common scents' on moths. Don't let moths feast on your wool coats, hats, and sweaters when they're tucked away during warm weather. Place whole cloves in coat pockets and in bags containing sweaters. Moths don't like the scent, and they'll avoid your wool. You can also put cloves in your dressers to keep moths from nibbling on your everyday clothes.

Season your clothes during the off-season. You want to put your winter clothes in storage, but you don't want them to turn into moth food. Just sprinkle some black pepper on your clothes before storing them. It will keep moths away.

Tidy up to topple pests. Keep your house clean if you want to prevent carpet beetles or moths. Vacuum regularly and make sure to suck up the dust from baseboards, corners, and other hard-to-reach spots that might harbor unwanted pests. When you're done, throw away the contents of the vacuum cleaner bag.

Ice beetles with freezer treatment. When carpet beetles or moths make themselves at home in a small item, you can get rid of them with one small step. Just put the item in the freezer for a week. The cold will kill the invading pests.

Curb moths with herbs. Safeguard your clothes from moths with a fragrant herbal remedy. Mix half a pound of rosemary, half a pound of mint, one-quarter pound of thyme, one-quarter pound of ginseng, and two tablespoons of cloves. Scoop the mixture into cheesecloth bags and put them in closets or drawers. Moths will stay away.

Snag moths with molasses. Set a sticky trap to nab moths. Just mix one part molasses with two parts vinegar in a yellow container. Moths will flock to the bright container and get stuck in the gooey mixture. Make sure you clean the container regularly.

Protect your family from poisonous pesticides

Pesticides kill pests, but they can also spell doom for humans. Keep all pesticides in a locked cabinet out of the reach of little ones. Make sure the cabinet is not too cold, too hot, or too wet. Know the danger of each pesticide by reading the label on the can. "Danger-poison" means even a taste can be deadly. "Warning" means one teaspoon can kill you, and "Caution" means two tablespoons or more is bad news.

Home in on pigeon control. No matter how much you enjoy "Romeo and Juliet," you don't want pigeons making a scene on your balcony. Bang on it occasionally if they seem to be getting too comfortable landing there. If they become a real nuisance, you can enclose your balcony with netting. Keep the areas under the eaves of your house clean so pigeons aren't tempted to nest there. And, no matter how cute you might think they are, never feed them. It only encourages them to return.

Uncover the mystery of the stinging nettle. The stinging nettle is a mysterious plant. It attracts beautiful butterflies to your garden and repels pests. Royal Admiral butterflies lay their eggs on the underside of the plant's leaves so their young can chomp on the leaves as soon as they hatch. If you look long enough, you'll probably spot some beauties. But you can also turn the stinging nettle into a powerful pesticide. Steep the stems and leaves in a bucket of water for 24 hours. Remove them and use the water, which now contains formic acid from the stinging nettle, to kill mites and aphids on your plants.

Evict raccoons from your garden. Raccoons sure are cute, but not in your garden. To keep them from eating your produce, spread dog hair around the edges. Raccoons will think a fearsome beast lives there and think better of eating his food.

Chase roaches with a cucumber. It's easy to repel roaches without dangerous pesticides. Just combine cucumber skins with chopped bay leaves. You'll end up with a natural roach repellent. Sprinkle the mixture around the cockroaches' usual hangouts. They won't stick around for long.

Make a lethal snack for roaches. To control cockroaches in your home, combine equal parts oatmeal, flour, and Plaster of Paris. Put the mixture in dishes where cockroaches are likely to hide. Just make sure children and pets don't eat the mixture. Or mix two tablespoons of flour, four tablespoons of borax, and a tablespoon of cocoa. Leave this deadly treat on dishes around your house. Make sure you keep borax out of the reach of children and pets because it will poison them.

Silence cockroaches with mums. Chrysanthemums look pretty – unless you're a cockroach. That's because these flowers double as natural insecticides. To put mums to work for you, let them dry out before slightly shredding them. Then sprinkle some wherever cockroaches hang out – in your garage, under appliances, or in storage areas.

Maximize boric acid's power. You might know boric acid kills cockroaches. But here are some tips on how to use this powerful substance more effectively. Toss a few pennies or pebbles into the bottle to prevent the powder from caking and clumping. And don't apply it from a container that's more than two-thirds full. Otherwise, it's tougher to squeeze out the powder. Lastly, leave a thin, barely visible layer of boric acid for the cockroaches to walk through. They will avoid a big, obvious pile.

Cockroaches drink as well as slink

Cockroaches are called "born inebriates." That means they like to get drunk. Bar owners often find these critters in partially empty beer bottles. You can take advantage of this habit by soaking a piece of bread in some beer and leaving it as bait.

Go fishing for silverfish. Silverfish rarely show themselves in the day. If you want to stop them, you have to attack their hiding spots. Pour boiling water down the drain in your bathtub and sink. Use the nozzle on your vacuum cleaner to get at holes and cracks. Aim a hair dryer or fan heater into known silverfish hangouts. Keeping your house cool and dry also helps discourage these pests.

Attack attic pests with mothballs. Your attic, with all its boxes and papers, makes an ideal playground for silverfish. One way to help control these pests is to put some mothballs in the boxes in your attic.

Intimidate silverfish with lemons. Silverfish can put you in a sour mood. Do the same to them. Stash slices of lemon wherever these critters tend to hang out. The silverfish should pucker up and retreat.

Polish off silverfish with cinnamon. No one wants to use dangerous pesticides in their home, especially in the kitchen. So how do you get rid of those annoying silverfish? Just put a little cinnamon inside your drawers and cabinets. Although silverfish eat everything from glue to clothing, they hate cinnamon and will stay away.

Nighttime is the right time for silverfish

Your house might contain silverfish, but it's hard to find them. These small, soft, wingless insects are nocturnal, meaning they function during the night. If you manage to spot one during the day, chances are the critter will be too fast for you to catch. Here's another interesting tidbit – a silverfish can live for up to a year without food.

Think 'stink' when battling skunks. You've heard the expression "fight fire with fire." Well, the same thing applies to getting a skunk out of your garage. Only, in this case, it's "fight odor with odor." Fill a large, flat pan with ammonia and set it in your garage. Leave the door slightly open so the skunk can slink out, but make sure the ammonia smell is trapped inside. The ammonia will eventually offend the skunk's nose, and the skunk will leave the premises.

Say no to skunk nests. To keep from playing host to a nest of skunks or other critters, put fencing around the base of raised porches or low decks. Use fencing that complements your home, like a nice latticed wood. Whatever you choose, be sure to secure it several inches below the ground to keep wily animals from digging their way in.

Shake birds with fake snakes. Mischievous little kids love to scare their squeamish playmates – or unsuspecting mothers – with toy snakes. But toy snakes don't just scare humans, they also scare woodpeckers and other birds. Dangle some toy snakes around the eaves of your house. Make sure they can move when the breeze hits them. The birds that were pecking holes in your roof will quickly reconsider.

Boot out squirrels in birdfeeder. Tired of squirrels getting all the food you put in your birdfeeder? Try this. Cut a pole-size hole in the bottom of an empty, plastic, gallon milk jug. Then put the birdfeeder pole through the jug, moving it up near the food, and placing the pole back in the ground. Squirrels won't be able to climb over the jug without slipping off, and the birds will finally enjoy their feast.

Take the termite test

Relax. That critter you just spotted might not be a termite after all. Winged ants are often mistaken for winged termites. Here's how to tell them apart. Ants have bent antennae, thin waists, and longer front wings than back wings. Termites, on the other hand, have straight antennae, thick waists, and front and back wings that are equal in size.

Trick ticks with Vick's. You probably keep a jar of Vick's VapoRub in your medicine cabinet in case you or someone in your family gets sick. But Vick's does more than clear up congestion. It keep ticks away. Smear some on your legs and pants before walking in the woods.

Become less tasty to bugs. Vanilla might be the most popular ice cream flavor, but it doesn't rate well with ticks and mosquitoes. Cover your skin with a mixture of equal parts vanilla and water to ward off these pests.

Waylay wasps with sugary trap. Don't let wasps ruin your next backyard barbecue. Generously cover a grapefruit with sugar and leave it in a dish outside. The wasps will be too busy attacking the sugar to bother your guests.

Offset wasps with onions. There's no mistaking the smell of onions cooking on the stove, even if you're a wasp. These flying pests will stay away if you heat some onions in a saucepan. Warming up vinegar the same way also works. Or you could mix some lemon slices with cloves. Just set these smelly things out on a dish, and wasps will steer clear of the area. And never tempt wasps by leaving your food or drink uncovered.

Foil hungry wasps with vinegar. Don't let pesky wasps steal all the sweet stuff from your hummingbird feeder. Soak a cotton ball in vinegar and place it near the feeder. The wasps will fly away in search of more pleasant fare.

Wipe out wasps with ammonia. Give your wasps a housewarming present they won't forget. Attach a hose-end spray bottle filled with ammonia onto your garden hose and turn on the water. Then soak the wasps and their nest. The ammonia shower will kill the wasps at once and eventually topple the nest.

Wasps are unsung heroes

Everyone hates wasps, but they do serve a useful purpose. Wasps catch other harmful insects and feed them to their young. In fact, a wasp colony can kill about 4 1/2 pounds of insects each day.

Muffle a woodpecker's peck. You know it's a woodpecker, but it sounds more like 12 drummers drumming. Give yourself the gift of peace and quiet. Fill the hollow space the bird is drumming on with caulk. The noise will no longer resonate throughout your house.

Stave off woodpeckers with suet. Give woodpeckers something to munch on besides your house. Fill a birdfeeder with suet and hang it away from your home. It might lure the woodpeckers – and keep your house free of holes.

Use a box to outfox woodpeckers. Hang a wooden box somewhere on your property. Maybe the woodpecker that's been tapping on your house will choose to tap on the box instead.

That way, everybody is happy. The woodpecker gets some wood, and you get some peace and quiet.

Put a new spin on woodpecker control. Pinwheels entertain kids, but they frighten woodpeckers. Tape, nail, or pin some on your house wherever woodpeckers are pecking. Make sure the pinwheels can spin around in the breeze. Woodpeckers will find somewhere else to do their thing.

Move woodpeckers with mirrors. People who live in glass houses shouldn't throw stones – or have woodpecker problems. Put a magnifying shaving mirror on your house, right where the woodpecker usually sets up shop. The bird will get startled by its own reflection and fly away.

Deflate woodpeckers with balloons. Decorate your house with colorful balloons. Not only will they make your house look festive, they will also scare off woodpeckers. Hang the balloons close to where the woodpecker usually taps, and make sure they can blow in the breeze. If regular balloons seem too friendly, you can also find inflatable owls, hawks, or snakes at some garden shops.

Try music to scare woodpeckers. Woodpeckers can make noise – they just can't take noise. Drive these pecking pests away from your home by turning up the volume. Place your radio in a window near the woodpecker and play it loud. You can also get more sophisticated by playing recorded bird calls of owls, hawks, or other birds of prey. This can be especially effective if you also have inflatable birds guarding your house.

Techniques & tips for
personal safety

Save dinner from going up in smoke. If you frequently forget about food cooking in the oven, wear a timer around your neck. Set the alarm so even if you snooze you'll know it's time to take your dinner out of the oven.

Don't let kitchen fires pan out. Reach for a cookie sheet when you have a pan fire on your stove. Smothering the fire with the sheet will extinguish it faster than you can say "chocolate chip."

Use a 'spyglass' to spot broken glass. Save your hand from a gash the next time you're fishing for broken glass in a soapy sink. Stick the bottom of a tall, clear drinking glass into the water. It will help you see through the suds.

Soften your floor to cushion dropped glass. Install a softer floor in your kitchen to lower your risk of harm from broken glass. Vinyl flooring is a good choice. Ceramic tile, on the other hand, is very hard, and it can be very slippery when wet.

Shake, rattle, and put out the fire. Always keep a super-size shaker of salt, baking soda, or baking powder on your stove to help put out small cooking fires.

Make your bathroom safer. You're asking for trouble if you have an all-white bathroom. White makes the edges in the room harder to see and easier to crash into. Instead, cut down on your chances of falling by attaching bright stickers or tape to the walls, tub, and sink.

Hang a towel for bathroom safety. Hang a towel over the top of your bathroom door when you have little ones around. The towel will prevent them from locking themselves in.

Immobilize thieves with home lighting. Outside lights are a burglar's worst enemy, since they give the good Samaritans in your neighborhood a clear view of suspicious activity

248

around your house. Faced with good lighting, most robbers will give up on breaking into your house without even trying.

Uncover robbers' favorite hiding places. Trees and shrubs add more than beauty to your home. They also give robbers a place to hide. That's why it's important to keep your shrubs trimmed below 3 feet, especially the ones around doors, windows, and walkways. It's also a good idea to trim trees so they don't block your neighbors' view of windows and doors. And trim limbs that could provide thieves easy access to your second-story windows.

Plant obstacles to discourage burglars. To set up a natural security system around your ground floor windows, plant bushes or trees with thorny, thick branches, like hawthorn. Put down loose gravel or pebbles between the bushes. They will make a racket whenever someone steps on them. To build a natural fence around your yard, plant sharp, dense shrubs, like barberry.

Secure your home with a phone trick. Don't let strangers know you're not home. Turn off your phone ringers. People walking by your house won't hear your phone ringing and no one answering.

Pretend you're at home. A quiet air conditioner on a steamy summer day is a good tip-off for would-be robbers that no one is home. Before you go away, set your air conditioner at a higher temperature so you won't waste energy, but don't turn it off.

Avoid alerting thieves to expensive purchases. Whenever you make a major purchase, don't advertise it to roving thieves by leaving the box on the curb. Fold the box or cut it up and put it in the garbage.

Scare burglars with vegetables. For a homemade security alarm, line up food cans along the insides of your doors and windows. If someone tries to break in, they'll make a racket knocking over the cans. That will give you time to escape, and it might even scare off the burglars.

Use old work boots to fool thieves. Let strangers think a burly man is living in your house while you're away. At your local thrift store, buy a pair of large men's work boots. Stomp them in some mud to make them look as if they were just used. Then leave them on your front steps.

Drive robbers crazy with this trick. Keep robbers guessing by having your neighbor park her car in your driveway while you're away. The trick will work even better if she moves the car regularly.

Install deadbolts on outside doors. Sturdy deadbolts are a must on every outside door in your house. By itself, a knob lock provides very little security.

Secure your sliding glass door. Sliding glass doors are an open invitation to robbers unless you lock them securely. Either have a lock bar installed or jam a broom handle or dowel in the inside track.

Fend off fire with the right bulb. Ceiling fixtures and recessed lighting can be a fire hazard if you use bulbs with too high a wattage. Extra heat from the bulbs builds up and can ignite a fire. So follow the light manufacturer's instructions on bulb wattage, or stick with bulbs that have no more than 60 watts.

Watch out for space heater dangers. Space heaters top the list of home fire hazards, but you'll be safer if you follow these tips. Keep the heater at least 3 feet away from anything flammable, including furniture, rugs, clothing, and curtains. Dangerous liquids, like gasoline or kerosene, should be used and stored far away from the space heater. Avoid plugging it into an extension cord, but if you must, make sure it's the correct wire gauge size and type. Lastly, turn the heater off and unplug it any time you're not using it and when you go to bed.

Light a fire with spaghetti. Instead of burning your fingers with a regular match, light a deep candle, gas grill, or fireplace with a stick of raw spaghetti. Spaghetti stays lit a long time, so you won't have to rush to light your fire.

Wash away slippery steps. Save yourself from falling on treacherous ice by pouring a solution of warm water and dishwashing detergent all over your steps. The warm water will melt the existing ice, and the soap will prevent the water from refreezing.

Stay on your feet with the right shoes. To avoid falls in the winter, wear sturdy, low-heeled shoes when venturing outside. Thin-soled shoes are best if you have poor circulation in your lower extremities. They'll give you better traction and feeling. If you have arthritis and sore leg joints, try thick-soled shoes for better support.

Add traction to ice with cornmeal. When your outside deck turns into an ice skating rink, sprinkle cornmeal for traction. And don't worry – the cornmeal won't damage the wood or your yard, and you can easily sweep it away once the ice melts.

Stop pussyfooting around icy sidewalks. Toss cat litter onto your icy sidewalks instead of salt. The litter will provide traction, but it won't damage the pavement, unlike salt.

Stay alert when you're dog tired. Instead of guzzling a pot of coffee, try a piece of peppermint candy. The strong sensation will help keep you alert.

Prepare a fire safety kit. If you live in a high-rise apartment building, it's a smart idea to pack emergency supplies. First, have a blanket handy to use as a smoke tent until help arrives. And keep aluminum foil and duct tape within reach. You'll need them to seal off vents and cracks from smoke. Complete your kit with a flashlight, first aid supplies, and a flag or cloth you can hang out the window to alert firemen of your location. Most importantly, have an escape plan and practice it with your family.

Save a life with a cooler. Always take a foam ice chest with you on boating trips. Not only is it a cheap way to keep your beverages and food cool, it'll double as a spare life preserver if somebody goes overboard.

Point the finger at a two-way mirror. Do this mirror test to see if someone is spying on you. Place the tip of your finger against the mirror's reflective surface. If it's a regular mirror, you'll see a gap between your real finger and your reflected finger. If your real finger directly touches your reflection, it's a two-way mirror.

Conquer darkness with a spool. Tired of groping around in the dark for a dangling light switch? Paint an empty thread spool a bright or fluorescent color and tie it to the end of the string. You'll have something bigger to grab – and it will be easier to spot.

Skip a trip on electrical cords. Keep electrical cords out of your way by taping them to the walls or floor. It's a bad idea to run them under carpets, where they're likely to get worn and short out. Stapling or nailing cords along your wall is also dangerous since you can damage the cords' insulation. Tape is the safest bet.

Step up to safer steps. Paint your outside steps white so you'll have no trouble seeing them at night, no matter how poor the lighting is.

Halt slick steps with bathtub strips. Those nonslip strips you stick in your bathtub are also a great idea for painted porch steps. They'll keep you from taking a tumble in wet weather.

Light up your stairs for safety. Dark stairways can be treacherous. Give yourself a clear view by cleaning light bulbs and fixtures. If that doesn't work to brighten the stairway, add a night light. As a last resort, install another light fixture.

Head off stair climbing injuries. If the low overhang of a staircase is a hazard in your house, attach a mirror to the front of it. When people see their reflection coming at them, they'll know to duck.

Paint bottom step white. Never miss the last step of your dark basement stairs again. Paint it with white enamel. Even if your basement is a dungeon, you'll see it coming and avoid a fall.

Tape your handlebars for a sure grip. For a cushy feel and a sure grip on your walker's handlebars, wrap them with friction tape.

Batten down your throw rugs. Make throw rugs less of an obstacle for your feet by sewing rubber jar seals underneath. The jar seals will keep the rugs – and you – from slipping and sliding. These rubber seals are easy to find in kitchen supply stores.

Add contrast to walls to avoid falls. Paint your walls a different color than your floor if you want to protect yourself from falling. Making your floor the lighter of the two colors works best.

Give yourself an extra hand. A plastic grocery bag will help you carry everything you need, even though you have both hands on your walker. Just tie the bag to the front of your walker. For a fancier look, try a fabric bag.

Wrap sharp corners to prevent injury. Falling is the second-most-common fatal accident. To protect young children and the elderly, buy foam pipe insulation at your local hardware store. The foam pipe is already slit and comes with adhesive strips. Cut it to fit around the edges of your tables and counters. To wrap the piping around corners, cut a V-shaped notch in the insulation at the corner.

Photocopy credit cards for extra protection. Always keep photocopies of your credit cards with the rest of your financial information. If your cards are ever lost or stolen, you'll have your account numbers and expiration dates handy. That means no problems reporting the incident. When you travel, make two copies – one to bring with you and one to leave at home.

Stash your valuables securely. Hide your spare cash, jewelry, and other valuables somewhere less predictable than under your mattress. Be creative. Try stuffing them inside an empty frozen vegetable box in your freezer. Or put them in an empty cereal box on your pantry shelf. Cut out a portion of some of the pages in a book you don't read, or stuff your valuables inside a full tissue box. The inside of your vacuum cleaner bag, a stuffed animal, and a tennis ball make great options, too.

Know the key to hiding valuables. Stash important keys – like to a safe or a cabinet – in an aspirin bottle.

Label property to discourage thieves. Make it easier for the police to recover your stolen property. Write your name on your belongings with a special pen that can only be seen under ultraviolet light. Or borrow an engraver from your local police station.

Take stock of household possessions. Keep tabs of everything in your home in case of a fire or robbery. If you can, videotape every room, as well as the outside of your home. Take pictures of your most valuable possessions and keep a copy of the receipts. Make a list of all your property, including its worth. Store these important documents in a safe-deposit box.

Make muggers think twice. Split your valuables between your two front pockets. In one, hold your cash. In the other, keep your credit cards and identification card. If you are mugged, hand over the cash.

Keep tabs of important papers. To file insurance claims after a disaster, you'll need documents to prove you're actually you. Keep important documents in a safe location, like a fireproof strong box. And make copies of these documents and store them in a safe-deposit box or at a relative's house. Include these documents – car insurance cards, birth certificates, car registrations and titles, checking account numbers, deeds, drivers licenses, investment records, life insurance plans, wills, marriage license, medical insurance, military records, social security cards, and five years of tax returns. Old photos of you and your family are also a good idea.

Secure online credit card transactions. When you're online, only send personal information if you are on the Web site of a reputable company. They usually have adequate security to guard against Web thieves. Look at the URL, or Web address, of the site. If the URL begins with "https://" you are on a secure page. If it starts with just "http://," you aren't safe.

Handy help for
your green thumb

Leave a shine on houseplant leaves. Clean most houseplants, except those with fuzzy leaves, like African violets, with a solution of one-half cup of baking soda to a gallon of cold water. To give them an even brighter shine, rub the leaves with a little bit of mayonnaise.

Take control to keep plants pretty. To keep your houseplants from losing their pretty shape as they grow toward the light, rotate them one-quarter of a complete turn each time you water them. Pinch back new growth for a bushier plant, and prune any misshapen or straggly branches. Remove brown or discolored leaves. If only the tip of a leaf is brown, trim it at an angle with scissors.

Clear the air with houseplants

Surrounding yourself with houseplants not only beautifies your home, it might protect you and your family from harm caused by household chemicals. Research shows that one spider plant can reduce the amount of formaldehyde in a sealed room by 85 percent within 24 hours. Other plants are good at cleaning the air of carbon monoxide and nitrogen dioxide. Scientists say as few as 15 plants in the average-size house could make a significant difference in the air you breathe. If that seems like a lot of plants, think of what it's worth to have healthy lungs.

Water without making a mess. Are you tired of cleaning up puddles when the water runs straight through your houseplants? A neater way to water them is to toss a few ice cubes on top of the soil and let them dissolve slowly. Not only will it make less mess, the roots get a better chance to absorb the water.

Serve soda to your plants. Don't pour out club soda that has gone flat. Save it to water your plants. They thrive on the chemicals it contains.

Water plants while you're away. With this practical tip, you won't have to worry about your plants drying out while you take a vacation. Just poke a small hole in the side of a plastic bottle, near the bottom, and fill it with water. Place it on the soil beside your plant. The slow drip will provide steady moisture while you're away. Use a 12-ounce bottle for small plants. For large houseplants or outdoor plants, use a 2-liter bottle.

Soak houseplants in the shower. Put your houseplants outside on a rainy day, and let them enjoy a good soaking. When there isn't a cloud in the sky, use your bathroom shower instead. Make sure the water temperature isn't set on hot, and then give your dry plants a nice, gentle shower. When you turn off the water, close the door to hold in the remaining humidity as the plants drain.

Check for dryness with a pencil. You know that overwatering can drown your plants. But how do you know how much is too much? Here's a simple test. Take a pencil and push it into the soil. When you pull it out, if there is dirt on it, don't water just yet. If it's soil free, go head and give it a good soaking.

Listen to your plants. If you listen to your potted plants, they will tell you when they need water. Just hold the container to your ear and thump it. If you hear a thud, the soil probably still holds some moisture. If it sounds hollow, it's time to get out the watering can.

Rub out aphids with milk. Are aphids sucking the life out of your plants? Fight back with a simple and inexpensive solution. Mix powdered milk and warm water in a spray bottle. Spray your plants' leaves and let the mixture dry. As it dries, the milk will kill the aphids.

Cut plant care time in half. You can dust your houseplants in half the time if you wear an old glove and wipe both sides at once.

Hang it high with lighter soil. When potting a new houseplant in a hanging container, begin by filling the bottom with pieces of Styrofoam. It won't be so heavy and will drain easily.

Group houseplants for higher humidity. Place several houseplants together to increase humidity. Or cover the bottom of a low pan with water, put in a layer of small stones, and place containers of plants on top. As the water evaporates, it will provide the extra moisture most plants love. If you have to be away for a few weeks, water the plants well, fill the pan with water, and slip it all inside a plastic dry cleaning bag. Your plants should be just fine when you return.

Take a vacation from your plants. Going on a trip or just don't like to water your houseplants? Here's an easy way to ignore them. Run a soft cotton rope, a length of nylon hose, or a few strands of yarn from a large container of water to the soil around your plants. The water will move by capillary action from the container to the plant, providing a steady drink.

Curtail care of houseplants in winter. Houseplants don't grow very much during the short, dark days of winter, so they generally need less care. Too much water can kill them, and only plants growing under special artificial lights need fertilizer. You can increase the amount of available natural light by placing reflective aluminum foil under the pots. Just be sure water doesn't collect under the foil where it can rot wooden surfaces.

Peek in the pot before you transplant. If you're not sure if it's time to repot a houseplant, here's a quick and easy way to decide. Place some newspaper on a table. Lay the flowerpot on its side and tap it. Gently pull the plant out. If roots are wrapped around the outside of the dirt, it's time to move it to a container that's an inch or two bigger. If you see more soil than root, there's still room to grow, so just slide it right back in the pot.

Discourage gnats with dry soil. You might be doing too good a job watering your plants. If your plants are too wet between waterings, the damp soil invites fungus gnats. These pests need damp soil to breed. To counter fungus gnats, put some stones at the bottom of your plants' pots so the soil drains quicker. Another good strategy is to let your plants dry out completely between waterings.

Rub out mealybugs with magic wand. Find the ultimate weapon against mealybugs right in your bathroom's medicine cabinet. Just dip a cotton swab in rubbing alcohol, and you have a magic wand to make mealybugs disappear. Examine your plants for these pests, and touch each mealybug you find with the cotton swab. They will die and drop off the plant. When you're done, wash your plant with warm, soapy water and rinse.

Nab gnats with sand. Your new plant might come with some uninvited guests. Fungus gnats love fresh potting soil and are more likely to breed in it than in older soil. But you can thwart these pests with a simple tactic. Just add a half-inch layer of sand to the top of your fresh potting soil. This dries out any fungus gnat eggs and prevents adult gnats from getting out.

> ### Plants – just what the doctor ordered
> People often send plants to family and friends to make them feel better emotionally. But researchers at Washington State University discovered that plants can also reduce physical pain. In this study, more people could stand to keep their hand in a container of freezing-cold water for five minutes if plants were nearby.

Chase cats from potted plants. To keep your feline friends from using your houseplant container as a litter box, add white vinegar to the water you use to mist the plants. Pine cones or horticultural charcoal around the base of the plant will also keep cats away.

Bag some moisture for your houseplant. Line the bottom of the container with used tea bags before potting a houseplant. It will help hold in moisture and add nourishment to the plant.

Let spuds do double duty. Potatoes boiled in their skins can provide a lot of nutrition, not only for you but for your houseplants, too. After boiling some potatoes, let the water cool and use it as a tonic for your plants. It's full of nitrogen, phosphorus, and potassium.

Fish for more moisture. Are your houseplants suffering from dry air? Place them near your fish tank where there's higher humidity.

Save money on seedling starters. Get an early start on your spring garden and save money, too, by using egg cartons as starter trays for your seedlings. Just fill the cups with soil, plant your seeds, and keep them in a sunny window. If you use cardboard cartons, you can separate the cups and plant them directly in the soil when the threat of frost has passed. If you use Styrofoam cartons, remove the seedlings from the cups before you transplant them. If your small plants or seedlings need protection from the weather, grab a plastic milk jug or soda bottle. Cut off the bottom and place it over your plant. Leave the top off for air and water.

Nurse your seedlings in a bottle. Create a mini greenhouse from a plastic 2-liter soft drink bottle to give your garden plants an early start. Cut a 3-inch-wide flap in one side of the bottle, beginning at the neck and stopping several inches from the bottom. Punch some drainage holes in the opposite side. With the bottle resting on its side, lift the flap and put in a few inches of potting soil. Plant and water your seeds, and place the bottle in a sunny window with the flap closed. Moisture held inside will help the seeds sprout, but you can open the flap to adjust the humidity as needed. If established plants grow too large before it's time to transplant them, you can cut the flap away to give them more room.

Soak seeds for speedier sprouting. Seeds will sprout twice as fast if you soak them overnight before planting. Mix the tiniest ones with sand, and they'll be easier to spread evenly.

Wait for seeds to mature. Don't rush to collect the seeds as soon as your flowers die. Wait until the capsules turn brown. You'll know then the seeds are fully ripened.

Get a jump on spring. If you want to start your garden before the last frost, save your milk cartons and make covers to protect your plants. Cut away the top part of a half-gallon carton about 6 to 8 inches from the bottom. Turn it upside down and cut three sides of the bottom square to make a flap. Press the sides of the carton a few inches into the loose soil, and plant the seedling in the center. Open the flap to let in air and sunshine, but close it at night if there is danger of frost. After the plant grows tall and the danger of cold damage has passed, leave the open carton in place as a shield against cut worms.

Baby your seedlings with baby shampoo. Plant your seeds and then water them with a mixture of one teaspoon of baby shampoo and a quart of water. Your seedlings will find it easy to burst through the moist, soft soil.

Cushion your hands with handlebar covers. Don't let blisters from wooden wheelbarrow or rake handles spoil your fun in the garden. Head to the bicycle shop for some spongy handlebar covers. You may need to use a lubricant, like petroleum jelly or liquid dish soap, to get them to slide over the wooden handles. But once you get them in place, you'll love the way they protect your hands.

KO sticky hands with mayo. If you come in hungry after gathering evergreen branches, head to the refrigerator for the mayonnaise. But before you use it to make a sandwich, rub some on your hands to remove the sticky resin, and then wash up with warm, soapy water.

Clean and soften dirty hands naturally. Remove garden stains and soften your hands at the same time. Just rub them briskly with a paste of oatmeal and milk. If you don't have those ingredients on hand, try a mixture of two tablespoons of cornmeal, a tablespoon of water, and a little bit of apple cider vinegar.

Brush away garden grime. An old toothbrush is ideal for scrubbing your hands and fingernails after working in the garden.

Bar dirt with a bar of soap. Scrape your fingernails over a bar of soap before heading to the garden. It will block most dirt from getting under your nails and make it easy to wash away any dirt that does.

Empty gas from mower with kitchen tool. A turkey baster makes a simple tool for removing gasoline from your lawn mower at the end of the grass-cutting season. Buy one and keep it with your gardening tools.

Store tools for a round of gardening. An old golf bag makes a terrific caddy for your long-handled garden tools, like rakes and shovels. And your gloves and hand tools fit neatly in the side pockets.

Keep knees clean and comfortable. Digging in the dirt can be hard on your knees, but old computer mouse pads can help cushion your joints. They'll keep your pants clean, too.

Recycle a broken rake. Don't throw out that old garden rake just because the handle is broken. Attach the metal part to the wall of your toolshed and hang tools from the teeth. And use the handle as a stake for tall plants.

Soothe hands with smooth handles. As wooden handles on wheelbarrows and tools weather and age, they can be rough on your hands. Sand them and rub with linseed oil to prevent splinters.

Remember rosemary

Some say scholars in ancient Greece wore wreaths of rosemary to improve their memory. Today, there are other good reasons to grow a pot of this aromatic herb. It's delicious on grilled fish, and it adds flavor to many vegetable dishes.

Hasten new herb growth. After you plant herbs in pots, put them into an indoor window box and fill it up to the pot rims with soil. In an attempt to reach the outer soil, the plants will send roots through the hole in the bottom. In the process, the herbs will grow faster.

Solve pest problems naturally. Don't drown your garden vegetables in toxic pesticides. Instead, repel aphids, slugs, and other destructive pests simply and naturally with these solutions. To drive away aphids, combine two tablespoons of minced garlic, one-half cup of parsley flakes, and three cups of water. Boil it down to two cups, then strain the mixture and let it cool. Take one cup of the mixture, put it in a hose-end sprayer, and spray your plants. To stop slugs, fill a small bowl with half beer and half water and put it near plants the slugs enjoy eating. They will be attracted to the smell and fall in and drown. To kill a variety of bugs on your plants, mix a tablespoon of liquid dish detergent with a gallon of water.

Transplant for faster results. Most gardeners find some plants grow too slowly to start from seeds. Tomatoes and peppers take six weeks or longer to reach the transplant stage. You'll probably do better buying those as transplants, especially if you live where the growing season is short.

Sow some seeds directly in the garden. While some plants grow best from transplants, others, like squash, pumpkin, melons, and carrots, do best when seeds are planted directly in the ground.

Mute hornworms with marigolds. Sick of seeing your tomatoes being eaten by tomato hornworms? Plant marigolds around the tomato plants in your garden. It's an easy and natural way to keep those crawling green caterpillars away.

Plant tomatoes along a fence. You won't need to stake your tomatoes if you plant them along your chain-link fence. Just tie them to the fence with pantyhose or use strips of clear plastic dry cleaning bags. Plant enough so you can share the tomatoes that grow through the fence with your neighbor.

Pick pests off produce with vinegar. Growing your own produce often means picking off your own bugs. To get bugs off your fresh vegetables, rinse the vegetables well. Then soak them in a solution of one cup of vinegar and a gallon of water. Five minutes later, you'll be able to pick the bugs off much easier. And you won't ruin the taste of your produce.

Weed out worms with marigolds. Let marigolds protect your produce. Nematodes, a type of worm, and other insects love to munch on beans, spinach, tomatoes, and celery. But the roots of marigolds produce a chemical that kills nematodes. So plant some marigolds among your vegetables for a worm-free garden.

Guard your garden with garlic. Onions and garlic add flavor and aroma to many delicious meals. But these members of the leek family also deter Japanese beetles from munching on your garden. Make sure to plant plenty of onions and garlic for a zesty source of natural defense.

Nail those naughty cutworms. The hardware store has just what you need – ten-penny finishing nails – to keep cutworms from feasting on your prized tomatoes. Press a nail into the soil beside the stem of each tomato, leaving the head about an inch or so above ground. It will make it impossible for the cutworm to wrap around the stem and eat away at your tender plants.

Grow unmatchable peppers. For the best sweet peppers ever, bury a book of matches in the soil with each pepper plant. These acid-loving veggies will thrive on the sulfur that will be released. Peppers also need magnesium. When the first blossoms appear, dissolve two tablespoons Epsom salt in a gallon of water and give each plant a pint of this liquid.

Raise a stink over doggy-do. Doggy-do messing up your garden? Mix up a brew that will keep Fido and friends – with their sensitive noses – out of your yard for good. Chop up a clove of garlic and the most pungent onion you can find. Mix these and a teaspoon of Tabasco sauce, a tablespoon of cayenne pepper, four teaspoons of dried oregano, and a quart of warm water in a large pail. Let sit overnight, and then sprinkle in areas where dogs like to rest or dig. Once they smell this concoction, you won't see them in your yard again. If you think this mixture will be too strong for your human nose, here's an alternative. Brush or spray a mixture of two cups rubbing alcohol and a teaspoon of lemon grass on the areas you want treated. This also repels cats.

Keep uninvited animals away. Don't let cats and squirrels trash your yard or garden. Fight back. In a large bowl, mix five tablespoons of flour, two tablespoons of cayenne pepper, and two tablespoons of powdered mustard. Slowly add five cups of water and five cups of vinegar and continue mixing. Use a funnel to pour the mixture into a spray bottle and label it. Squirt the mixture wherever animals are disturbing your yard. They won't be back for seconds.

Pepper your plants to stump squirrels. Turning squirrels away from your garden is a breeze. Make that a sneeze. Just sprinkle some cayenne or black pepper around anything the bushy-tailed pests might eat. They'll think twice about coming back.

Make your cat 'rue' the day. If your cat constantly digs up your garden, try planting some rue. This strong-scented shrub, which grows 2 feet tall, can deter cats from trespassing.

Discourage cats with pungent mixture. Cats won't treat your yard as an outdoor litter box if you spread a pungent mixture of orange peels and coffee grounds around your plants.

Repel rodents with Epsom salt. Keep nosy raccoons and woodchucks out of your garden or garbage can. Just sprinkle a few tablespoons of Epsom salt around those areas. The rodents hate the salt and will steer clear of it. Plus, the salt acts as food for your plants. Don't worry – it won't harm the animals, either. To make sure the Epsom salt trick keeps working, you'll have to replace it every time it rains.

Attack gophers with ammonia. Are gophers ruining your lovely lawn? Go on the offensive with a mixture of ammonia and water. Add a cup of ammonia to two gallons of water, open a hole, and pour the mixture down into it. Then cover the hole with dirt. Repeat if necessary.

Beat burrowing animals with a drum. When moles and other burrowing animals find your tulip bulbs too tasty to resist, it's time to take action. Bury the drum from an old washing machine in your flower garden with the top even with the ground, and plant your bulbs inside. The metal keeps moles and other underground pests away from their feast. And since the holes in the drum allow for drainage, your bulbs won't rot in soggy soil.

Make a snake feel at home. Snakes are good for your garden. They eat mice, grasshoppers, slugs, and other pests. If you want to attract one to your garden, provide pools of water and a few planks, rocks, or other hiding places.

Use soap to cope with deer. Get the deer that are chomping at your garden to clean up their act. Hang a bar of deodorant soap in a pair of old pantyhose. That should discourage them from trespassing anymore.

Steer deer clear of your garden. You like Bambi as much as the next fellow, but not when he's eating your crops. Spray your plants with a mixture of two raw eggs, a cup of milk, two tablespoons of liquid detergent, two tablespoons of cooking oil, and two gallons of water. Or protect up to a whole acre of land by mixing 18 raw eggs with five gallons of water. The scent will keep deer away, but it won't bother humans.

Chase caterpillars from cabbage patch. This smelly spray will send caterpillars crawling in the other direction. Just mix two shredded onions and their juices in a gallon of water. Let it sit overnight, strain, and spray the liquid on your cabbage plants. You might need to spray the plants twice.

Liquidate slugs with a beverage. Placing a dish of beer in your garden will take care of slugs. But you don't have to run out and buy beer or waste the beer you already have on a slug. You can use soda, fruit juice, or sugar water and get the same results. A more elaborate trap involves cutting off the upper part of a soda bottle, then sticking the section you just cut off back in the bottle, neck first. Tape the two parts together, fill half the bottle with one of the beverages mentioned earlier, and bury the bottle in your garden so the entrance is level with the ground. It should fill up quickly with dead slugs.

Make things rough for slugs and snails. Crawling through sand is no day at the beach for slugs and snails. They can't stand the feel of coarse substances. Guard your garden by spreading a bed of sand around your plants. You can also use eggshells, sawdust, or human or animal hair. Slugs and snails will stay away.

Slay slugs with salt. Here's a simple way to get rid of slugs. Just sprinkle salt on them. When they come in contact with salt, slugs shrivel and die.

Stop slugs the natural way. You don't need fancy or dangerous pesticides to conquer slugs. A number of natural substances will help keep them away. Try using prostrate rosemary, garlic, wormwood, or sawdust to stave off slugs.

Plant some protection from slugs. Add onions and marigolds to your garden, and you will subtract slugs. These common plants act as natural slug deterrents.

Stymie snails with garlic spray. Garlic wards off snails, caterpillars, and aphids. Make a homemade garlic concoction to protect your garden. Mix three heads of garlic and six teaspoons of mineral oil in a blender, and let the mixture sit at room temperature for two days. Then add the garlic mixture to a combination of one pint hot water and one tablespoon of oil-based soap, and refrigerate it in screw-top jars. When you go to spray your garden, combine two tablespoons of the refrigerated mixture with four pints of water. It should do the trick.

Outsmart cutworms. Sprinkle crushed eggshells on the ground around the stems of your tomato plants. Cutworms won't crawl across them, even for the most luscious tomatoes.

Keep bugs away with garlic. Bugs and worms will keep their distance if you bury a clove of garlic in the soil around your indoor and outdoor plants.

Wipe out bugs with milk jug. Turn a harmless, plastic milk jug into a deadly bug killer. Just toss in a cup of sugar, a cup of vinegar, and a banana peel. Leave the jug open, and hang it from a tree or set it in your garden. All the bugs that have been munching on your fruits and vegetables will be lured to the milk jug – and their doom.

'Dew' in worms with baking soda. Get rid of pesky worms the scientific way. In the late afternoon, sprinkle some baking soda on your cabbage or broccoli plants. When dew forms on the plants, it combines with the baking soda to create an enzyme that kills worms but will not harm humans. Just rinse your plants with water the next day to clean them.

Whisk away whiteflies. Whiteflies are true pests. They suck the juice from your plants and weaken them. They also multiply quickly, so it seems like they're always around. But they have a weakness – they're lazy. Sneak up on them while they lounge in the early morning and evening. Vacuum the leaves of your houseplants and suck up the unsuspecting whiteflies.

Attract birds to your yard. Want to attract more birds to your yard? Don't get overzealous in your fall yard and garden cleanup. Be sure you leave plenty of plants – like thistle and milkweed – that provide flossy material for nests in the spring. One way to find out what the birds in your area like to use is to take apart a few of last year's nests and examine the building materials.

Scare birds away from fruit trees. To keep birds from eating your ripe fruits and berries, cut strips of mylar from old party balloons and tie them to the tree branches.

Prevent fruit theft with pantyhose. If the birds eat your grapes while you are still waiting for them to ripen, this trick should stop them. Cover each cluster of grapes with a leg from an old pair of pantyhose.

Guard fruit trees with giant 'scarecrow.' Don't let birds eat all the fruit from your trees before you can harvest it. Turn your fruit tree into a giant scarecrow by hanging plastic bags on it. When the wind blows, the bags will rustle and scare off the feathered thieves.

Use scare tactics on invading birds. After a lot of hard work, you might think gardening is for the birds. But that doesn't mean you want the birds to eat all your crops. Take some precautions to scare birds out of your garden. It takes more than a simple scarecrow – unless it can sing and dance, like the one in "The Wizard of Oz." Try a variety of devices. Pinwheels, aluminum pie plates, balloons, and ribbons all work well. Stretch ribbons between two poles so they'll make a roaring noise when the wind blows. Make sure to alternate the devices and change their location every few days. And hide the devices that aren't being used. Otherwise, the birds will just get used to them. Keep things unpredictable. Start using the scary props about two weeks before your crop will start tempting the birds. If you start too soon, the birds will be too familiar with your props to be scared. If you start too late, the birds will be too familiar with the taste of your crops to be driven away.

Protect your grapes with drapes. Keep birds and other hungry animals out of your fruit vines and berry bushes. Cover the vines and bushes with old sheer curtains. The curtains will thwart any animal invaders, but they won't harm them or the plants.

Garden after rain if allergic to pollen. If you are allergic to pollen, a good air-cleansing rain is your friend. On the other hand, if your allergies are caused by mold, wait until everything dries out to return to your gardening.

Breathe easy in your garden. With a few precautions, gardening and lawn work don't have to be off limits even if you have allergies. Just cover your nose with a mask, wear long sleeves and pants, and wash your clothes right away when you come inside. Keep your grass short and your garden weed free. And stay indoors during early morning and late afternoon hours, when pollen counts are highest.

Reduce allergies with low-pollen posies

Perhaps you like to garden, but struggle with allergies during the growing season. If so, stick with plants that produce bright blossoms. Since they attract insects to spread their pollen, they need less of it. On the other hand, plants that depend on the wind for pollination produce a lot more of the stuff that makes you sneeze. Azalea, hibiscus, oleander, pyracantha, and yucca are some shrubs that shouldn't aggravate your allergies. Other plants you are likely to be comfortable with include cacti, chrysanthemums, crocus, daffodils, ferns, hyacinths, irises, lilies, orchids, roses, and tulips. If you have allergies, trees to avoid during pollen season include elm, sycamore, oak, walnut, maple, birch, ash, willow, and pecan. Some trees you won't need to avoid are fir, magnolia, palm, pear, redbud, and yew. Some other plants you may also want to watch out for are privet hedge, Bermuda grass, bluegrass, artemisia, amaranth, and sorrel.

Learn the secret to fabulous cut flowers. Don't throw out that flower arrangement before you have had time to enjoy it. A surprising sweet-and-sour combo will keep your bouquet looking absolutely gorgeous. To a quart of water, stir in two tablespoons of sugar for plant food and add two tablespoons of white vinegar to keep your flowers fresh.

Lengthen short flower stems. Don't let short-stemmed, cut flowers slide too low in your bouquet. Instead, give them a boost by slipping them into soda straws before adding them to your arrangement. Just be sure to use an opaque vase so the straws won't show.

Keep clouds away from your bouquet. Cloudy water in a clear vase can ruin the beauty of your cut flower arrangement. But a teaspoon of liquid bleach added to each quart of vase water will keep it clear and sparkling.

Help cut flowers keep their cool. You can prolong the beauty of fresh cut flowers by placing them in a cool 65 to 72 degree location. Just remember to keep them out of direct sunlight; away from fans and heating or cooling vents; and off televisions, radiators, and other appliances that give off heat.

Turn your flowers a different color. You can turn yellow daffodils green and white carnations blue. To work this magic, just place the stems in warm water and add a few drops of food coloring. Watch the flowers change color as they suck this solution up through their stems. Experiment with colors and different kinds of flowers for variety in your bouquets.

Clear the way for long-lasting blossoms. If your floral arrangement gets droopy too quickly, air bubbles in the stems could be preventing the flow of water to thirsty blossoms. To avoid this problem, hold the stems under cold water. Then, using sharp scissors, cut the stems at an angle. They're now ready to be placed in a vase.

Prolong the life of cut flowers. You can prolong the life of freshly cut flowers by adding a dash of salt to the water in the vase.

Dump water to deter bugs. Insects breed in stagnant water. Just don't give them a chance to do it in your house. When your fresh flowers die, make sure to dump out the water in the vase. Otherwise, the standing water will lure all sorts of critters.

Sweeten the pot for fresher flowers. The secret to cut flowers that last weeks longer is to drop a shiny copper penny and a cube of sugar into the vase of water.

Divide and conquer perennial problems. You'll have fewer pest and disease problems if you give your perennials plenty of room to grow. Fall is the best time to divide crowded plants. When you dig them up to separate them, be sure each clump has plenty of roots and one or more healthy growing tips. Give your transplants a boost with some rich compost in the soil, and you'll have beautiful, healthy plants come springtime.

Add pizzazz to your landscape. Annuals provide a lot of color in the garden. They show off their beauty best when planted in groups of the same kind, rather than interspersed with other colors and varieties. Some of the best bloomers that require the least amount of care are nasturtium, coleus, marigold, dusty miller, impatiens, periwinkle, zinnia, spider flower, sweet alyssum, and yellow cosmos.

Store bulbs in oatmeal boxes. Save your oatmeal boxes to store bulbs over the winter. Punch a few holes in the sides and fill with dry peat moss and a few bulbs. Place them in a cool, dry place until spring. When storing different varieties, be sure to label them.

Give unwanted bamboo the boot. Bamboo blowing in a gentle breeze makes a pretty addition to your garden. But it can get out of hand quickly if you leave the new shoots unchecked. Fortunately, if you act while the shoots are still tender, you can easily break them off at ground level with your foot.

Protect bamboo with a little neglect. Do you like the look of bamboo fences, trellises, bean poles, and tiki torches in your garden? If so, chances are you try to protect them against decay, only to get discouraged when the varnish or polyurethane flakes off. The secret is to let bamboo weather for a year. The wind and rain will wear away the outer surface, which is hard and smooth like glass. When it gets a little porous, you can stain it the color you want and apply a protective finish.

Build a fence with bamboo. If a patch of bamboo is taking over your yard, why not use some of it to build a trellis or fence? Begin by selecting stalks that are 3 to 5 years old. They will have lost their bright green color for a more golden tone. The lower and middle parts of the stalk are strongest. The upper sections may be too weak for these projects. Make your top cut just above a node, which is solid all the way through. You'll have a natural top, so rain can't rot the stalk.

Learn the secret of drying hydrangeas. Blue, pink, or purple hydrangeas make attractive additions to your dried flower arrangements. For best results, pick them when their color peaks before the first frost. And use your parked car as a drying oven. On a sunny day, leave flowers inside with windows rolled up for 24 hours. You can tell they are dry enough when you rub the petals and they make the sound of rustling tissue paper.

Recycle water from wading pool. When the kids finish playing in the wading pool, use a garden hose to drain it onto your thirsty plants. Just put one end of the hose in the bottom of the pool and suck air from the other end until the water starts to flow. To avoid swallowing dirty water, make a fist around the end of the hose and suck with your lips against your hand. You will be able to feel the water pressure and move your mouth before the water gets to it.

Soak dry roots in a tub. Just watering your hanging plants may not be enough during a hot, dry summer. If the water runs quickly through, that means the roots are too dry to take up enough moisture. You may need to immerse them – pot and all – in a tub of water for a few minutes to give the roots a good soaking.

Grow strong plants with Epsom salt. Get your garden off to a good start with a cup of Epsom salt mixed into every 100 square feet of soil. Stalks will be stronger and leaves greener. And to keep your vegetables and flowers healthy, give them another dose every two to four weeks.Feed individual tomato plants and rose bushes one teaspoon per foot of height, and sprinkle one tablespoon over each 9 square feet of the root zone of azaleas, rhododendrons, and evergreens. Lawns like Epsom salt, too. Apply 6 pounds per 2,500 square feet. Feed houseplants, as well, with one teaspoon per gallon of water.

Treat thirsty roots to a long drink. Newly planted trees and shrubs require lots of water. You can save time and water with a system that gets it right to the roots where it's needed. Just take an 18-inch length of PVC pipe and drill a number of half-inch holes about an inch apart. When planting, place the pipe in the hole near the root ball with the top even with the ground. Place the garden hose into the pipe and let water run slowly so it will be absorbed into the soil.

Fish for houseplant fertilizer. Are you searching for a good organic fertilizer for your houseplants? Look no further than the dirty water in your fish tank. Not only does this water contain nutrients that plants love, it is free of chlorine and other chemicals. So when it's time to clean the tank, dump the water on your plants, not down the drain.

Don't leave footprints in your grass. If you leave a path of footprints when you walk across your lawn, it's time to turn on the sprinkler. Dry turf doesn't bounce back the way grass that's had a good soaking does. And be especially careful not to walk on grass just before you mow it. You won't get an even cut if parts of it are flattened.

Slow snails with ashes. Not only are ashes good fertilizer, they also make a good insect repellent for your plants. Slugs, snails, and other soft-bellied creatures won't crawl across a ring of ashes. Keep the circle a few inches from the plants, as ashes can harm the stems if they touch them.

Make a handy rain gauge. After it rains, you may wonder if your garden got enough water or if you need to turn on the sprinkler. To solve the mystery, place empty coffee cans here and there in your garden. When the rain stops, just measure the depth of the water in the cans. If you have at least an inch, there's no need for additional watering.

Feed your plants a tin-can tonic. Add iron to your garden by watering your plants from rusty tin cans.

Give your roses a tea party. You don't have to read tea leaves for the secret to bigger, more beautiful roses. And you don't have to slave under the hot sun for hours either. Just sprinkle tea leaves on the ground beneath your rose bushes. The tannic acid is really their cup of tea, especially in midsummer when production starts to slow down. Ferns also like tea. You can water them occasionally with the beverage or mix wet tea leaves into the soil around them.

Fasten your climbing plants with floss. A good way to attach your climbing roses or other trailing plants to a trellis or fence is with mint-flavored dental floss. It's strong and weather resistant, and the green color will blend with the green vines and leaves.

Fertilize your plants with coffee grounds. After you make a pot of coffee, don't toss out the grounds. Save them to fertilize your roses, evergreens, azaleas, rhododendrons, and camellias.

Foil beetles with flour power. Pesky Japanese beetles can be a thorn in the side of your rosebush. Smother the pests by sprinkling your rosebush with self-rising flour.

Dress your deck for a beach party. Give your deck or porch a festive look by using a beach pail as a planter. Just put some rocks in the bottom and set a pot that's already planted inside. That way, you won't have to cut holes in the bucket for drainage, and you can still use it when you head to the beach.

Keep planters portable with cans. Large planters can be moved more easily if you reduce the amount of heavy soil inside. To make them lighter, fill one-third to one-half of the bottom with aluminum cans. Finish filling with soil and add your plants. The aluminum cans, which won't rust or decay, will also help your planters drain well.

Pick a petite pot for your plant. Don't put your plant in a pot that's too big if you want thick, lush greenery. It will work so hard filling the extra space with roots, there'll be little energy left for growing foliage.

Spruce up your patio with a recycled planter. A coat of paint and a few flowers or vines planted inside are all it takes to turn an old barbecue grill into an attractive planter for your patio.

Winterize terra cotta pots. Winter rain and freezing temperatures can destroy your pretty terra cotta flowerpots. That's why you should empty the contents and bring them inside, or at least find a dry place to store them. While you're at it, check for traces of white salts that have built up from fertilizer or water. Scrub these away with a wire brush and soak in a solution of one part bleach to 10 parts water to kill any organisms that might be harmful to your plants next season.

Help clay pots hold moisture. Terra cotta flowerpots have an appeal the plastic variety just can't match. Unfortunately, soil tends to dry out much faster in clay pots. You can slow the evaporation by lining the inside with newspaper before planting.

Plant more value into your landscape

Not only do the trees around your house add beauty and shade, they give your property more monetary value. One study found that people were willing to pay 15 percent more for a house with two red oaks, each just 2 inches in diameter.

Don't fail to water in the fall. You would never neglect watering your hollies, magnolias, and other special deciduous trees during a hot, dry summer. But it's easy to forget their needs when temperatures cool down. Fall, however, is when roots grow the most. So your trees may need regular watering to keep them strong against winter damage, even after they drop their leaves. As the temperatures fall, you can water them less often.

Spread borax for abundant fruit. Fruit trees need a trace of boron. If yours are not producing fruit, this might be the reason. Correct it by sprinkling a pound of borax under each tree.

Stamp out small stumps. You cut down a small tree, but before you knew it, new growth appeared. If you want to get rid of it for good, you must kill the roots. For the stump of a tree no more than 2 inches in diameter, cut a deep cross with a saw or hatchet and fill the open space with baking soda. Leave it for 20 minutes and then pour vinegar into the space. This will destroy even a tough stump, like mesquite.

Give fruit trees a good 'whupping.' It's not just an old wives' tale – beating your fruit trees will increase your harvest. Just take a rolled up newspaper and smack the trees up and down their trunks. This causes the vessels that carry the sap to the leaves and buds to loosen up, resulting in more fruit. According to the old wisdom, the best time to do this is by moonlight in early spring. But you might prefer a dark night so you don't have to explain what you're doing to your neighbors.

Remove moss from tree trunks. Moss growing on trees won't hurt them. But if you don't like the way it looks, here's how to get rid of it. Mix half a cup each of bleach and liquid dishwashing soap in a gallon of warm water and pour over the moss. You may need to do this a few times to completely kill it.

Prune your trees with ease. Dead, damaged, and diseased branches should be the first to go when pruning trees and shrubs. Next, cut out the weak ones and those that cross each other, and your job is done.

Protect your hands from thorns. When pruning roses or other thorny plants, wear oven mitts rather than regular gardening gloves.

Turn leaves into mulch. You can quickly turn dry leaves into mulch or organic material to add to your compost bin. Just fill a plastic garbage can about half way with leaves. Turn on your string trimmer and run it up and down inside to shred the leaves.

Prevent weeds with a newspaper. Put layers of newspaper in your garden to block the sunlight so weeds can't grow. When you're ready to plant, just cut slits in the paper. It's porous enough for water to soak through, yet holds moisture in. For a more attractive appearance, you can cover it with mulch.

Foil attacks against your new lawn. Your dreams of a lush, green lawn evaporate quickly when you see birds flocking to eat your freshly planted grass seeds. Frighten them away with strips of aluminum foil twisting in the breeze. Tie foot-long strips about every 18 inches along lengths of string that will reach across the seeded area. Position the decorated strings in a crisscross pattern and tie them to stakes placed along the border.

Aerate while you mow. How can you aerate your soil and cut the grass at the same time? Easy. Just wear your spiked golf shoes while you mow.

Save grass from salty ice. Salt works great to melt winter's ice and snow. When spring comes, however, you may find the grass along your sidewalk is brown. Instead of melting the ice, you could use sand, sawdust, or cat litter on top for traction. But if you prefer to melt it, use calcium chloride, which is far gentler to plants than sodium chloride.

Recycle shells from seafood feast. Seafood shells – lobster, shrimp, and crabs – are full of calcium. Crush some up and sprinkle them over your lawn to feed the grass.

Hammer out weeds. A plain, old hammer can be a useful tool for weeding your garden. Slam it into the soil, catching the weed between the claws, and pull it up, just like you would with a nail.

Kill weeds with boiling water. Get rid of weeds that are ruining the appearance of your cement or flagstone walk by pouring boiling water on them. You may have to repeat the process from time to time.

Wipe out weeds without emptying your wallet. Kill bothersome weeds easily by pouring vinegar and salt directly on them. Your neighbors who pay an expensive lawn-care company for this service will be green with envy.

Zap poison ivy with salt and soap. There's a natural way to get rid of the poison ivy that comes creeping around. Just stir 3 pounds of salt into a gallon of soapy water and spray it on the leaves and stems.

> ### Rake away pounds
>
> Raking leaves can also double as a workout. A 130-pound woman, for example, burns up 190 calories an hour doing this chore.

Pickle your posies for more blooms. Give your sweet-smelling gardenias a sour treat, and watch for an astonishing increase in snow-white blossoms. When you finish a jar of pickles, just pour the liquid on the ground under the bush.

Visit the henhouse for houseplant helper. Every time you prepare boiled eggs, you make the perfect tonic to perk up your droopy or dying plants. The calcium that remains in the water is good for all kinds of plants, so when it's cool, give them a drink. A little milk also gives plants a boost. Rinse out your empty milk bottle or carton and use that water on your plants as well.

Find free fertilizer in your fruit bowl. Whatever you want to grow – yummy vegetables or fabulous flowers – will thrive with hearty helpings of potassium and phosphorus. And you hold these minerals in your hand each time you eat a banana. So forget expensive fertilizers. Just save those peels, air dry them until crisp and crumbly, and store in an airtight container at room temperature. At planting time, mix the dried banana peels with garden soil and watch the prettiest plants in your neighborhood grow big and strong.

Add a rusty nail for iron. African violets, just like people, need iron to be healthy. A simple way to be sure they get it is to push a couple of rusty nails into the soil beside them.

Let transplants rest on a bed of eggshells. You can add lime and provide drainage for your potted plants with eggshells. Wash the empty shells thoroughly and crush them. Then place the shells in the bottom of the pot before adding soil.

Mend a broken stem. Act quickly when a plant or flower stem gets bent or broken. Make a splint with a toothpick, and wrap it securely with adhesive tape.

Organize chores with a garden calendar. Keep a loose-leaf notebook that includes a calendar to record when planting, fertilizing, and other garden chores should be done. At the beginning of each month, copy what needs to be done that month on the family calendar and check things off as you do them. This keeps the master calendar clear for referral year after year. You may need to make some new pages in your master calendar from time to time, as you add or remove chores.

Make gardening like child's play. If you're looking for an easy way to move tools and supplies around in your garden, buy a child's plastic sled. It can carry a great deal of weight. And since it's low to the ground, it's convenient for planting and other on-the-spot gardening chores.

Guard your knees against hard ground. When your bed pillow loses its fluffiness and is no longer enough padding for your head, give it a new life as a kneeling pad in your garden. But, before you do, wrap it in plastic and tape it closed to keep your new pad clean and dry.

Dump ashes in your garden. For bigger, brighter blossoms, add wood ashes from your fireplace to the soil in your flower beds at the beginning of the growing season. But keep them away from acid-loving shrubs, like azaleas and rhododendrons.

Age your garden with moss. You don't have to wait years for your new garden to acquire that mossy, old-fashioned look. You can quickly grow moss on patio surfaces, planters, and fountains. Just mix any amount of moss, buttermilk, and water in a blender, and apply it wherever you want moss to grow.

Place moisture-loving plants near puddles. Take advantage of those low areas in your lawn where water is slow to drain after a rain. Mint, lavender, hostas, and other plants that require a lot of moisture will be happy in those damp spots.

Support your local plants. Make a plant support from an old lampshade. Just remove the fabric and place the wire frame around your plant.

Give your woodpile a summer makeover. When the weather is warm and you are no longer using firewood, let cucumbers, squash, or climbing flowers crawl over your woodpile.

Rx for bug bites

When you spend a lot of time in the garden, you not only have to battle bugs on your plants but on yourself as well. Here are some natural home remedies for those bothersome bites and stings.

Chiggers	Paint bite with clear fingernail polish
Itchy bites	Cotton ball soaked in vinegar
Itchy bites	Spray starch
Itchy bites	Thick bar soap paste
Sting	Paste of meat tenderizer and water
Sting	Slice of onion
Sting or bite	Paste of baking soda and rubbing alcohol

Extra special ideas for
special occasions

Trim a tree for Easter. A decorated tree adds a magical feeling to the Christmas holidays. So why not decorate trees for other holidays? If you own a big houseplant – like a ficus – decorate it with red ribbons and heart-shaped ornaments for Valentine's Day. Glue loops of ribbon to plastic, colored eggs to hang for Easter. Or twist red, white, and blue crepe paper into a garland and add little stars for the Fourth of July.

Serve a 'hearty' breakfast for Valentine's Day. Show your feelings on Valentine's Day by making a heartfelt breakfast. Break out the red tablecloth and arrange a few red roses in a pretty vase. Fry eggs in heart-shaped, metal cookie cutters. Then clean the cutters and use them to cut bread into hearts for toast.

Color 'egg-citing' Easter eggs. Do your grand kids love to dye eggs for Easter? Try this fun way to make really unique designs. Save all sorts of rubber bands – wide ones, thin ones – and cut some of the thicker ones into wavy or V-shaped patterns. Cut small ovals into a thick band by pinching the elastic at intervals and cutting half circles. Once you have a variety of shapes and sizes, dress up your eggs with the rubber bands and toss them into the dye. When you pull the bands off, you'll have plenty of interesting designs. For a two-toned effect, dye plain eggs a pastel color, then put the bands on and dye a darker shade.

Help little hands color eggs. Even a very young child can dye Easter eggs with a little help. Place a hard-boiled egg in a resealable plastic bag along with the food coloring. Once you're sure the bag is completely sealed, let the little tyke gently shake it. He'll be delighted with the results.

Ban boring Easter baskets. When the Easter Bunny visits your home, give children something that will last longer than the candy. Use a bike helmet, ball cap, jewelry box, purse, or any number of fun containers to hold the loot.

Honor dad on his day

People in the United States have been celebrating Father's Day as far back as 1910. But it wasn't a nationally recognized holiday until 1966 when President Lyndon Johnson officially proclaimed the third Sunday of June the day to honor dads everywhere.

Get your home ready for Halloween. On Halloween night, you not only have to make your house safe for trick-or-treaters, you have to protect it from people looking for not-so-clean fun. Don't forget – keep sidewalks clear of objects and leaves. Make sure your outside lights are working, and leave them on all night. And lock your car inside the garage.

Try this bright idea for Halloween safety. Your child will be delighted to carry a flashlight next Halloween if you make it fun. Using a paper lunch bag, cut out a jack-o'-lantern or other scary face in the bottom. Place a flashlight face down in the bag and wrap a rubber band around the outside. When your tot turns on his flashlight, he'll see a spooky design everywhere he shines it.

Carve spooky jack-o'-lanterns. Don't pay a lot of money for ceramic jack-o'-lanterns. You can make Halloween decorations out of real ones. Working from underneath, hollow out tiny pumpkins and gourds. Then carve scary faces on them with a small, sharp knife. Using a string of battery-operated Christmas tree lights, tuck one light under each little face. Arrange the spooky heads on a tray of fall leaves and dim the overhead lights for extra drama.

Put a monster in your punchbowl. Crank up the fear factor this Halloween by freezing some green soda or punch in a scary-looking plastic mask and a pair of clean rubber gloves. Once frozen, gently cut the gloves away and place the formed hands palms up in your punchbowl. Ease the face out of the mask and into the bowl between each hand and stand back. You're sure to hear at least one bloodcurdling scream.

Hang on to old clothes for Halloween. There's no need to spend $40 on a Halloween costume your child will quickly outgrow. Instead, save old formal dresses, hats, gloves, belts, jackets, and purses and use them to create costumes. An old, fancy dress and purse paired with glittery costume jewelry will appeal to many girls, and a yellow sweat suit can be the basis for a tiger costume for a boy. Simply draw stripes with a magic marker, fasten a piece of rope for a tail, and add whiskers with an eyebrow pencil.

Carve pumpkins safely. Carving a jack-o'-lantern can be a scary job. Make it safe and fun by using a potato peeler. Scratch in a face with a sharp knife, then use the potato peeler to finish the job.

Skirt high price of Christmas tree skirts. Don't pay a lot of money for a skirt for your Christmas tree. Watch for sales on holiday linens and buy a small, round tablecloth in a pattern you like. You'll find a much wider selection in tablecloths than tree skirts, and the prices are better, too. Trace a dinner plate at the center of the tablecloth and cut out the circle. Now cut straight from one edge to the hole in the center, and you've got a beautiful tree skirt. Hemming usually isn't necessary. Just put the opening in the back of the tree.

Zap sticky tree sap. You finally got the Christmas tree to stand up straight in the tree stand, and it looks great. But your hands are another story. You can get that sticky sap off your fingers by rubbing shortening on them and wiping it off with a paper towel. Now wash your hands with soap and water, and you can get back to admiring your tree.

Take the hassle out of hanging lights. Every year you spend a frustrating hour or two untangling the Christmas lights before you can hang them. Save yourself the hassle next time by wrapping each strand in heavy-duty aluminum foil before putting them away. Crunch the foil around the bulbs, and you'll prevent tangling and broken bulbs. Next year, you'll be whistling carols while you decorate.

Play Santa to a child. Did you know that many post offices keep letters written to Santa? This year, ask for a few from a low-income neighborhood. You can buy gifts from a child's wish list and include some extra toys in case there are other children in the home. Purchase a gift certificate from a local grocery store and tuck it in a card with an encouraging message. Send the package anonymously and enjoy your secret all year.

Avoid being 'needled' by your tree. If the Christmas tree you picked out this year is particularly prickly, use giant paper clips to hang your ornaments. Twist the clip open in the shape of an "S," and fasten the ornament to the smaller end. Holding the paper clip in the middle, carefully hook each ornament on a branch.

Toast a classy centerpiece. With a little know-how, four wine glasses can make a classy holiday centerpiece for your table. Here's how. Fill the glasses half full with red or green dry gelatin. Next, place short, red votive candles in each glass. Use transparent tape to secure holly cuttings around the glass stems. When your guests arrive, light the candles, stand back, and enjoy the compliments.

String lights on your palm tree. Ho, ho, hold on a minute. How are you supposed to decorate for Christmas now that you live in a year-round warm climate? Don't sweat it. Gather up leaves of citrus and eucalyptus trees and place them on mantles and tables. You can even fashion a wreath of the leaves and add a big holiday bow. Use your imagination to turn local flora into holiday decorations, and you'll have a holly, jolly Christmas after all.

Create cranberry Christmas ornaments. Use cranberries to make stunning, old-fashioned tree ornaments. Buy various sizes of foam balls from a craft store and spray each with dark red paint. When they're dry, hot-glue a small loop of cranberry-colored ribbon on each ball for hanging, then glue cranberries all around the balls until they're covered. For a completely natural look, use a garland of strung popcorn to complement your new ornaments.

Deck the halls – and the plants. Decorate ordinary objects at Christmas to give your home extra holiday spirit. Turn throw pillows into decorations by tying ribbons around them as if they were presents. Wrap plant pots in rich fabric or colored tissue paper tied up with colorful ribbons. Little touches like these will make your house sparkle during the festive season.

Make your own holiday pillows. If you buy fancy holiday pillows, you'll clean out your wallet and then have to clean out a closet to stash your regular pillows. That just doesn't make sense. Buy holiday fabric in January when it goes on sale, and use it to make slipcovers for the pillows you already have.

Turn a CD into a frozen pond. Ever notice how the shiny, flip side of compact discs look like glass – or ice? Make a miniature winter wonderland by gluing a CD to a piece of cardboard. Glue cotton balls all around it to look like snow, and place an interesting rock in the center hole. Add a tiny sled to the "ice," and your frosty scene will be complete.

Reflect the holidays in your mirrors. Spray-on snow isn't just for windows. You can use it on mirrors throughout your home to celebrate any holiday. At Christmas, outline mirrors using stencils of snowmen, pine trees, or presents. Try heart stencils for Valentine's Day. Unlike ornaments that have to be carefully packed away, spray-on snow wipes off for easy cleanup.

Light your walk with luminaries. If your holiday luminaries fall apart every year, try this. Cut the top off an empty 64-ounce juice carton. Then cut out designs in the sides and decorate it with paint and other trimmings. Place a candle holder and candle inside. These sturdy containers will light up your holidays for years to come.

Restore satin ornaments. Do your satin-covered ornaments have the frizzies? You can easily fix that by smoothing down the threads and zapping them with a bit of hair spray.

Fill in tree with forgotten ornaments. Save those old, inexpensive tree ornaments that have seen better days. Hang them deep inside the tree and on the bottom branches where they won't be obvious. Display your best ornaments on the outside branches – especially at eye level. You'll create the illusion of having a richly dressed tree.

Toss the tree, save the scent. Before you haul away your Christmas tree, consider this. Many trees have needles that will keep their scent for months. Use scrap material to sew little bags to fill with needles. They'll lend a woodland scent to bathrooms, closets, and dresser drawers.

See your room in a new light. Warm your home during the holidays by replacing white lampshades with amber-colored ones. The shades will cast a cozy glow despite the dipping temperatures.

Make ornaments from film canisters. Recycle film canisters into Christmas ornaments your grandchildren will love. Use a hot glue gun to add sequins, beads, lace, or anything else to decorate the containers, and glue a loop of ribbon to each top. Fill the canisters with treats, such as tiny toys, candy, or money, and hang the ornaments on your tree. Invite young visitors to choose their favorite and see what's inside.

Put CDs to work as reflectors. Here's yet another use for freebie compact discs that come in the mail. Use them as reflectors for Christmas lights to line your front walkway. Place some stakes in a row and lay a string of large-bulbed lights on them. Once the lights are in place, unscrew each bulb and place the CD over the socket before putting the bulb back. The CDs will help the lights reflect better and cast an interesting glow.

Hide special treats in walnuts. If the long winter days are making you feel a little squirrelly, try making these nutty crafts for your family. Split several walnuts in half and clean out the shells. Place a tiny slip of paper inside each one stating a prize – a favorite dessert, control of the television remote one evening, choice of the restaurant the next time you go out to eat. You get the picture. Then carefully glue the walnut halves back together, being careful not to let glue seep inside the shells. Lay the shells on newspaper and spray them with a touch of gold or silver paint. When dry, place them in a pretty basket, and let your family choose from them as part of your holiday festivities.

Pick the perfect poinsettia. Every year you buy a poinsettia plant and take it home. And every year it dies soon after the Christmas decorations are put away. It could be you're not choosing healthy plants. Look for a plant with dark green leaves and large flowers with little or no pollen visible. Have the plant wrapped to protect it from the cold and get it indoors as soon as possible. During the winter months, keep it away from drafts and near a sunny window. Water it whenever the soil is dry, but don't give it too much water. If leaves are turning yellow and falling off, you're overdoing it.

Celebrate holidays by saving money

Shopping during national holidays has become a national pastime. That's because people have less and less free time, and they must take advantage of an occasional day off to make their purchases. Retailers, anxious to make sales, significantly discount their goods on those days. Especially good sales appear New Year's Day, Memorial Day, Independence Day, and Labor Day. But don't be too free with your money at Thanksgiving and Christmas. Retailers know most people like to buy presents around these holidays, so you won't get the very lowest prices.

Pop these fun gifts in a stocking. Here's another fun way to recycle the cardboard tubes from paper towel rolls. Cut the cardboard into three equal-sized tubes. Fill the tubes with small wrapped candies, bubble gum, and little toys. Then wrap the tubes with a length of wrapping paper that extends a few inches past the tube on each end. Tie the ends closed with small pieces of ribbon. Put them in your children's Christmas stockings, and tell them to yank both ends at the same time. They'll love the popping sound they make, as well as the candy that spills out everywhere.

Wrap up shopping early. You won't panic at gift-giving time if you jot down gift ideas all year. Record in a notebook the names of everyone you buy for. When you see an appropriate gift for someone on your list, make a note of the item and where you saw it. Make your decisions early, and leave plenty of shipping time for catalog purchases. When special days arrive, you'll have a gift that says "I was thinking of you" instead of "I bought this on the way over."

Give baskets of homemade soap. A basket of little soaps makes a great gift for a woman. Form them yourself to save money and add a personal touch. Start with two bars of non-deodorant, white soap. Place a drop or two of food coloring into a cup of warm water. Use a cheese grater to grate two cups of the soap into the warm water. Knead the soapy "dough," adding a bit of warm water as you go, until all the soap is mixed in. Roll the soap into small, compact balls, and lay them on wax paper to dry for 24 hours. When dry, put the soaps in a small basket or pretty dish and wrap with colored plastic wrap tied with a ribbon.

Make gifts that warm the hearth. Empty toilet paper rolls aren't good for much more than tossing into the fire. So put them to work there. Save empty rolls all year, and collect plenty of dry leaves in the fall. Stuff the rolls with the leaves, and cover them with a rectangle of newspaper about 4 inches longer than the roll. Twist the ends of the newspaper closed and cover the newspaper with wrapping paper, twisting the ends once more. Place your decorative fire starters in a nice basket and give them as gifts. They'll look great on someone's hearth.

Shop for Christmas in January. Don't wait until the last minute to do your Christmas shopping, when there's little left in the stores to choose from. Instead, write out your list of people to buy for early in the year. Then watch for sales on the exact item you want for them. When you find the perfect present, wrap it and label it with a gift tag as soon as you get home. You'll be able to get all your holiday shopping done long before the malls get crowded and the merchandise disappears.

Give teachers what they really want. That ceramic apple might seem like the perfect Christmas gift for your child's teacher, but chances are good she already has an attic full of them. Give her something she can really use – materials for the classroom. Send a grade-appropriate book, magazine subscription, or educational game. Your gift will enrich the lives of many children, which is exactly what teachers want.

Return misfit gifts quickly. Return that "interesting" gift you can't use within a few days of Christmas. If you wait too long, the item may be marked down during post-holiday sales. Unless you have the receipt, you'll only be refunded the reduced sales price.

Make emergency kits for gifts. If you're tired of ties, scarves, and fruitcakes for Christmas, try giving practical gifts this year. Make emergency kits for your loved ones to keep in their cars. Fill a plastic storage box with a first-aid kit, a flashlight, a flare, and an insulated blanket. Add some bottled water, a can opener, and packages of factory-sealed and canned foods to feed someone for several days. Your gift could come in very handy someday.

Fall for this autumn menu. Throw an autumn dinner party your guests will never forget. Hollow out a large pumpkin to use as a festive tureen for delicious pumpkin soup. Carefully cut in half and clean out smaller pumpkins for soup bowls, and make a centerpiece of interesting gourds and beautiful fall leaves. After your favorite entree, serve hot cider with cinnamon sticks in hollowed out Rome apples.

Entertain the easy way. For a more relaxed way to serve a large number of guests, try a buffet. You can serve anything from finger sandwiches, chips, and drinks to a variety of fancy foods. Decorate the buffet table according to the season, and place utensils, plates, and napkins before the food. Your guests will appreciate the casual atmosphere, and you'll feel free to mingle and enjoy yourself.

Pack a picnic in a tray. Pack picnic lunches in bags that double as trays. Instead of small lunch bags, place each person's food in large, paper, grocery bags. To create a greaseproof barrier, line the bottom of the bag with a sheet of wax paper. When you reach your picnic site, simply roll down the sides of the bags to create individual trays.

Design a lovely centerpiece. Some of the best centerpieces are made from the simplest items. Visit the grocery store and feast your eyes on the array of interesting fruits and vegetables available. Choose an assortment of complementary colors and textures – artichokes, lemons, brussels sprouts, radishes – and arrange them in a pretty glass or wooden bowl. Toss in a few pine cones or ornaments to add a holiday flavor.

Bag boring place cards. Turn a plain, white, paper lunch bag into a cute place card at your next luncheon. Write a guest's name toward the bottom of the bag and fold the top down neatly a few times. Place a nice cloth napkin in the bag and let it drape gracefully over the edges. Now fill the bag with an assortment of delicious breadsticks to go with your lunch menu.

Turn the tables on drab dinners. Variety is said to be the spice of life. And like spice, it helps perk up an otherwise drab dinner. Gravy, for example, doesn't have to be served in a clunky, white gravy boat. For a change of pace, serve it in an antique, glass measuring cup or a quaint pottery crock. Use your imagination – and your sense of humor – to add interest to your dinner table.

Plan for trash at parties. If you're having an informal get-together and using paper plates and cups, your kitchen wastebasket might soon be overflowing. Instead of leaving the party to empty the trash, line a large box with a garbage bag and place it in an obvious location. When your guests leave, you'll only have one bag to take out.

Take the stress out of holiday baking. Make baking for the holidays effortless this year. Beginning in September, start freezing half a dozen cookies every time you bake. Do the same with candies and any other treat you create. When your holiday guests arrive, you'll have a wide variety of goodies to serve them, and you won't be stressed by last-minute baking.

Make holiday baking fun. Instead of spending hours baking several types of cookies for holiday guests, organize a cookie exchange. Here's how it works. Invite friends, relatives, and neighbors to bake their favorite cookies for an exchange party. Let everybody know how many people will be attending. Instruct them to wrap the cookies in batches of a dozen and to bring enough for everyone invited, plus a small plate of samples. Brew a pot of coffee and serve the samples at the get-together. You'll get to visit with your friends and relatives, and everyone will take home a nice variety of cookies to serve during the holidays.

Send cookies, not crumbs. You spent a whole day baking pretty cookies to send for the holidays, but they arrived at their destination a pile of crumbs. Next time, pack them in plastic sandwich bags, three or four to a bag, and place the bags in a small, sturdy box or cookie tin. Fill in any air pockets in the box with extra plastic bags. Your cookies should arrive looking as good as they did when you packed them.

Bake perfect gingerbread

Winter festivities call for gingerbread men and gingerbread houses. For best results, use baking soda for soft, delicious cookies. But for building, use baking powder in your recipe. That way, the pieces of your gingerbread house will be firm enough for quality construction.

Make your ice cubes sparkle. You go out of your way to make fresh-squeezed lemonade for special guests. Don't ruin it with cloudy ice cubes that look like they were chipped out of the pond last winter. For crystal clear ice cubes, simply boil water, let it cool, then pour it into your ice cube trays. Boiled water freezes clearly because it contains less oxygen.

Punch up your holiday party. Make a splash at your next party with an eye-catching bowl of punch. Find a fancy punch bowl and ladle, and use your favorite punch recipe. But forget those little ice cubes that water down drinks way too fast. Fill muffin tins with some punch and toss a maraschino cherry into each one. You'll have classy ice cubes that will keep the punch cold instead of diluting it.

Toast friends in style. This New Year's Eve, raise a glass to friendships that have weathered the years. In honor of your treasured friends, dress up your stemware with ribbons, tiny ornaments, beads, or dried flowers. These fanciful trimmings will make your toast – and the night – truly memorable.

Carry drinks with confidence. Carrying a tray of drinks through a crowd of people can make the steadiest hand sweat. Ditch the trays at informal get-togethers. Use your muffin tins instead. Place a drink in each space for no-spill carrying even when little ones are underfoot.

Dress your table for cold weather. Does your dining room table seem cold and impersonal? Warm it up with a colorful quilt. You can use a quilt with a holiday theme or special colors to make a dinner more festive. Choose a color from the quilt and match cloth napkins to it for a coordinated look. Just be sure to use a quilt that's washable and not a family heirloom.

Use pine cones for place cards. Give your winter dinner party a special touch. Spray pine cones with paint or fake snow and use them as place card holders. Write each guest's name on a bit of birch bark or ribbon to tuck into a cone. Your table will look like a winter wonderland, and your guests can take home their pine cone as a memento of the party.

Share a love of gardening. Here's a great dinner party idea for a group of friends who share a love of gardening or cooking. Decorate your table with a centerpiece made of dried herbs and flowers. At each guest's place, set a small, potted herb with the person's name on a garden marker. It's a clever way to direct people to their seats, and each person can take home their plant as a lovely memento of the party.

Trim your table with cranberries. You don't have to spend a lot of money to adorn your coffee table for the winter holidays. A small, decorative dish filled with cranberries will add just the right color. Or try floating cranberries in an elegant bowl with a little water. Add a small, floating candle for a classy touch.

Favor guests with flowers. Put together a centerpiece that comes apart easily for party favors. Fashion a small bouquet of flowers for each guest by wrapping a bit of twine around small bunches of flowers. Arrange the posies together to form a centerpiece, and present one to each person at the end of the evening.

Host a beach bash. Make a splash with a beach party. Cover your table with clean, brightly colored beach towels. Buy plastic toy pails, shovels, and rakes – the kind kids use at the beach. Use the tiny shovels and rakes for utensils, and serve side dishes in the pails. Clean and dry different-sized shells to use as condiment holders. Regardless of the weather outside, your party is sure to sizzle with fun.

Announce the season with sweets. Match your centerpiece to the season or holiday. Use any clear glass container and fill it with candies that reflect the holiday or season, like hearts; red and green M&Ms; candy corn; and red, white, and blue jawbreakers. "Plant" fresh or dried flowers, and you've got a fun and festive focal point for your table.

Deck the dining room, too. Don't forget to dress up your dining room for the holidays. Get out your lacy tablecloth, and hang Christmas ornaments on your chandelier. Drape a garland over a buffet table, and set a few extra special ornaments on top. Place a single, white-bulb candle in each window for some old-fashioned holiday charm.

Make your own trivets. Large ceramic tiles – available at most home improvement stores – make great trivets for protecting your table. Best of all, they come in all sorts of colors and cost very little. Pick up a few in holiday colors, or colors that complement your china. Glue felt rounds onto the four bottom corners for added protection.

Watch this centerpiece on New Year's Eve. Make a memorable centerpiece for a New Year's Eve party. Place all sorts of time-telling devices on the table – clocks, watches, calendars, hourglasses, egg timers, and whatever else you might have. Set the alarm clocks for exactly midnight for a timely reminder to celebrate.

Decorate simple place mats. Turn ordinary place mats into holiday luncheon mats by fastening strips of ribbon across the width and length of the mat. Use tiny pins to secure the ribbons to the back of the fabric. Add a stick-on bow in a corner, and your place mat will look like a wrapped present.

Lock card tables together. If you've placed card tables together for a large dinner party, you run the risk of the tables separating and a plate of food crashing to the floor. To keep that from happening, lock together adjoining table legs in large coffee cans. Cover the tables with long tablecloths, and no one will be the wiser.

Shower her with recipes. You can perk up a bridal or baby shower by asking each person to bring the guest of honor a favorite recipe. For new brides, an easy-to-prepare meal is a winner. For new moms, a tried and true "recipe" for calming a crying baby will be much appreciated. Put the recipes in a pretty box, and toss in an instant photo taken at the shower.

Fill the pantry of a bride-to-be. Forget the lingerie shower for the bride-to-be. Give her something she really needs – recipes. Mail a recipe card to each person invited to the shower. Ask them to copy a favorite recipe, sign the card, then shop for all the nonperishable ingredients required. At the shower, each person presents a "meal" to the future bride. For those who can spend more, place the supplies in a Dutch oven, set of mixing bowls, or other handy item.

Create your own Christmas cards. Make your own Christmas cards using a photo of your family at a holiday dinner, your home blanketed with snow, or a beloved pet surrounded by holiday decorations. Have copies made of your favorite photo, and use spray adhesive to glue the pictures to the front of blank cards. Use a fine-tip marker to write a message inside. Far-flung friends and relatives will treasure their holiday "visit" to your home.

Turn a greeting card into art. Sometimes greeting cards qualify as works of art. When you see one you love, frame it and set it out each holiday season as part of your decorations. Let your children pick out a few of their favorites to be framed, too. They'll love seeing them year after year.

Grace gifts with handmade tags. Personalize gift wrapping by making your own gift tags this year. Cut out interesting or seasonal pictures from magazines and glue them to business cards or small pieces of cardboard.

Unstick tape with a button. Wrapping gifts wouldn't be so bothersome if you could only find the end of your roll of tape. Here's a simple way to do just that – stick a button on it. As you use the tape, keep moving the button.

Wrap big gifts easily. Think outside the box when wrapping an oversized package. Don't waste a roll of pricey wrapping paper trying to piece together a covering. Instead, buy an inexpensive, festive, paper tablecloth. A few pieces of tape, and you're all set.

Make bows that make 'cents.' You can pay over a dollar each for pretty bows to adorn presents for your grandchildren. But that just doesn't make sense. Instead, accordian-pleat a dollar bill, secure the middle with a piece of ribbon, and fan it out like a bow. The kids are sure to enjoy these practical decorations.

Bank a boodle of buttons. Colorful buttons make great additions to packages, wreaths, and ornaments. Watch for sales throughout the year at craft and fabric stores and buy gold, silver, red, and green buttons in bulk.

Wrap tiny gifts with flair. Some holiday paper napkins are almost too pretty to wipe your hands on – despite the fact they only cost a few pennies each. Use them creatively to wrap small gifts or to tie up little bags of sweets for an exchange. Add a bit of ribbon, and you'll have an attractive-looking gift.

Top a present with tinsel. Use colorful, wired tinsel to customize gift wrapping. Shape the tinsel into stars, hearts, trees, or whatever you like. You can even spell out the person's name or initials for a personal touch.

Iron wrinkled tissue paper. Save the tissue paper that goes flying over your grandson's shoulder as he unwraps his toys. If you iron it on a low setting, it'll be good as new for next year.

Rough up the wrappings for boys. Don't waste ribbons and pretty paper on your burly teenage grandson. Wrap his gift in something he'll appreciate. Try the Sunday comics as an interesting alternative to fancy wrapping paper. Or use rough material like burlap and tie the package with twine. If he's athletic, pack his present in a gym bag he can use for his gear.

Make emergency wrapping paper. It's Christmas Eve and all the stores are closed. But you have one more present to wrap and no more wrapping paper. Take a deep breath. Now look around. You probably have small, irregular pieces of wrapping paper all over the place. Take several of the bigger pieces and cut them into the largest squares possible. Taping from the inside of the paper, make a patchwork quilt of the leftover pieces. Your present will not only be wrapped, it will be wrapped with flair.

Wrap presents with precision. You probably waste a roll of wrapping paper each year by cutting pieces a bit too short or much too long. Eliminate the guesswork by using a length of string to measure the object before cutting the paper.

Wrap a present with music. Create wrapping paper sure to delight a music buff. Photocopy sheet music from one of her favorite composers, and wrap the gift with the title and opening bars clearly visible. The paper will put a song in her heart and a smile on her face – even before she sees your present.

Hide your wrapping paper to keep it neat. You saved all your leftover wrapping paper from last Christmas, but it managed to unravel and tear in the storage box. Next year, unroll all of the paper, then roll it tightly to fit inside the cardboard tube. Your paper will be in perfect condition for the next season.

Save money with glue sticks. Wrapped presents will look designer perfect if you use a glue stick instead of tape. Unlike regular glue, a swipe of the stick dries almost immediately. And compared with the expense of tape, it will cost only pennies to wrap your gifts.

Stop buying wrapping paper. Does it make you wince to see wrapping paper thrown away every Christmas? You can save paper – and money – by sewing oversized sacks for your presents. Use velvet or a plush material and sew as you would a giant pillow-case. Decorate the sacks any way you wish, and use fancy curtain tiebacks with tassels to tie them up. The beautiful sacks will look every bit as charming as wrapped presents under your tree, and they'll become permanent keepsakes for your loved ones.

Drum up new packaging ideas. Did you buy someone a collection of little things for Christmas? Toss them into a coffee can, and wrap the can – not the lid – with red paper. Draw a "W" pattern around the can with a thin, black marker, and your present will look like an adorable little drum.

Make your own gift bags. Gift bags look great, but they're expensive. Make your own with a little help from a cereal box. Using heavy wrapping paper, loosely cover a cereal box without actually taping the box. Gently pull the box out, and use a hole punch to make holes at the top of the bag for handles. Fashion the handles out of matching yarn, and tie a knot in each end on the inside of the bag. You'll have a fancy-looking gift bag for pennies.

Strengthen parcels with soggy string. Worried that your package won't arrive in one piece? Put your mind at ease with this trick grandma used. After you wrap and tape a parcel, wet a long piece of string and tie it around the middle of the package. Secure the string in the back and wrap it in the other direction to form a cross on both sides of the parcel. Knot it well, and when it dries, the string will shrink a bit and hold your package securely.

Fend off foam peanuts with fabric softener. Does it feel like you're being attacked by foam peanuts when you're sending or opening a package? Before you handle those pesky peanuts, put a little liquid fabric softener on your hands. It will cut down on the static cling.

Welcome a baby with a wreath. Give a decorative and useful gift to a friend with a newborn. Buy a colorful wreath and tuck baby gifts into the branches. Insert a baby spoon, a rattle, a teething ring, a pair of little socks, and any other tiny thing for a tiny person. After removing the small gifts, your friend can hang the wreath in the nursery.

Wax nostalgic with candles

It's a bit of a mystery where candles originated, but they go back at least as far as biblical times. Historians think grease-soaked rushes were probably the first candles. These burning weeds smelled terrible and gave off a lot of smoke, but they were easy to make and cheap. Eventually, the idea of a wick evolved into hand-dipped, wax candles similar to the ones used today.

Protect tablecloth from dripping wax. A little greenery wound around the base of your candles lends a bit of elegance to a table. But that's not all it does. Carefully placed holly or magnolia leaves also protect your furniture and tablecloths from wax drippings.

Fit candles into smaller candleholders. If your candles are too fat to fit in your candleholders, don't throw them out. Candle stores sell shavers, which are similar to pencil sharpeners. Simply shave the base of the candle until it fits.

Enjoy a fire without the heat. Don't pass up the fun of a crackling fire on Christmas morning just because you live in Miami. Place a collection of red and green candles in your fireplace and toss in some tinsel and a few ornaments. Your hearth won't give off much heat, but it will still warm your spirit.

Make a special candle last forever. If you have a large, lovely candle you treasure, you probably have mixed feelings about burning it. Here's a way to use it indefinitely. Light the candle and let it burn until there is about a two-inch crater in the middle. Then place a small, votive candle in the space and burn that instead. Just keep replacing the small candles as they burn down, and your special candle will last forever.

Slide votive candles from holders. Ever notice how hard it is to change a votive candle once it has burned down and melted all over the holder? You can avoid this by adding a few drops of water to the candle holder before putting the new candle in. When it's time to change candles, the old one should pop right out with a little help from a butter knife.

Hold birthday candles with candy. Keep candles from disappearing into the frosting by placing them in colorful, ring-shaped candies. Depending upon how old you are, they can add quite a lot of interest to the cake.

Protect wine bottle from dripping wax. Wine bottles make interesting candle holders, especially when they get covered with wax drippings. But if you want your bottle to stay wax free, make a wax-catching collar by snipping the bottom off a small paper cone and placing it in the mouth of the bottle. You can jazz up the paper with paint and glitter if you like. The wax will collect in the collar, and your bottle will stay clean.

Save money sending flowers. You can arrange to have pretty flowers delivered monthly to a friend or relative, but it'll cost you a pretty penny. If the person lives within driving distance, why not give the gift of flowers and a visit from you? On your way to visit each month, stop at the grocery store, where flowers are inexpensive, and buy a new bunch. Your special someone will feel even more special when you visit, and you'll save on the high cost of delivery.

Add flowers to your grocery list. You love the look of fresh flowers, but with the prices the florist charges, you have to limit yourself to special occasions. Now you have another option – the local supermarket. Most large supermarkets have floral departments with a wide variety of lovely flowers and plants for much less than you'd pay at the florist. And if you provide your own vase, it will cost even less. So put flowers on your grocery list and start enjoying them year round.

Add color to cut flowers. Amaze your friends with two-color flowers you create yourself. All you need are white carnations, food coloring, and two vases. Position the vases next to each other, and fill them with cool water. Add a different food coloring to each. You can experiment with colors until you get two shades you like. Try red and green for Christmas, or two shades of green for St. Patrick's Day. Trim the stems of the carnations with a sharp knife, then slit the stems in half lengthwise to within a few inches of the flower. Place half of each stem in a vase. If you have trouble keeping the divided stems in their vases, use tape or a paper clip to anchor them. Gradually, as the stems pull in the colored water, you'll get a most unusual, two-toned flower.

Stock a craft box for kids. Grand kids coming for a visit? Start filling up a craft box now. Save scrap material, ribbons, buttons, pipe cleaners, tissue boxes, cardboard, and any other interesting items you might have. Add some poster paints, scissors, and glue, and the kids will amaze you with their creations.

Make squirrel-size knitting baskets. Help your grandchildren make these adorable tree ornaments. Halve and hollow out walnuts. Then glue a 5-inch piece of ribbon to the inside of the shell to form a loop for hanging. Take several long pieces of yarn in different colors and wrap each one tightly to form a little ball. Glue the balls into the walnut shell and stick two straight pins in one of the yarn balls to look like knitting needles. The ornaments will look like tiny knitting baskets hanging on your tree.

Personalize a pencil holder. Help your grandchild make this personalized pencil holder for a parent, sibling, or teacher. First cut out a magazine picture of something interesting. Find a clean, clear, glass jar and cut the picture to fit inside. Using white, paper glue, paste the picture to the inside of the jar so it shows through the glass. Be sure it's completely glued to the glass without any air bubbles. When the glue dries, paint the inside of the jar a complementary color with acrylic paints. Tie a ribbon around the rim, and your pencil holder is ready for giving.

Turn softball into a splash-fest. Score big points with your grand kids this summer. On a hot day, supply them with water balloons to replace balls in traditional games, such as softball or volleyball. Even a simple game of catch becomes exciting when the ball threatens to explode with icy water.

Dig these garden party ideas. Dress up your patio for an evening garden party. Put pretty, glazed flowerpots on the table and set candles in them with a bit of modeling clay. Buy shiny, new garden trowels to use as serving utensils, and hide your ice bucket in a fancy planter. And, of course, arrange plants and flowers on every available surface.

Give a 'tasteful' gift. Give a gift from the heart that gladdens the taste buds. On nice note cards, write recipes for favorite family meals or desserts. If there is any history behind the recipe, include it on the back of the card. Tie the recipes with a pretty ribbon, and hand them out on special holidays.

Give a gift of favorite recipes. Is your child or grandchild moving out on her own soon? Send her off with a scrapbook of family recipes. Explain the origin of each recipe and rework a favorite family meal so it will feed two. That way she'll have some leftovers to eat instead of fast food. Or who knows — maybe she'll invite you for dinner.

Delight dieters with potpourri. Giving edible gifts this Christmas? Be kind to loved ones dieting. Instead of food, delight their sense of smell with a potpourri kit. Include an orange, a lemon, four cinnamon sticks, six cloves, a bay leaf, and the following recipe: Put three cups of water in an uncovered cooking pot. Add the cinnamon sticks, cloves, bay leaf, and the fruit cut into quarter-inch slices. Bring the water to a boil, then reduce the heat so it simmers. Add water as needed.

Picture this at your party. Give your party guests a lovely memento to take home – a snapshot. Use an instant camera to take photos of each guest near a special decoration, such as a Christmas tree or chatting with other partygoers. Hand the pictures out during the festivities, and they'll also spark conversation. Your guests will remember your party for years to come, and they'll appreciate your thoughtful touch.

Preserve newspaper clippings like an old hand. Make a sensational gift for someone who has been written up in the newspaper by preserving the article from aging and yellowing. Simply mix a quart of club soda with two tablespoons of milk of magnesia and refrigerate the solution overnight. Using a clean, shallow pan, lay the clipping in enough solution to completely cover it. After an hour, remove the clipping and lay it on a stack of ink-free paper towels. Once it has dried a little, place it on a clean countertop to finish drying. Now you can frame the clipping and present it to your achiever, who will be able to enjoy it for years.

Give a scrapbook of memories. Turn your shutterbug shenanigans into personalized gifts for friends and family. Fill a scrapbook with photos of the person in all sorts of settings throughout the year. Nothing says I care for you like a scrapbook full of happy memories.

Take advantage of this photo opportunity. The corrugated cardboard packaging that came with your new light bulb has done its job. Your light bulb is safe and sound, shining from its new home in your lamp. But now what can you do with the packaging? Assign the light bulb cover another mission – to protect your photographs. Fold it flat and slide your photos inside. When you send them through the mail, they won't get damaged.

Give a unique antique. Consider antiques and collectibles the next time you're shopping for unique gifts. Personalize a beautiful, old cufflink case by having your friend's initials engraved on it. For a costume jewelry collector, you can buy lovely, used pieces of jewelry for a fraction of what they would cost new. If you have a good idea what your friends like, you're sure to put smiles on their faces at gift-giving time.

Give free phone time to a friend. Give a prepaid phone card to a friend on a fixed income. Many discount department stores display them at the checkout counter in various dollar amounts. Your gift will take some of the pressure off your friend at bill-paying time, and you might hear from her more often, too.

Make pretty candy rosebuds. Can't decide whether to give candy or roses? Give both with this clever craft idea. You'll need chocolate kisses, pink plastic wrap, green tissue paper, green floral tape, and green pipe cleaners. For each "rosebud," tape together two kisses, back to back. Wrap both of the kisses in a 4-inch square of pink plastic wrap, starting at the top of one of the kisses. Twist the bottom end closed, then wrap a pipe cleaner around it to form a stem. Cut pieces of tissue paper to form leaves on the stem and secure them with floral tape. Place the roses in a pretty vase and present them to your sweetie.

Create clocks from CDs. Those free compact discs that come in the mail are good for more than serving bagels. You can turn them into clocks with a $5 clock kit from the craft store. Flip a CD to its blank side and personalize it with paint. When the paint dries, arrange the numbers on the CD, then add the hands. You'll find the hole in the middle is just the right size for the hardware. Computer geeks will love these folk art clocks.

Work fragrances into wreaths. Tuck bits of fragrance into your holiday wreaths. Add sprigs of eucalyptus, rosemary, or bay leaves, or fasten cinnamon sticks to a wreath with a bit of hot glue. Wreaths that look great and smell good will make a lasting impression.

Recycle old holiday tins. The tin you got as a holiday present was great when it was filled with popcorn. But now that the snack is gone, don't just throw it out. Since most of these tins come decorated in a holiday theme, it could make a pretty and easy-to-find storage bin for your ornaments.

Toast this ornament holder. Keeping special ornaments safe during the off-season doesn't have to cost lots of money. Go to a nearby liquor store and ask for a small box with the bottle dividers still in it. These boxes make perfect vacation homes for each little treasure.

Find storage space for decorations. If you're short on closet space, store your Christmas wrapping paper, bows, tags, and other items in a long, shallow storage box that will fit under your bed.

Color code storage boxes. Oh, no. It's time for the Easter Bunny to make an appearance, but every box you open is full of Santa stuff. Avoid this mix-up in the future by color-coding your storage boxes. Use a pastel one for Easter goodies, green for Christmas, and orange or black for Halloween. Clearly label each holiday on the sides and tops of boxes to make your job easier.

Sock away delicate ornaments. Don't discard those unpaired socks your dryer occasionally spits out. Save them to cushion delicate Christmas ornaments. An old, heavy sock is especially good for protecting a treasured ornament in a storage container.

Pack ornaments in air. Each year you lose a precious ornament or two to packing mishaps. Keep all your Christmas ornaments safe until next year by storing them in sealable plastic bags. Place one ornament in each bag and use a straw to blow air into the bag while sealing it. Pack the bags loosely in a sturdy storage box. The air will help cushion your treasures.

Find your tree stand fast. You're tired from a long afternoon of picking out the perfect tree, and the last thing you want to do is dig through storage boxes to find your tree stand. You can avoid this yearly hassle by boldly labeling one box "open first." In this box, put your tree stand, extension cords, and anything else you'll need to kick start the holidays.

Record the stories of your ornaments. In your box of special ornaments, tuck a little notebook listing the memories associated with each trinket. You don't have to write an essay, just enough information to jog your memory. Jot down things such as "ice-skating mouse, 1965, gift from father the year I left for college." When children and grandchildren help trim the tree, they will relish the stories your ornaments tell.

Creative notions for
sewing & crafts

Archaeologists dig up very old beads

Some people's fascination with beads knows no bounds. The 28,000-year-old remains of a man and two children were found in Sungir, Russia, in 1986. All three were draped in thousands of ivory beads. The 60-year old man was wearing 2,936 large beads, while the children were each wrapped in about 5,000 smaller beads. What was most surprising was the time required to make each bead – about one hour. It would have taken the whole community over a year to prepare the beads for this burial.

Ease the strain of bead sorting. Separating the wheat from the chaff is hard enough, separating pearls from seed beads is even harder. To simplify sorting small from large beads, pour them into a fine mesh colander. The tiny seed beads will fall right through the mesh, while the larger ones rest innocently inside.

Restrain scampering beads. Stop chasing bouncing, rolling, jumping beads. When you work on a beading project, spread a towel over your work space. The beads will get caught in the pile, and they won't roll in every direction. You can clean up and transport your project with ease by simply moving the towel. If you use a light-colored towel when you work with dark beads, they will be easy to find and remove at the end of the project.

Think before repairing brooch. To reattach a pin to the back of a brooch, make sure you position the clip no further than

1/4 inch below the upper edge of the piece. This will keep the brooch from sagging forward when worn. If the piece is long and narrow, glue the pin on lengthwise, with the clasp at the top.

Glop on alternative to jeweler's cement. The next time you have to reattach an earring post, try a cheap alternative to jeweler's cement found in your local hardware store. Called plumber's epoxy, it's easy to apply and will hold metal, ceramic, and plastic jewelry pieces together.

Twirl yarn scraps into gifts. Don't toss out yarn scraps. Dip them in starch and blot until just damp. On a sheet of wax paper, arrange the yarn into tightly curled swirls, ovals, hearts, or knots. Let the starch dry and mount your designs on small pieces of cardboard. Glue a magnet to the back and you've got a decorative refrigerator magnet. Or attach a pin back for designer costume jewelry.

Design your own dazzling jewelry. Accessorizing is effortless with these easy-to-make beads. Before you throw out small wallpaper scraps, rip them into long, triangular or rectangular strips – 1/2-inch wide and 12-inches long – and dip them in glue. Starting with the wide end, wrap the moistened strips around a wooden skewer and let them set. When your new beads begin to get stiff, take them off the skewer and let them dry. For a shiny finish, coat the beads with clear nail polish. String them on beading thread or dental floss. Experiment with different shapes and colors of paper for fun jewelry you and your friends will love.

Thread a needle in a flash. Instead of jabbing repeatedly at the eye of your needle with a limp thread, spray some hair spray on your fingers and twist the end slightly. When the thread is dry, it will be stiff enough to easily spear your needle.

Cut bias binding blunders. Finding a bias line is hard enough, but when all the stretching and tugging is done, it's difficult to hold the fabric in place. To simplify the process, use masking tape to mark the bias. And for straight strips, cut the fabric down both sides of the tape. Carefully remove the tape when you are ready to sew on your binding.

Control slippery fabric. Discover a whole new side to table pads by flipping them over and using the felt surface to cut out a pattern. The felt should cling slightly to the material, keeping it stable as you snip along the seam allowance.

Mend a sleeve using a magazine. It's hard to mend a hole when the fabric is loose in your hands. To make sure your seams are straight and smooth, roll up a magazine and slide it into the shirt sleeve or pant leg you are working on. The magazine will unfurl enough to hold the fabric in place while you sew.

Step up to pain-free hemming. Don't strain your knees bending and kneeling to pin up your daughter's skirt hem. Instead, have her stand a few steps above you on the landing. The stairs will provide a comfortable place for you and your notions to sit.

Discover the secret to a great hem. The right hem can make a dress or skirt hang better. When sewing a hem, keep in mind that different skirt styles require different hem widths. In general, narrow skirts should have wider hems, while fuller skirts hang better with a narrow hem.

Duplicate a pattern with wax paper. Many sewing patterns have multiple sizes on the same sheet. To protect the original pattern, trace the size you need using wax paper.

Recycle old socks. Wait! Don't throw those old socks out! The ribbed binding can be cut and reused as cuffs for the wrists and ankles of homemade pajamas. If you like, dye the socks to match your material.

Sew buttons to last. Instead of securing four-hole buttons in one pass, try sewing only two holes at a time. Anchor two of the holes, knot and cut the thread, then anchor the other two. Your button will be more secure, and you won't lose it if one of the threads comes loose.

Dispose of pins and needles safely. Keep broken needles and pins from coming back to haunt you. Put them in an empty, childproof medicine bottle before throwing them away.

You'll never have to worry about rubbing up against your garbage bag or maiming the garbage man.

Bag sewing patterns for safekeeping. Instead of squeezing pattern pieces back into the original envelope, store your favorites in individual, zip-lock bags. The plastic allows you to see the illustrations and keeps the delicate pattern pieces safe. Add a swatch of each sewing project to your bag for a quick record of your sewing history. You may be surprised how many memories these patterns bring back.

Steer clear of crafty scissors. If you find it hard to keep track of small scissors, keep an empty dental floss container in your knitting basket. The thread blade is useful for cutting yarn, and you'll never accidentally hurt yourself on a sharp blade again.

Give tired fingers some help. Don't give up on needle-work because your hands get tired. For a slip-free grip on smooth crochet hooks and knitting needles, wrap thick rubber bands around them where your fingers rest. If you have arthritis, this added padding can spell relief for your strained fingers.

File away blunt tips. Nail files can sharpen, as well as smooth. Revive a dull needle by filing its tip with an emery board.

Thread a needle the easy way. Sometimes threading a needle can be as hard as pushing an elephant through a doorway. To simplify matters, hold your dark thread against a light background, and your light thread against a dark one.

Try tape to make a thimble fit. If your finger slips and slides inside your thimble, wrap a piece of masking tape, sticky side out, around your finger and push it into the thimble. The tighter fit and traction should help your finger guard stay put.

Shrink a sweater to make mittens. Don't throw away that 100-percent wool sweater you accidentally shrank. Make a pair of mittens. Wash the sweater in hot water and dry it on high heat one more time. Meanwhile, trace the outline of your hand on paper or cardboard, adding an inch all around. Cut four layers of this dense, tightly woven wool according to your template and blanket stitch the edges together. These mittens are not only soft and snugly, they're well-insulated.

Make pinning hems a snap. Before you begin pinning a hem, slip a rubber band around your ruler at the measurement mark. You won't have to strain your eyes to see a faded number when the mark is clearly defined.

Drop a cloth to protect a table. Try this to protect the finish on your table from scissors. Lay an old vinyl tablecloth or plastic dropcloth on your work surface before you start cutting out patterns. The scissors will glide easily over the plastic, and your table won't sustain any war wounds.

Mend gloves using marbles. Drop a marble into the finger of a glove before you mend it. The marble will give you a smooth, hard surface to surgically repair tricky holes.

Steam a seam for professional look. For a professional finish on your handmade garments, be sure to steam press your seams open. Simply use the point of the iron to separate the two selvages and press them flat. For seams that won't stay put, dampen them with a little water and then steam press.

Stop your hem from falling. A stitch in time saves nine, but how about a knot in five? Knot your thread every 3 to 5 inches whenever you hem anything. If the thread breaks, you'll only have to hem a short stretch of seam.

Shed some light on the subject. Tracing patterns, drawings, or lettering can be a real chore without a light table. Before you invest in one, take a look at your dining room table. If you can remove one of the central leaves and replace it with a sheet of Plexiglas cut to size, you can set a lamp under the table. The extra "leaf" can easily be stored under the couch or beside the refrigerator for quick access.

Back your embroidery with dryer sheets. Used dryer sheets work perfectly for backing sewing and embroidery. They sew on smoothly and pull off easily when you're done.

Use tape to determine right from wrong. Sewing was simpler when you could tell the right side and wrong side of fabric just by looking at it. Now, many fabrics look the same on both sides until they are sewn together. To keep right sides together, mark the wrong side of the material with a small piece of tape right after you cut out a pattern piece.

Secure knots with nail polish. To keep thread knots from coming undone while you're working on your cross-stitch, dab them with a drop of nail polish. The knot will stay firm even when you wash and frame the finished piece.

Try floss for color harmony. Next time you don't have the right color thread to sew a button on your coat, ransack your cross-stitch project for embroidery floss. When you find the right color, separate one thread from the six and enjoy instant thread matching. Double the thread for extra-strength mending.

Match your thread with markers. If you need black thread and all you have is white, run your thread over the tip of a black permanent marker until it is entirely coated in black ink. This will work for any color marker, just make sure the ink is permanent or it will come out in the wash.

Sponge away tangled floss. Valuable time is wasted untangling knots in embroidery floss. Instead of mastering the correct tug to loosen an existing knot, avoid them altogether by running one strand of floss at a time over a moist sponge. Once the floss dries, it's straighter and less likely to tangle.

Mark your fabric with soap. Tired of seeing your carefully marked darts disappear in a cloud of dust? Use soap slivers instead of expensive tailor's chalk. The dry soap will leave a distinct mark on your fabric that will stay put as you sew. Best of all, it will disappear in the wash, leaving your new project clean as a whistle.

Iron out problems before buying fabric. Steer clear of creased material at a fabric store and save yourself frustration at the ironing board. Fabric near the end of a bolt usually has a deep crease, formed when the fabric was rolled on the bolt. This crease will not iron out. Don't pay for fabric you can't use.

Serve your heirlooms coffee. Tea-dyeing is a well-known trick to make new linens look old. Unfortunately, the tannic acid in tea will destroy your heirloom in 30 to 40 years. As an attractive alternative, dip your linens in coffee. The rich brown color will give your cloth an antique look without damaging the fabric.

Buy notions and fabric together. Don't make several trips to the fabric store if one will do. Buy matching thread, buttons, zipper, and binding at the same time you buy your fabric. Keep all the notions in a plastic bag so you'll be ready to sew when the urge hits.

Be picky when buying fabric. Don't start what's not worth finishing. If you don't like the look or feel of a piece of material, don't spend time sewing it into a garment. Chances are you won't like it enough to wear it anyway.

Banish grease on fabric with shampoo. If you notice a grease stain on your new fabric, treat the spot with shampoo made for oily hair before pre-washing.

Turn knitting needles into rulers. To gauge your progress as you knit, mark your needles every inch with nail polish. As you finish a row, you can measure how far you have come, and calculate how far you have to go.

Smooth knitting needle flaws. Nicked knitting needles will snag yarn worse than a chipped fingernail. To smooth your tips, coat needle ends with nail polish. Your yarn will thank you.

Stiffen crocheted pieces with glue. To stiffen a piece of crochet, dip it in a mixture of equal parts water and white glue. Stretch the piece and pin it to Styrofoam or cardboard covered with plastic wrap. If you want to add sparkle, sprinkle with glitter while the glue is still wet. Let the piece dry for 24 hours and enjoy.

Untangle yarn with a straw. You've finally worked out that complicated two-tone sweater pattern, but the two balls of yarn keep getting tangled. To knit or crochet in peace, string each ball of yarn through a straw. The straw sleeve will keep them from snarling, and let you pull the yarn freely as you work.

Keep hands smooth as a baby's bottom. Sprinkle your hands lightly with baby powder when you knit or crochet baby gifts. Not only will your hands stay dry and silky, your finished garment will smell as sweet as a newborn babe.

Dress up your phone book. Can't find a spot for that ugly, yellow phone book? Grab some leftover wallpaper and dress it up. Using the original cover as a guide, cut the wallpaper, glue it in place, and trim to fit. Be creative and make your book an object to display, not hide.

Create an elegant doorstop. You can easily turn a brick into an elegant doorstop. Wrap the fabric from an old evening bag or tapestry pillowcase around a brick, tacking it down on the ends. You may be surprised how pleasurable it is to enjoy your discarded accessory in its new form.

Wrap your gift in flowers. Gifts for people with green thumbs are easy to find but hard to wrap. Whether it's a plant or a special tool, present your gift in true gardener's style. Save empty flower seed packets and seed catalogs. Cut out and glue your favorite blooms onto a plain paper bag. Use the front cover of a seed packet as a centerpiece and surround it with paper roses, daffodils and tulips. And don't forget to make a gift tag for your earth friendly bag.

Blow bubbles to jazz up paper. This easy alternative to marbled paper will blow you away. Mix poster paint with water and a little liquid soap. Pour it into a shallow bowl and use a straw to blow air into the mixture. The paint will soon froth, the colorful bubbles growing until they tower over the edge of the bowl. Lay a clean piece of paper over the bubbles to create a pattern of intersecting circles. Continue to blow bubbles and move the paper until it's covered with a pleasing pattern. When the paper is completely dry, use it for cards, gift tags, wrapping paper, or book covers.

Marvel at designer pencils. Why settle for plain yellow pencils when designer pencils are easy to make? To prepare your pencils for painting, lightly sand off their shiny surface and protect the eraser with a piece of masking tape. On a piece of wax paper, swirl together two or three colors of acrylic paint and fold the sheet over, smoothing it out to marble the colors. Unfold the sheet and roll your pencils in the paint. Let them dry on wax paper. These pencils make great stocking stuffers.

Preserve pictures of your ancestors. Passing down family portraits is a time-honored tradition, but sometimes there are more relatives than copies. When you need to reproduce a photo, don't photocopy it. The light from a copy machine can ruin the finish on a picture. Instead, have a professional photofinisher make a negative of your original and create copies from this negative.

Show off your dog in style. Make this charming frame to proudly display your favorite dog. It's easy. Just gather some bone-shaped doggy treats, a flat frame, and some polyurethane spray. Spray the treats to seal out moisture and let them dry. Remove the glass and backing from the frame and glue the bones nub-to-nub around it. Carefully spray the frame again with polyurethane and reassemble it. Your dog's face can now be displayed in true canine style.

Steer clear of leaky photos. If you crop your Polaroid photos to fit into your scrapbook, they may leak chemicals, and your pictures will be destroyed. This doesn't mean you have to settle for square images in an otherwise imaginative book. Use die-cut mats or cut your own to draw attention to the focal point of each picture and hide its telltale frame.

Photocopy newspaper clippings. Mounting newspaper clippings in a photo album can be hazardous to your photos' health. The acid in newsprint causes the paper to yellow and may ruin your photos. To keep your pictures safe, make a photocopy of your clippings on acid-free paper and add it to your album. Hold on to the original clippings in a separate "brag book."

Ease photos off sticky paper. Magnetic photo albums have a reputation for not letting go of pictures. If you need to loosen the bond between photos and paper, use the lowest setting on your hair dryer to warm the adhesive. Just make sure you don't get too close to the pictures. When the paper is warm, gently lift off the photographs.

Move scenery photos to the sidelines. Boring pictures make a boring album. Use landscapes and crowd scenes to create a border around your best pictures. Trim the images so only the interesting features remain.

Produce a memory movie. Create an irreplaceable record of your family's year. Slowly flip through your photo album with a video camera trained on the pages. Narrate the events of every picture to make them pop off the page. You can send this video to family instead of spending extra money and time creating a copy of your scrapbook. Best of all, it's easier to ship and store on the other side.

Resolve to organize family photos. Is organizing photo albums your New Year's resolution? Get a jump start on last year's buildup by starting early on New Year's morning. Pull out all the photographs taken during the past year and ask your loved ones to help create a family album. You can spend the whole day reminiscing about days gone by, cutting, pasting, journaling, and creating new memories for the year ahead.

Rewrite your photo history. Who said pictures need to be arranged by date? For a fun diversion, create a theme timeline. Follow your hairstyles or skirt lengths, your loved one's string of cars, choice of eyeglasses, or receding hairline. Group together relatives, holidays, or special events to show, in a glance, how things have changed. You can even use unflattering photos for these short journeys, since the focus is on the theme, not the person in the photo.

Add interest to album with ordinary photos. Pictures of zoos, old buildings, flowers, and sunsets seem to multiply in photo boxes. If you have lots of unsentimental snapshots, crop them to form letters and fun shapes, like hearts and stars, and use them throughout your album.

Wedding quilt folklore

Many years ago, brides-to-be were often presented with a wedding quilt at their bridal shower. It
was a custom for the bride and her fiancé to lay
the quilt on the floor and sit all the single guests
around it. A nervous cat was then placed in the
center of the quilt. According to tradition, the first
person the cat jumped over in its mad scramble for
safety would be the next to be married.

Turn discarded jeans into a quilt. A quilt made from
discarded jeans will become a treasured possession. To make one for
someone special, cut several pairs of jeans into squares and stitch
them together to form a patchwork quilt. Use a sheet for the lining
and embroider the recipient's name on a corner. This quilt will stand
up to repeated washings.

Avert a sewing catastrophe. Do you remember the
white socks – now pink – that accidentally got washed with your
new red sweater? The same thing could happen to the quilt you
spent weeks piecing together. To avoid ruining your project, wash
the fabric before using it. Cloth straight off the bolt is not preshrunk
and will leach dyes when washed for the first time. Washing and
drying your fabric will remove the loose dye and shrink cotton to its
normal size.

Protect delicate fingertips when quilting. Hand
quilting is incredibly taxing on sensitive fingertips. To protect your
fingers from pokes and prods, wear a finger guard. Leather thimbles
will grab the needle and conform to your finger, but they may not
completely shield your skin. For full protection, use metal thimbles
with deep indentions. Look for the kind with a fingernail slit to air
out sweaty fingertips.

Pick the perfect quilting background. Don't be shy. When you are choosing background fabric for a quilt, feel free to unroll a section of the bolt to compare color combinations. Stack other fabric bolts on top to make sure the colors and patterns work together. It's better to risk the annoyance of a salesperson than find out your swatches don't match when you get home.

Use special thread for quilting

Making your first quilt? If you're using regular thread, you're probably having a rough time. Because quilts are heavy, quilters use waxed thread that glides easily through all the layers of material. Buy some waxed quilting thread and make your life a little easier.

Oil your brush to lift out lint. Little dust bunnies in your sewing machine will run and hide from the static electricity in your cleaning brush. To make your brush more attractive to dust, rub it with sewing machine oil and lightly brush the dust away.

Change needles for better sewing. Sewing silk with a needle made for jeans will leave a trail of damaged fabric. To make switching needles on your sewing machine easier, mark the tips of the needles with nail polish, a different color for each size. Now when you start a new project, you can tell at a glance if your needle needs to be changed.

Practice sewing for perfect seams. If you're a sewing machine novice and want to practice your technique, rip out several pages from an old coloring book and sew along the lines – without using thread. The next time you have a complex sewing project to tackle, you'll be ready to handle your fabric and machine like a pro.

Don't mix memory and magnets. Don't erase your sewing machine's memory. Be careful to keep magnetic pincushions away from your computerized sewing machine.

Blow dust away with a squeeze bottle. Save your lemon juice squeeze bottles and clean them out. Dust your sewing machine bobbin, camera lens, or any other hard-to-reach or delicate surface with short bursts of lemon-scented air. Make sure the bottle is dry before squeezing because moist air will trap dust.

Speed your pine cone's bloom. Do you want to make a pine cone wreath, like the ones pictured in decorating and craft magazines, but picked your cones too early for the full-blown effect? To open closed cones, warm them for an hour in a 250-degree oven. Open the oven door when the smell of fragrant pine fills your house, and you will discover fully opened cones. Be sure to shake out all remaining seed pods before using them for your craft project.

Stay in touch with popsicle notes. Here's a great idea for keeping in touch. Line up 10 to 12 clean popsicle sticks and attach them to a strip of masking tape. Write a message on the sticks, continuing each line on the next stick. Remove the tape and slide the sticks into an envelope. Your friend will be in for a pleasant surprise when she solves the puzzle and decodes your message.

Outsmart your hot glue gun. Don't scar your hands with hot glue. Hold the objects you need to glue down with the end of a popsicle stick and keep your fingers away from the heat.

Sweeten your home with spices. Don't let musty smells dampen your day. Mix up a batch of fragrant ingredients to sew into a handkerchief or make into a sachet for your closet. Combine half a cup of lemon zest with one tablespoon each of coriander, nutmeg, and whole cloves. Add lavender buds for bulk and one teaspoon powdered orris root for a longer-lasting scent. To fill out your sachet, add an unscented material, like cornstarch. Your sweet-smelling home should make you the envy of your neighbors.

Turn trash into treasure. It's easy to make loving keepsakes from old sewing scraps. Sew small pillows and fill them with potpourri. Sew quilt scraps into tea cozies, hot pads, or oven mitts. Piece small scraps into crazy quilt pillows or baby quilts. Make a wall hanging from your loved one's ties. Use round scraps to decorate homemade preserve jars. Create little gift bags using scraps, pinking shears, and ribbon. Or glue some scraps to blank cards to make stationery.

Save time with pick-up-and-go tray. To avoid tidying up every time you complete a step in a complicated project, keep your pieces together on a cookie tray. You can easily slide the tray into a safe place, and cleanup is a snap. Best of all, you can quickly pick up where you left off the next time you have a few minutes.

Build an organizer for supplies. Don't pay high prices for desktop organizers. Make your own out of an empty tissue box and toilet paper rolls. Slit the cover of a tissue box from the opening to each of its four corners, fold the sides down, and glue them in place. Cut the toilet tissue rolls the height of the box and arrange them in rows inside. Glue the cardboard rolls in place and use them to hold brushes, pencils, markers, glue, scissors, and paper clips.

Turn a clothespin into a magnetic note clip. Trying to keep all your grocery receipts in one place? Make a magnetic note clip to attach to your refrigerator. Just gather together a magnet, a spring-loaded clothespin, and a silk flower. Glue the magnet to one side of the clothespin and the flower to the other side. Now when you bring receipts home, they won't get lost.

Store supplies in candy dispenser. Who said candy dispensers are only good for candy? Reuse flip-top breath mint boxes to store beads, needles, buttons, or nails. The clear plastic makes it easy to find what you need, and the flip top allows you to take out only what you want. You can even store these little boxes in hardware organizers for easy access. Best of all, they are portable, free, and still smell like refreshing mint when you open them.

Stand your brushes at attention. Keep the tips of your paintbrushes dry and undamaged when they are not in use. Flip a plastic berry basket upside down and organize your brushes in the plastic grid, handles down.

Let egg carton lend a hand. Prop up round objects in an empty egg carton while you work. This will keep your fingers free, and you can let your project dry without disturbing it. For smaller objects, turn the carton over and use the crevices between the egg cups to hold slippery marbles, beads, and baubles.

Create a disposable paint palette. Instead of buying an expensive paint palette, mix watercolor or acrylic paint in an empty, foam egg carton. The egg cups can hold standard tube paints while you mix your custom colors on the attached lid. Cut out one of the egg cups to make a handy finger insert for your disposable palette.

Store your paint in the freezer. Use a clean, Styrofoam meat tray as a palette for your oil paints. Then when you're done painting for the day, slip the tray into a zip-lock freezer bag, blow some air into the bag, and store it in your freezer. Since oil doesn't freeze, your paint will be ready to use when you feel like painting.

Immortalize your summer blooms. Why pay hothouse prices for a winter bouquet when you can enjoy one from your own garden? In the summer, trim the buds off your favorite daisies and violets and flatten them carefully between two paper towels. Choose a variety of small blooms and greenery, making sure they are fairly flat and not wet with dew. Dry them for six to 10 weeks between the pages of a large book. Come winter, you can spend many a cozy hour creating cards, bookmarks, and framed posies from your dried treasures. You can even use them to decorate candles and lampshades in true Victorian style.

Wrap up summer in time for winter. Here's a great way to use the summer blossoms you discover sandwiched between the pages of a book. Arrange them attractively on a piece of wax paper. Dab some glue on the back of each bloom, letting it dry slightly before carefully securing it in place with tweezers. Peel a piece of clear contact paper and gently smooth it over the flowers, making sure you don't disturb the arrangement. Grace a frame, card, bookmark, or photo album with one of these little posies. They will never lose their sunny charm.

Remember fall all year long. The colors of autumn are breathtaking. Here's how you can enjoy the beauty of the season all year. Gather the most colorful leaves you can find and spray them with hair spray. Arrange some in a pretty basket or decorate a table or sideboard. The leaves will maintain their color and shine for weeks, well into the cold and dreary winter.

Pick flowers to make unique place mats. If you're expecting a large crowd for dinner and don't have enough place mats, make your own with treasures from your garden. Pick small, flat flowers and leaves and arrange them artistically on a sheet of wax paper. Carefully lay another sheet of wax paper on top and iron gently in place. Your guests will be impressed with these unique place mats. You can even use this decorative paper to wrap gifts or make gift bags.

Flip stamp pad for better ink flow. Don't be fooled by a dry stamp pad. When you put pressure on a stamp pad it forces the ink to drain to the bottom. To keep your stamp pad fresh, keep it upside down when not in use. When you're ready to use it, simply flip it over and coat your stamp with fresh ink.

Save money on stamping supplies. Don't spend extra money buying specialty sponges for your stamping crafts. Dime-a-dozen cosmetic wedges work exactly like their market-savvy cousins, but at a fraction of the cost.

Give stuffed toys personality. To add a joyful noise to a stuffed animal or ball, place small bells or dried beans in a plastic Easter egg or film canister and glue it securely closed. Insert the rattle when you add the stuffing.

Store beads in film canister. To keep the pieces of a broken necklace together until you can restring it, put the beads in an empty film canister and tape one of them to the outside. These handy containers are wonderful catchalls for many small items, like buttons, coins, confetti, and thumbtacks, that are easily lost.

Turn an old platter into a treasure. You can create an interesting, inexpensive mirror from an old silver platter. Polish the tray until it shines. Take the platter to a local glass company and have them cut a mirror to fit inside the platter and secure it in place. Attach a small hook to the back of the platter and hang it in a special place.

Tackle gold leaf tackiness. You want to coat your mirror with gold leaf, but the thin sheets seem to like your fingers more than the tacky surface of the frame. To keep the gold leaf from sticking to your fingers, lightly powder your hands with talc and watch the attraction fizzle.

Master scrapbooking basics. You don't need to invest in expensive accessories to make a keepsake album, just remember these basics. Stick to acid-free paper and pens, which will last forever. Clue others in to the subject of each page by providing a title. Write the names of the people in each photograph around the frame. Add some tidbit of history, a personal memory, or a poem and write it in your own handwriting for a personal touch. Remember, it's your thoughts that make an album something more than just a place to keep your photos.

Travel proof your photo project. Make scrapbooking a lap craft you can take on vacations and doctors' visits. Keep photos, paper, scissors, punches, glue, and templates in the pockets of a diaper bag. Or use an old briefcase as a traveling workstation. It will keep things flat and clean and serve as a worktable in a pinch.

Be choosy when arranging photos. Deciding what goes in and what stays out is one of the hardest parts of scrapbooking. Look at your photos and plan what you can crop. Move a template over your picture until you find the perfect fit. Make sure the subject of your photograph dominates the final shape. Leave anything that may have historic significance, the name of a site, a skyline, or a temporary event or exhibit, in the picture. Crop uninteresting elements, like the stranger waving in the background or the telephone pole in the foreground. Don't leave sharp corners. Round them with decorative scissors, a punch, or even a horizontal cut. Finally, arrange your photographs so the background space is attractively filled, and make sure you leave some room for journaling.

Give hot pots the cold shoulder. Big shoulder pads might not be in style anymore, but they're still taking up space in your closet. Tackle the problem by sewing those old shoulder pads together to make a potholder.

Spruce up party invitations. Ask at your local hardware or paint store for outdated wallpaper sample books. They are usually free. Then using a dismantled envelope as a template, cut the wallpaper and fold it to make your own unique envelope. Seal with a sticker or a bit of colored wax. If you have scraps left over, cut out a wallpaper motif and glue it to a blank card to create matching stationery.

Update Christmas dough ornament recipe. Make traditional dough ornaments for Christmas, but try something new. Update your recipe by adding oatmeal, cornmeal, or coffee grounds. Mix one cup each of water and flour with two cups of oatmeal for a wonderfully textured dough. Add a small amount of cornmeal or coffee grounds to the dough for extra texture, as well as color.

Extraordinary ideas for
ordinary outdoor activities

Encourage birds to take a bath. Birds won't take a dip in your birdbath if it's covered with green, slimy algae. To clean it, drain all the water. Soak paper towels with bleach and lay them on the bath. Wait about 30 minutes, then rinse and air dry. To prevent algae growth in the future, change the water and scrub your birdbath every week. Consider cleaning it every day if your birdbath is a bird hotspot.

Feed your feathered friends a feast. Give hungry birds a treat during the winter by coating pine cones with peanut butter and leaving them outside. For a tasty dessert, smear hardened bacon grease on pine cones and roll them in birdseed.

Treat the neighborhood birds. Make a special treat this winter for your neighborhood birds. Take one cup of crunchy-style peanut butter and melt it into one cup of lard. Stir in two cups of instant oats, two cups of cornmeal, one cup of white flour, and one-quarter cup of sugar. Pour about an inch of this mixture into several containers. Harden it for several hours in your freezer and serve.

Beautify your birdbath. To make your birdbath the hottest landing pad in your neighborhood, drop a few colorful marbles in the water. Birds will flock to them.

Feel good about your birdfeeder. If your birdfeeder is dirty, it could be spreading disease and parasites to your feathered friends. Here's how you can give it a good cleaning. Start by rinsing and scrubbing the inside. Then dunk the feeder for two minutes in a mixture of 1 quart chlorine bleach and 9 quarts lukewarm water. Rinse it again and let it air dry. Finally, clean the ground underneath your birdfeeder with a broom and a shovel. If you don't want to spend time cleaning a birdfeeder, plant berry bushes around your house. Birds love to feed on them, and they don't require any cleaning.

Recycle an old tablecloth. Hold onto that old, plastic-coated tablecloth. It might not be nice enough for your dining room table anymore, but it will do just fine for your next picnic. When you're roughing it, a plastic window shade or shower curtain will work well, too.

Make your own blocks of ice. Chill out at your next party with big blocks of ice made from old milk cartons. Clean out the cartons, fill them with water, and tape them shut. After a few hours in the freezer, you'll have ice blocks big enough to build an igloo.

Defend your picnic from ants. Protect your picnic table from an ant invasion by placing the table legs in old coffee cans filled with water.

Prepare piping hot food for picnics. If you're bringing a hot dish to a picnic, keep it warm by tightly wrapping the container in several sheets of newspaper. Tape it closed and then carry it in a paper bag.

Protect candles from wind. For picnics that run past sunset, make a windshield for your candle. Cut off the top and bottom of a 2-liter soda bottle. Save the middle portion, making sure it's taller than your candle. Carefully place the shield over it.

Get your grill ready for great food. A red-hot grill is essential for great outdoor cooking. If you're using wood as fuel, the embers should be bright red and orange before you start cooking. If you're using charcoal, wait until the coals are grayish-white.

Save some bread on guitar picks. If you're all out of guitar picks, don't spend money on new ones. Dig up a plastic, bread bag clip instead.

Soften your hands for better guitar playing. Before you pick up your guitar, soak your hands in cold water and rub them with moisturizing cream. That will keep your fingers from making those distracting squeaks when they strum up and down on the strings.

Mark your spot with free bookmark. Even bookworms need a break from reading. To mark your place, cut off the corner of an old envelope and slip it on your page.

Help your books find their way home. Place an address label on the inside cover of all your books. That way, when you lend books to friends and family, they'll always remember to return them to you.

Clean your guitar with rice. Clean the inside of your acoustic guitar with uncooked rice. Just toss in a few grains, jiggle them around, and dump them out.

Tackle a crowded tackle box. You can have everything you need on your next fishing trip without having to trawl around a whale-size tackle box. Divide your gear by the types of fishing you do, or by the season, and put it in separate boxes. For instance, keep your fly-fishing equipment in a different box than your deep-sea fishing tackle.

Cover up fishing lure scents. Lure scents and dyes can ruin the rest of your tackle if you're not careful. Keep these secret weapons to themselves in a resealable bag.

Grab a mint and save the tin. After you're done freshening your breath, use that empty mint tin to store your small hooks and weights in one easy-to-find place. Then maybe you won't get stuck fishing for them at the bottom of your tackle box.

Save time by organizing hooks. A rubber band is an easy way to organize your hooks. Sort your hooks by size and wrap one around each bunch. To use a hook, slide it out carefully, and the others will stay in place.

Give the hook to a messy tackle box. Make organizing your hooks, weights, and other fishing equipment a snap by storing them in plastic film canisters.

Separate lures to protect them. In your tackle box, make sure to separate your soft plastic lures, like your worms, from your other lures. Otherwise, they could be damaged.

Think safety when taking kids fishing. If your wee ones are tagging along on your next fishing trip, stash your dangerous hooks where only you can get at them – old childproof aspirin or medicine bottles.

Fool fish with phony bait. Even the biggest catch in the lake won't be able to resist this homemade bait – a small piece of sponge coated with petroleum jelly.

Fish for worms in your yard. Two wooden boards and a pail of dishwater are all you need to nab a day's supply of earthworms. Pour the nutrient-rich dishwater over a spot in your lawn where you've seen worms before and cover it with the boards to keep in the moisture. The next day you'll have a whole gang of fish friendly worms underneath the boards. Or try laying down a whole newspaper soaked with water to attract worms.

Liven your worms with coffee. Keep your worms wiggling all day long with a cup of coffee – grounds, that is. Mix the coffee grounds into the soil in your bait box and dump in the worms. They like coffee, and it helps them live longer.

Keep hooks rust free with rice. Put a few grains of uncooked rice in your tackle box to prevent your hooks from rusting.

Nab a free fishing net. Put together your own fishing net using a coat hanger and a mesh onion bag. Twist the hanger into a circle the size of the bag's mouth and attach the bag to the circle. For the longest, fish-grabbing reach, wrap the end of the hanger around a broom handle or dowel stick.

Scale fish with bottle caps. For a heavy-duty fish scaler, nail metal bottle caps to a block of wood. Rub the contraption against the grain of the fish's scales, and you'll be eating your catch in no time.

Keep your bait alive. A resealable, plastic bag makes a great storage container for live bait if you can't find a coffee can. And remember – leave a little moist earth in with the worms. And on a hot day, always store the bag in a cooler.

Whiten your golf balls. Get your golf balls as clean as they were on their first putt. Dip them in a mixture of one cup water and one-quarter cup ammonia. Let them sit until they are clean, then rinse and dry.

Chip dirt off your golf clubs. Give your metal golf clubs a bath in a bucket of water and laundry detergent. Soak your clubs for no longer than a minute and then towel them off. The laundry detergent contains the same active ingredient as fancy, store-bought club cleaners.

Personalize golf balls inexpensively. Never get your golf balls mixed up with somebody else's. Make a dot on them with a touch of nail polish. This is a great idea for tennis or racquet balls, too.

Dry soggy boots with newspaper. Don't spend a whole weekend hiking in soggy boots. Stuff them with newspaper at the end of the day. When the newspaper gets soaked, replace it until your boots are warm and dry again.

Chase away wet feet with plastic bags. If you plan to hike in wet country, put plastic bags on your feet before putting on your boots. They'll keep your tootsies warm and dry. And when you need to pack your wet boots after your hike, store them in the plastic bags. It will keep them apart from the rest of your clothes.

Whittle your own walking stick. A walking stick can make any hike easier and safer. Whittle your own from a fresh tree branch that's 1 1/2 to 2 inches thick and about 5 to 5 1/2 feet long. Make sure both ends are free of cracks and splits. Hard wood from a leafy tree is better than sappy and soft wood from an evergreen. Once you have the perfect stick, shave away the bark with a pocketknife and carve in whatever design you fancy. To finish it off, protect the bottom tip with a 1-inch-long piece of copper piping. Use quick-drying epoxy to make sure the piping stays on.

Try this new trick for a new wick. Lengthen the life span of your propane lantern wicks. Just soak them in vinegar for several hours and let them dry. Not only will they burn longer, they'll also give off more light.

Shed more light on your campsite. It's easy to make a windproof camping lantern. Just partially open a clean, dry tuna or cat food can and bend the lid straight up. When you put a candle in the can, the lid will block the wind. On top of that, the reflection from the metal will make the candle shine even brighter.

Multiply your matches. If you're running short on matches, get out the ones you have left and slice them down the center, lengthwise. That will double your supply.

Get the most 'juice' from flashlight batteries. Save your flashlight for when you really need it. To stop it from accidentally being jostled "on" during your day's hike and wasting power, turn your batteries around and put them in backward. When you need the flashlight, put the batteries back in the right way, and you'll have all the juice you need.

Scoop up some camping gear. Deep ice cream cartons (1.25 gallons) can carry your garbage on a camping trip, and their plastic lids make excellent cutting boards, too. They work best if you slice off half of their rim so they're more flexible.

Camp with great balls of fire. Before you go camping, smear petroleum jelly on a bunch of cotton balls and seal them in a plastic bag. They're fail-safe fire starters if you get stuck in the rain or can't start a fire for some other reason.

Cook creatively over an open fire. Stop lugging around a heavy, propane camping stove and get a griddle. It doesn't take up much space, and you can easily fix hamburgers, chicken, eggs, bacon, pancakes, toast, and veggies.

Leave bulky utensils at home. Substitute a small square of clean window screen for that bulky colander on your next camping trip. The screen is much easier to carry, and it strains just as well. Find a piece that's big enough to cover the top of your cooking pot, and tape its rough edges with duct tape.

Waterproof your matches. Anyone who has camped in the rain knows that waterproof matches come in handy. Make your own by dipping match heads in candle wax.

Clean your lint trap and feed a fire. Take along a ball of laundry lint with you on your next camping trip. On days when you can't find dry tinder, the lint makes a great substitute.

Start a roaring fire with a condiment cup. A little sawdust, candle wax, and paper condiment cups are all you need to start a roaring campfire. Just fill the little cups with sawdust, top with melted wax, and light for a surefire blaze.

Cook with recycled cans. Gallon-size vegetable and fruit cans have many uses on a camping trip. You can use them for boiling water, cooking corn on the cob, and carrying water. To make a water bucket, drill a hole in each side of the can and tie a cord through them. The cans shouldn't be hard to find. Check your favorite wholesale store or ask at a local restaurant or school cafeteria.

Demolish soot on camping pots. Coat the bottom of your camping pots with a thin layer of bar soap before you put them over an open fire. It will make cleaning off the soot a cinch.

Spice up camp cuisine. Dinner at the campsite doesn't have to be bland and boring. Before you leave home, remember to fill several plastic film canisters with your favorite spices. The airtight canister will keep the spices fresh and make them easy to pack.

Eliminate foul odors from your canteen. Dump three teaspoons of baking soda and a little bit of water into your canteen and shake it around. After an hour, dump this mixture out and rinse your canteen thoroughly. It will smell as fresh as a mountain stream.

Bowl over your camping buddies. Cut off and clean out the bottoms of empty, plastic soda or milk containers and pack them in your backpack. They'll make great cereal bowls on your next camping trip.

Crack your eggs and shake. Went camping and didn't bring your beater? Don't worry. You can still have scrambled eggs. Crack the eggs into a plastic bag, seal it up, and shake. This will "scramble" them just right.

Sleep in a clean, dry tent. A painting dropcloth is a must for your next camping trip. Bring one the same size as the floor of your tent and set your tent on top of it. It will protect you and your tent from wetness and dirt.

Prolong the life of your tent. As soon as you get home from a camping trip, set up your tent. Airing it out for 30 minutes will get rid of moisture and prevent mildew.

Loosen sap with margarine. If you camped under the wrong tree and got sticky sap all over your tent, get out your tub of margarine. Work some into the spot until the sap loosens. Then scrub the spot with a wet, soapy cloth. This technique is gentle enough to protect your tent's water-resistant finish, yet still gets the job done.

Discover the secret to a clean tent. To prolong the life of your tent, keep it away from your washing machine. Instead, give it a gentle hand washing with a mild, detergent-free soap, using as little water as possible. Then rinse the tent, being careful not to soak it. When you're finished, let it air dry in direct sunlight.

Get tough on tent mildew. Mildew is one of your tent's worst enemies. As soon as you see it growing, hand wash the tent with a gentle, detergent-free soap, using very little water. Then sponge the mildew spot with a half-cup of disinfectant cleaner in a gallon of warm water. Dry the tent in direct sunlight. If the mildew has caused your tent to start peeling, treat it with a stronger solution – one cup of salt plus one cup of lemon juice in a gallon of hot water. After the tent dries in the sun, peel off the damaged, flaking sections of the tent's coating and cover these spots with a new layer of water sealant.

Zap a stuck zipper. Don't get trapped in your tent because of a stuck zipper. Make it an easy slider by rubbing it with candle wax. In a fix, lip balm will work, too.

Sleep soundly using unusual pillow. If you're up a creek without a pillow, make sure you have a few large, sealable, plastic storage bags handy. Blow them up with air and you've got great camping pillows.

Steady your tent on a windy day. A few spare coffee cans can steady your tent in a strong wind. Pour 2 inches of wet cement into as many coffee cans as your tent has poles. Before the cement dries, stick a foot-long, hollow pipe in each can. The pipes should be wider than your tent poles. Finally, punch a hole in each can about an inch from the top. The next time you put up your tent, place the poles in the cemented pipe and tie the pole string through the can hole.

Take a milk jug camping. Nature calls in the middle of the night. It's dark and as you walk along – ouch! – you stub your toe on a tent stake. Next time you're camping, protect your toes by cutting off the tops of milk cartons or jugs and putting them on top of the stakes.

Add pantyhose to camping gear. Old pantyhose makes great rope. It's easy to find space for it in your camping gear and strong enough to bundle together your sleeping bag or cooking utensils. You can even use it to hang your food in a tree to keep it safe from animals.

Unstick sap with baking soda. To get tree sap off your hands, reach for baking soda instead of soap.

Feel clean without water. On long camping adventures, sometimes bathing isn't an option. To feel clean and refreshed, wash yourself with flat cotton pads soaked in witch hazel.

Protect your privacy at campsite. Privacy on a camping trip is possible if you bring along a hula-hoop and an opaque shower curtain. Attach the curtain around the hula-hoop and hang the contraption from a branch. Inside the curtain, you'll be able to dress – and even shower – in peace.

Carry a bathtub into the woods. If you're tired of smelling like the Great Outdoors, bring along an inflatable kiddy pool on your next camping trip. It's like your own personal tub.

Turn a bread bag clip into a clothespin. Plastic bread bag clips make great clothespins when you're camping. They'll hold up wet clothes just as well as regular clothespins, and they'll take up a lot less space in your backpack, too.

Save your valuables from sinking. When you're boating, place your valuables in a resealable, plastic bag. Before you close it, blow into it and fill it with air. That way, if the bag ends up in the water, it will float.

Bail out your boat with a milk jug. If you spring a leak in your boat, a plastic milk jug can help you stay afloat. Turn it into a scooper by cutting off the bottom. Just make sure the cap is on tight.

Evict musty smells from sleeping bag. Stick a fabric softener sheet in your sleeping bag before you roll it up and put it away. That will keep it smelling springtime fresh the next time you use it.

Plump up your sleeping bag. Don't store your sleeping bag in the sack it came in. Being scrunched in that cramped space can let the air out of your bag's padding and leave it less warm and comfortable. Try a king-size pillowcase instead, or store your sleeping bag under your bed or hanging in your closet.

Snuggle up to a squeaky clean sleeping bag. Unless you camp in the mud, washing your sleeping bag should only be a once-a-year chore. For best results, head out to a Laundromat and use a large, front-loading washer. Dry cleaning or washing your sleeping bag in a smaller, top-loading washer could damage the lining. When you move it to the dryer, be careful it doesn't stretch. Put the dryer on low and pump in the quarters. It could take several hours to dry.

Freshen your sleeping bag. If you put a bar of soap in your sleeping bag and leave it there for the entire camping season, your sleeping bag won't smell musty.

Take the dings out of Ping-Pong balls. A heated Ping-Pong match can leave dented balls in its wake, but those balls can be as good as new for the next battle. Just submerge them under hot water for 20 minutes. Enough pressure will build up inside the ball to pop them round again.

Soften up a new mitt. For breaking in a new baseball glove, this is one of the oldest tricks in the book – a little petroleum jelly rubbed into the palm.

Refresh tired board games. Don't toss away your family's treasured board games just because they've lost some of their luster. When you see a board wearing out, attach its bottom to plywood so it will last longer.

Sharpen your darts with sandpaper. If you want your steel-tipped darts to hit their mark and stick, sharpen them regularly. It's easy with a little sandpaper. Just rub the darts lengthwise on the sandpaper while rotating the darts between your fingers. Or try the all-natural way – sticking the darts into a raw potato.

Protect your wall from wild darts. Don't ruin your walls with dart holes. Make your own dartboard backing with spare plywood and rolled corkboard. First, figure out how big you want the backing to be. Then cut the corkboard and the plywood the same size. Use woodworking glue to stick the two pieces together, making sure they're flat against each other. Put a few heavy books on top and let dry. When the backing is finished, hang it according to dart rules. The middle of the board – where the bull's-eye will be – should be 68 inches from the floor. Mark your throwing line on the floor 7 feet and 9 1/4 inches from the wallboard.

Unstick puzzle cube with talc. If you haven't used that puzzle cube in a long time, its movable parts might not want to move. To get it twisting and turning smoothly again, sprinkle it with talcum powder.

Toss wet tennis balls in your dryer. If your tennis balls get wet, throw them in your dryer for a few minutes.

Stuff a sock to make a ball. Here's a softball that really is soft. Stuff a sock with old pantyhose and sew the end shut. It won't hurt your little ones or your furniture.

Win in the game of croquet. Colorful drinking straws can make croquet more fun and easier to play. Slide a straw onto each wicket leg before you place them in the ground. When it's your turn to shoot, you'll be able to find the wickets a lot easier.

Expose film to the cold. Keep rolls of unused film in the refrigerator until you need them. They will stay fresh longer that way.

Carpet your swing set. The ground underneath your little ones' swing can take a beating. Before their feet dig a trench there, lay down an old carpet remnant. One about 3 feet by 3 feet should be large enough to cover the area.

Grease up your skating gear. Before you teach your little one the art of roller-skating, get the squeak out of her wheels with a little petroleum jelly.

Cover skate blades with a hose. Slice open sections of an old garden hose to make great blade covers for your ice skates.

Wash your clothes in your trunk. Don't waste time on a road trip doing laundry. Before you hit the road, get your hands on a sealable, plastic bucket. Fill it with hot, soapy water and add your clothes. Secure it in a corner of your RV or your trunk. A day's worth of sloshing around in the bucket should be all it takes to clean your clothes.

Fly on a super sled. If you want a sled that's simple to make but wild to ride, pull out a large trash bag and wrap it around you like Tarzan's jungle briefs.

Bag your toys for the beach. A mesh bag is one of the neatest ways to take toys to the beach. When you're done for the day, dip the bag and its toys in the ocean or spray them with a hose. The sand and water will just drip away.

Protect valuables at the beach. An old film canister makes a great waterproof beach necklace. Just hot glue a strong cord to the cap, and you'll be able to take your keys and money in the surf. You won't have to worry about leaving them on your beach towel.

Rescue your car from beach sand. For your next trip to the beach, buy the largest, resealable, plastic bag you can find and fill it a third of the way with baby powder. Stick your hands and feet in the powder before you get in your car at day's end. When you take them out of the bag and brush off the powder, any leftover sand will come off with it. It's a great idea for your little ones, too.

Coax a bike inner tube with powder. Once you're done repairing the tube of a bike tire, douse the tube with talcum powder. It will squeeze back inside its outer casing without any trouble.

Simple solutions for
stress-free travel

Land a prime seat on next flight. Make sure you always get the safest and most comfortable seat on any airplane. It's easy – just ask for it. When you book your flight, ask to sit in the first row (the bulkhead) or an exit row. You'll have plenty of leg room. Keep in mind that, in case of emergency, certain responsibilities come with an exit row seat. If you don't think you can handle those responsibilities, choose an aisle seat in the row behind or in front of an exit row. That way, you'll have some leg room, and you're still close to an exit – but you won't have to open the exit door or direct people during an emergency.

Make sure you're paying the lowest price. Just because you've already booked your flight doesn't mean you should stop checking prices. Call and see if the price has come down. Even if you have to pay a $75 fee to change your ticket, you might end up saving money if the new fare is dramatically lower.

Shuttle for 'lots' of savings. You need to go to the airport to get on your plane, but you don't need to park there. Look for a private lot with shuttle service to the airport. Many times it's cheaper and safer than airport parking.

Get frequent perks as a frequent flier. Even if you're not really a frequent flier, sign up with airlines' frequent-flier programs. Besides free trips, you can earn discounts on hotels and car rentals. You might also be able to earn frequent-flier miles by using your credit card or switching your long-distance phone company.

Phone for flight changes. You're at the airport when you hear the awful news – your flight has been canceled. Don't panic and join the stampede of anxious travelers rushing to the ticket counter to rebook their flight. Simply find a phone, call the airline's reservation number, and ask to be placed on the next available flight.

Grab a cab the easy way. After a long flight and a long walk through a crowded airport, the last thing you want to do is wait a long time for a taxi. So don't. Simply exit the airport through the departures section instead of the arrivals area. You'll find all sorts of empty cabs, since they just got done dropping off passengers.

Outsmart jet lag with simple tactics. You can avoid jet lag by fooling your body. For example, if you're going to land in the morning, sleep as much as possible during your flight. If you're going to land at night, try to stay awake with your overhead light on while you're in the air. That way, your body will be adjusted to the new time zone.

Soothe swollen feet with elastic. Do your feet swell up during air travel? Ease the pain by substituting the shoelaces in your walking shoes with 1/4-inch braided elastic. Your feet will have a much more comfortable flight.

Beat airport stress in the restroom. Feeling overwhelmed by the long lines and flight cancellations at the airport? Find a peaceful, private spot to relax – a restroom stall. Just sit down, drop your bag, and take a few minutes to calm down. You can even read a magazine. No one will bother you.

Use common scents for air travel. Is it time to sleep or time to be alert? Your nose knows. Drip some lavender or vanilla essential oil onto a cotton ball and bring it on the airplane in an old pill bottle. Sniff it during your flight to help yourself relax and sleep. On the other hand, if you need help waking up just before the plane lands, sniff pine, peppermint, or citrus scents.

Land a quiet spot at the airport. You have lots of time to kill before your flight, but you'd rather spend it away from the noise of the busy airport. Find a gate where the plane has just taken off. Everyone will have cleared out, leaving plenty of empty seats. You can stretch out and snooze or get some work done in peace. When people start gathering at the gate again for the next flight, simply move to another empty one.

Steer toward safety and savings. Improve your driving skills and save money on your auto insurance premiums with a simple strategy. Just enroll in the AARP 55 ALIVE Driver Safety Program. The eight-hour course, which includes two four-hour sessions in two days, is designed especially for drivers over 50. You don't have to be a member of AARP to take the course, and there are no tests. It costs $10, but you might qualify for a discount on auto insurance when you complete the course. Check your state for details.

Hatch a plan to foil hunger. Hungry, cranky kids can make trips seem 12 times as long. Make them 12 times more fun instead. Clean out an old egg carton and fill each compartment with a different treat. You can put M&Ms in one, Cheerios in another, and so on. Put rubber bands over each end so the goodies don't spill, and pack the fun-filled egg carton in the car. When the kids start whining for food, let them dip into one of the compartments. Before the trip, the kids can have fun decorating the carton, too.

Wash up with ease on the road. There's no telling what kind of mess you might have to deal with during a family vacation. Be prepared for anything. Fill an empty plastic dishwashing liquid bottle with water and keep it in your car's glove compartment. Don't rinse out the bottle before filling it. Make sure you bring along some paper towels, too. You'll be able to clean up spills or wash your hands quickly and easily.

Pack coffee can to cope with smokers. Long car trips are bad enough without a smoker on board. If you're traveling with a smoker, here's an easy way to keep your car's ashtray and the air you breathe clean. Fill a 3-pound coffee can with three parts sand and one part baking soda. Your smoking passenger can put out his cigarettes in the sand, and the baking soda will absorb the smoky odor. The weight of the sand will also prevent the makeshift ashtray from tipping over.

Make pit stops during long trips. You're probably excited to escape the cold and get to your summer home in Florida or Arizona. But don't try to cover long distances all at once. Stop every two hours to rest and limit your driving to less than six or seven hours a day.

Fill the tank or empty your wallet. Even if a gas station is out of your way, make sure you fill up the tank before you return a rental car. If you read the fine print in your rental contract, you'll see the ridiculous price they charge you for gas. You could end up paying what it would cost to rent the car for a whole extra day.

Put the brakes on rental car insurance. When you rent a car, the rental company usually pressures you to spring for insurance, too. Don't just pay up without a word. Your regular car insurance might cover rentals. Check and see before paying for the same thing twice.

Find your map in a snap. Do you need a map to find your road maps? Keep them filed alphabetically by state in a folder or three-ring binder. Then, when you begin a trip, you can easily find the map you need. Folding it up again, however, might not be so easy.

Guard your maps from bad weather. If you plan to go for a hike – or just a leisurely stroll – while on vacation, pack your maps in a large zip-lock bag. That way, if it rains, your map won't get soggy and hard to read.

Hide your trail with disappearing ink. Travel wherever you want – then disappear without a trace. Just buy a disappearing-ink marker pen from your local fabric store. Use the pen to trace your route on your map. In a few days, the marks will fade away, and you'll be able to reuse the map for your next trip.

Make your suitcase stand out. Give your luggage a colorful makeover. Wrap some brightly colored electrical tape around the handle of your suitcase before you check it at the airport. That way, even if another passenger has the exact same suitcase and grabs yours by mistake, he'll realize he has the wrong one. You could also braid some brightly colored yarn and tie it around the handle.

Decorate your suitcase. Does your suitcase look like everybody else's? Transform your bland bag into a work of art. Paint flowers, stars, or any other design you can think of on your luggage. You can use stencils to make the designs or just express yourself freehand.

You definitely won't grab the wrong bag at baggage claim anymore. No passenger will take your bag by mistake, either. And no thief would think of making off with such a unique piece of luggage.

Store valuables in a diaper bag. You don't need to travel with a baby to carry a diaper bag. Use one as your carry-on when you fly. It's a great way to store camera equipment or other valuables. It also has plenty of outer pockets you can use to store your itinerary, snacks, or loose change. Besides, it's much less likely to be stolen than a normal bag.

Try layering your belongings. Feel like a smuggler with this exciting trick. Make a false bottom for your suitcase by tracing your bag on a large sheet of cardboard. Cut along the lines to form a cardboard shelf. As you pack, put your shoes, toiletries, and other hard items in the bottom of your suitcase. Then lay the cardboard shelf on top of the first layer and lay your clothes on top of the cardboard. Now you can easily lift the cardboard layer to add or remove items. It will also make things easier if airport security wants to inspect your luggage.

Double your bags to lighten your load. You've heard the expression, "Don't put all your eggs in one basket." Well, you might not want to put all your clothes in one suitcase, either. Instead of taking one gigantic, heavy bag on your trip, consider packing two smaller bags. They'll be easier to handle. And, if one of your bags gets lost, you'll still have some clothes to wear.

Cure musty suitcases with cat litter. If your suitcase smells like something the cat dragged in, try sprinkling cat litter inside. Leave the suitcase closed for a few weeks, then vacuum it out. That should get rid of the musty odor.

Send suitcase smells packing. As you prepare for your trip, you take your suitcase from the closet, open it ... and gag. Keep your suitcase smelling fresh with this simple trick. Fill a film canister or pill bottle with baking soda, poke some holes in the lid, and store the container in your suitcase between trips. This homemade air freshener will protect your luggage from unpleasant smells.

Fix luggage flaws with floss. When your luggage needs minor repairs, reach for your dental floss. Thread it through a sewing needle and use it to fix a ripped strap or torn seam. It's stronger than you think. For best results, use waxed dental floss, which slides through material easily. You can even camouflage the dental floss with a marker or some shoe polish so it blends into your bag.

Include ID inside your bags. Don't assume that the name tag on the outside of your luggage will stay on. In case it falls off, have a back-up plan. Write your name, address, and phone number on an index card, slip it into a zip-lock bag, and put it in your suitcase. Do the same for all luggage you're taking with you. The airlines check inside lost bags for ID.

Freshen your bags with fabric softener. It's time for one of your rare vacations. But you're dreading the prospect of packing because of your musty, smelly suitcase. Luckily, there's an easy way to protect your nose. When you store away your luggage, toss in a fabric softener sheet. Next time you travel, your luggage will smell fresh and ready to go.

Locate luggage with an index card. When your luggage is lost, you don't want to waste time stammering, babbling, and groping for details. Write a description of your bag on an index card and slip it in your purse before your trip. Include the make of the bag, color, and size. When you talk with the person at the lost luggage counter, pull out the index card. You'll make things a lot easier for both of you.

Treat your shoes like fruit. Next time you get ready to pack for a trip, head for the produce aisle of your grocery store. Not to buy fruits and vegetables, but to grab a few of those plastic produce bags. You can use them to wrap your shoes so they don't get the rest of your clothes dirty.

Bag shoes when packing. You don't need a separate bag for shoes when you travel. Go ahead and pack your shoes with your clean clothes. But first slip each shoe into a quart-size plastic bag. Your clothes will stay clean, and you'll be able to identify your shoes easily through the clear plastic.

Shield your shoes with sleeves. That old sweatshirt might not fit you anymore, but it still has a trick or two up its sleeve. Cut the sleeves off your old sweatshirt and use them to help you pack. Just slip your shoes inside the sleeves so they don't get the rest of your clothes dirty.

Make the most of luggage space. Stuff your underwear and socks into your shoes when you pack. It not only saves precious suitcase space, it also preserves the shape of your shoes.

Bring newspaper bags on your route. Chances are you recycle your daily newspaper. But you probably don't save those long, narrow plastic bags that come with it. Maybe you should start. You can use those narrow bags to pack your shoes or hairbrushes or to stash last-minute purchases on your vacation.

Bag wrinkles with packing secret. Clothes made of thin fabric can be a wrinkled mess when you take them out of your suitcase. Keep them wrinkle free with this simple secret. Save left-over plastic dry-cleaner bags and put them between folds of clothing as you pack.

Roll your way to wrinkle-free clothes. Roll, don't fold, clothing when you travel, and you'll arrive wrinkle free. For items on hangers, put them in a plastic dry cleaner bag and roll it up. You can also fold in the sleeves and collars of shirts and roll them with a layer of tissue paper.

Blow away wrinkles with a hair dryer. You brought the perfect outfit for your vacation. You just forgot to bring an iron. No problem. You can make do with your travel hair dryer. Just put it on the hot setting and wave it about 4 to 6 inches above your clothes with one hand, while you smooth out the wrinkles with the other.

Sew on a button with a matchbook. Turn an empty matchbook into a miniature sewing kit. Stick some needles and safety pins in the bottom, where the matches were. Then wrap a few different colors of thread around the matchbook. Your tiny sewing kit might come in handy during your travels.

Roll your ties to reduce creases. Are you fit to be tied over the way your ties look when you unpack them? Eliminate creases with this simple method. Tightly roll your tie backward, starting from the narrow end, around two fingers. Then slip a sock over it. When you unpack it and put it on, both you and your tie will look smooth.

Transform hangers with clothespins. When packing a skirt, throw two clothespins into your bag, too. Make sure they're the kind with springs. You can use them to turn a regular wire hanger, like you find in a hotel room, into a skirt hanger.

Count on clothespins during your travels. They don't take up much room, but clothespins can be a big part of your trip. Bring a few clothespins with you – you'll be amazed how handy they are. You can use them to hang up your clothes or wet swimsuit, clip your receipts together, and close partially eaten bags of chips or other snacks.

Pack a lightweight laundry bag. Your clothes are all nice and clean while you're packing them. But by the end of the trip, they won't be. Toss a plastic grocery bag in your luggage to store laundry until you have a chance to wash it.

Liquidate packing problem. Need a solid way to pack liquids on your trip? First, pour the liquid into a plastic container. Make sure you leave some space at the top. Press in the sides of the container as you put on the top to create suction. That way, it won't leak. Then store the container in a resealable bag.

Turn a lunch box into a toiletries bag. You don't need a fancy toiletries bag to go on a trip. Pack your cosmetics, lotions, and beauty aids in a child's plastic lunch box. It's a fun, easy way to keep all your toiletries in one place.

Pack your toothbrush in a pill bottle. You need to pack your toothbrush, but you don't have a toothbrush holder. Make a handy holder out of an old plastic pill bottle. Just cut a slit in the cap and slide the toothbrush handle through. Then snap the cap back on the bottle with the toothbrush bristles inside.

Remove nail polish remover from your bag. Your bags are heavy enough without tossing in a whole bottle of nail polish remover. Lighten your load by soaking a few cotton balls with nail polish remover and packing them in an airtight plastic bag. That way, you only bring as much as you need. Plus, you avoid the disaster of a broken bottle.

Keep your cosmetics bag on high alert. Cut down on packing time by keeping a cosmetics bag packed and ready to go. If you run low on something during your trip, write a note to remind yourself to pick up more of it when you get back home. That way, your cosmetics bag stays stocked and ready to travel at a moment's notice.

Curb shampoo spills with plastic jar. Did you ever open your suitcase to find your shampoo had spilled all over the rest of your stuff? Guard against the mess by packing your shampoo bottle in a plastic coffee jar. The plastic jar trick also works to protect other items – like a bottle of perfume – from breaking.

Save space with samples. Why bring bulky bottles of moisturizer, cleanser, and other beauty aids on your trip? Just grab a few samples that they give out at cosmetics counters in department stores. These smaller portions should last through your vacation without any problem.

Travel with disposable cloths in Europe. A European vacation has many charms. Unfortunately, an abundance of soft, cushy washcloths isn't one of them. Because European hotels and bed-and-breakfasts rarely provide washcloths, you could bring your own. But it gets tiresome lugging a wet, soggy washcloth in a plastic bag from place to place. Instead, buy a package of disposable cloths, like Handy Wipes. Cut each of them in half, and you'll have a fresh washcloth each night of your trip. You can even use it to wipe your shoes before tossing it out the next morning.

Make the most of a marker. Mark this down. Bring a thick, black marker on your vacation. You can use it to address packages if you mail souvenirs to family and friends. If your shoes get scuffed from lots of walking, you can also use the marker to polish them.

Unroll the many uses of electrical tape. Toss a small roll of electrical tape into your luggage. Its many uses will amaze you. You can use it to fix a skirt hem or remove lint from a dark sweater. You can also fasten souvenir items into your journal or securely tape a piece of luggage closed if you have to leave it in your room for a few days. And don't forget, you can also use it for packing and shipping gifts home.

Keep bugs away with cotton balls. Save precious suitcase space while saving yourself from mosquistoes and other pests. Instead of bringing a whole bottle of insect repellent, just moisten some cotton balls with the stuff and pack them in a small zip-lock bag.

Get the news about umbrella covers. Save those plastic bags your newspaper comes in for a rainy day. They make great umbrella covers. Shove a bag in your purse or pocket before you leave the house. When you enter a car or building, take out the bag and slip your wet umbrella inside.

Bank on this organizational tip. Check this out. Instead of throwing away those extra plastic checkbook covers your bank sends with each box of new checks, save them. You can use them to make your trip more organized. Store theater tickets, receipts, or even cash in a checkbook cover. Just make sure to keep it closed with rubber bands.

Dial for discounts. Curiosity may have killed the cat, but it also helps travelers save money. Get the phone numbers for state and local tourism offices in areas you plan to visit. Call and ask for any free material they can send you. While you have them on the line, ask about any discount coupons or booking services – all great ways to protect your "kitty."

Make your own money bags. Handling foreign currency during your travels can be difficult, especially if you pass through several countries on your trip. To help keep your money organized, slip some plastic sandwich bags in your purse or travel bag. You can use them to hold the various currencies and keep them separate from each other. If you pass through a country again on your way back, just reach for the appropriate bag.

Lighten your load with labels. Putting in a little extra time before your trip can save you both time and space during it, especially when it comes to keeping in touch. Instead of toting your entire address book with you, write the addresses of your friends and family on a sheet of labels and slip that in your luggage. When you buy a postcard, simply peel off a label and stick it on the card.

Organize more than shoes in shoe holder. A hanging shoe holder comes in handy if you're staying in one place for your whole vacation. You just fasten the holder's Velcro strap around your room's closet bar and let it hang there. But you don't have to use it just for shoes. The rectangular slots can also be used to store belts, underwear, socks, and pantyhose.

Help your bag find you. All is not lost just because one of your bags is. Increase your odds of having a missing bag returned to you during your trip. Photocopy your itinerary – where you plan to be on which dates – and include a copy in each piece of your luggage. That way, someone who finds your bag will know where to find you.

Stop scrambling for important info. A hole-puncher and a soft binder could make the difference between a smooth, well-organized trip and total chaos. Just punch holes in important documents – such as your itinerary, addresses of places you plan to stay, and phone numbers you'll need – and put them in a binder. Choose a brightly colored binder so you can spot it easily in your carry-on bag. Arrange the documents in the order you'll need them. You'll have all the information for your trip in one easy-to-find place.

Change the way you carry change. Too much spare change can be a hassle. But, when you're traveling, you might need dimes and quarters for bus or train fare or to make a call from a pay phone. Try storing your dimes and quarters in a used film canister. It'll cut down on the clanking, and you'll always know where to find change when you need it.

File away memories of your trip. Keep a record of your travels using a zip-lock bag and a file folder. Glue the zip-lock bag inside the folder and use it to hold small items, such as business cards, ticket stubs, and receipts, that you pick up during your trip. Use the main part of the folder for larger items, such as menus or maps. When you get home, take out the receipts, label the folder, and file it for safe-keeping. It comes in handy for scrapbooking or as a guide for some-one you know who is planning a trip to the same place.

Mix and match in a snap. Take some of the hassle out of packing. Tape an index card to each hanger in your closet that lists which garments you can mix and match with that item to complete an attractive outfit. Include accessories, too. When it's time to pack, you can throw a few outfits together in no time. On top of that, this organizing method also comes in handy for simply getting dressed every day.

Leave expensive camera at home. Buy a disposable camera to use on trips to countries where pickpockets and crimes against tourists are common. Save your expensive camera for pic-tures closer to home.

Dispose of high battery prices. Just because the camera is disposable doesn't mean the battery is, too. Make sure you remove and save the AA battery that comes with each disposable camera before you hand it over to the developer. Also, ask your local film lab if they'll sell you the batteries from other people's disposable cameras for a small fee, say 10 cents. Otherwise, the batteries just get tossed out with the rest of the camera.

Topple tangles with toilet paper roll. Do you spend most of your unpacking time trying to untangle your costume jewel-ry chains? Instead of tossing them in a jewelry case when you travel, wrap them around a cardboard toilet paper roll and secure them with tape. When you reach your destination, accessorizing is a breeze.

Grasp at straws when packing necklaces. After a long trip, your stomach might be in knots – but your jewelry doesn't have to be. To prevent tangled necklaces, thread each one through a plastic drinking straw and clasp it shut before packing. For long necklaces, use long straws. For shorter necklaces, cut a straw so it's exactly half as long as the necklace before threading the necklace through it.

Keep earrings in a safe place. Spend less time rummaging through your bags for your earrings while you're on vacation. Carry them in one of those lipstick cases with the flip-up mirror. You'll know where they are at all times, and they'll stay safe during your travels.

Use felt to store earrings safely. A quick trip to a fabric store might help you pack for your next trip. Buy a small square of felt, which should cost around 25 cents, and use it to transport several pairs of earrings. Just poke the earring posts through the felt, and fold the felt over them. Poke another pair of earrings through, fold it over, and so on. When you're done, you have a tiny roll of felt with a variety of earrings safely stored inside. Slip a rubber band over the felt roll so it doesn't come undone, and you're ready to go.

Remain loyal for travel benefits. If you had a pleasant stay at a certain hotel, seek out the same hotel on your next trip. That loyalty might pay off. Many hotel chains have frequent-stayer programs that offer discounts and other perks. Ask about the program when you book your room.

Feel welcome with hotel deals. Next time you're taking a trip by car, stop at a state welcome center. It's usually one of the first rest stops off the interstate once you enter a new state. Often, welcome centers offer discount booklets for hotels. You might be able to find a real deal.

Slap a shower cap on your shoes. Travel smarter from head to toe. Keep those free shower caps you get in hotels and use them as shoe bags. With your shoes in a shower cap, the clothes in your suitcase will stay nice and clean.

Feel at home with a scented candle. It doesn't take much to make yourself feel at home in a strange hotel room. Just bring along a scented candle. It will replace the sterile smell of a hotel with a pleasing and relaxing scent.

Don't discard drawstring bags. You don't have to use that hotel laundry bag just for laundry. Take the plastic drawstring bag with you and use it to hold your trash until you get to a garbage can. Or use it to sort your clothes when you pack. For example, you can shove all your underwear or socks in the bag. It's also a great way to tote a sweater so it doesn't snag.

Don't brake for breakfast. Breakfast might be the most important meal of the day – but it doesn't have to be the most expensive or most time consuming. Save both time and money on breakfast while you're on vacation. Pick up some juice and a muffin at night, and store the juice in your hotel room's ice bucket. The next morning, enjoy a quick, cheap breakfast before starting your day.

Resort to the Internet to browse menus. Before you head off to a big resort for vacation, head for the Internet. You might be able to view the menus of the resort's restaurants online. If you want, you can print copies of the menus and plan which restaurants you'll eat at during your stay. You might even pick out your entree before you set foot in the restaurant.

Drop a few coins for clean clothes. It's hard to return home to your regular chores after a fun, relaxing family vacation. And knowing you have all those dirty clothes to wash can really add to the dread. Why not take your dirty duds to a self-service laundry and use those big machines to make fast work of this unpleasant task.

Say 'bon voyage' to spills. The last thing you want to think about on vacation is laundry. But don't forget to bring a trial-size bottle of liquid laundry detergent with you. It comes in handy if you spill food on your shirt or if you run out of clothes and need to wash something by hand.

Turn your pillowcase into a hamper. Storing your dirty laundry in an airtight plastic bag while you're traveling might keep the rest of your clothes in the suitcase smelling better. But it could leave your dirty clothes moldy. Try tossing them in a pillowcase instead.

Stash trash bags in your luggage. Next time you pack for a trip, bring a few large garbage bags. They won't go to waste.

You can use them to store dirty laundry during your return trip. A garbage bag also serves as a waterproof layer inside your luggage to protect your stuff. You can even make an emergency raincoat out of a garbage bag by cutting slits for your head and arms.

Discover a 'cooler' way to travel. Here's a cool way to pack your carry-on luggage. Instead of a regular bag, use a small cooler. Pick a sturdy one with straps for easy handling. When you reach your destination, you can take out your toiletries and valuables and pack the cooler for a picnic or day trip. That way, you don't have to buy one of those cheap foam coolers that you throw away after a day's use.

Wash your clothes in your hotel room. You don't want to waste time at a Laundromat while you're on vacation. But you might need to freshen up your clothes a little, especially on a long trip. Pack an empty spray bottle and a few ounces of laundry detergent in a plastic travel bottle. Fill the spray bottle with water, mix in some detergent, and spray your clothes with the mixture. Rinse them in the shower and let them drip dry overnight. The next day, they should be ready to wear.

Protect posters with cardboard tube. The wrapping paper is all gone, but the cardboard roll it came on still has some value. When you go on a trip, cut the roll so it fits in your suitcase. If you buy a poster of the place you're visiting, you can roll it up and store it in the wrapping paper tube. As an added bonus, you can roll your clothes around the tube when you're packing to keep them wrinkle free.

Celebrate your birthday with free perks. Are you traveling to celebrate a special occasion? Maybe it's your birthday or anniversary. If so, let people know. You might get an unexpected gift. Many hotels and cruise lines offer free perks for these special occasions.

Plug in some protection. Groping through the darkness to find the bathroom in a strange motel room can be dangerous. To be safe, bring a night light with you on your travels. Plug it in before bed to shed some light on any nighttime bathroom trips.

Copy documents before you go. Besides making plans and reservations for your trip, you should also make some photocopies. Guard against theft or loss by making copies of your driver's license, passport, travel tickets, traveler's checks, and other important documents. Keep one set of copies at home and put another in your luggage.

Develop the perfect hiding spot. Carry a film canister with you on vacation, even if you don't have a camera. A film canister makes a perfect hiding spot for small pieces of jewelry, such as rings and earrings.

Outwit thieves with photocopies. Be prepared for the worst. Before you leave on a trip, photocopy everything in your wallet, front and back. Make two copies. Keep one at home and stash the other in your suitcase. That way, if your wallet gets stolen or lost, you'll know exactly what's missing and what telephone numbers you need to call to cancel credit or debit cards.

Make a splash with Velcro. Stick with this simple plan while you're on vacation. Get a fabric fastener, like Velcro, and sew or iron it onto the pockets of your swim trunks. That way, you can keep your keys and spare change safe while you take a dip in the pool or ocean. You can also use a fabric fastener on your regular pants to thwart pickpockets.

Buffer fragile items with Bubble Wrap. One minute you're bubbling with excitement over the delightful item you found in a store during your trip. The next, you're bubbling over with frustration because it's too delicate to bring with you on the plane. Prevent this problem by bringing a roll of Bubble Wrap and some masking tape with you on vacation. You can wrap the fragile item and put it in your carry-on bag.

Stop hotel intruders with doorstop. Feel secure in your hotel room. Bring along a small rubber doorstop and wedge it under your door from the inside. For added protection, use two doorstops. That should stop anyone from getting in.

Carry an umbrella and never get lost. A romantic getaway sort of loses its point if you and your spouse become separated on a crowded city street. Here's a simple way to reunite – if you don't mind attracting attention. Make sure you and your spouse carry matching, brightly colored umbrellas, the gaudier the better. When you lose sight of one another, open your umbrellas and hold them high above the crowd. You'll be back in each other's arms in no time.

Foil pickpockets with a rubber band. Keep tabs on your wallet during your travels. All it takes is a thick rubber band. Just wrap it around your wallet. If someone tries to slip it out of your pocket, you'll feel the rubber band rub against your pants.

Give your valuables maxi-mum protection. Camouflage your valuables from snooping thieves. Keep them in a tampon or maxi-pad box in your hotel room. No one will want to rummage through it. Leave half the tampons in the box and fill the rest of it with jewelry and other valuable items.

Add a pocket to hide passport. Look glamorous and be practical at the same time during your vacation. Sew some deep pockets onto a pair of cotton bike shorts and keep them closed with a fabric fastener, like Velcro. You can safely carry your passport, money, and other important documents in them. Then slip a long, elegant dress over the shorts and enjoy a night on the town.

Protect cash with pantyhose. Get a leg up on airport pickpockets. Cut a leg off an old pair of pantyhose and slide your credit cards and cash inside. Then tie the leg around your waist under your clothing. Since you don't need to access your credit cards or cash right away – and no thief will be able to get at them – you'll have a worry-free trip through a crowded airport.

Try a towel to prevent bathtub slips. Worried about slipping in a hotel bathtub? You don't have to take up precious suitcase space with sandals or flip-flops for the shower. Just lay a hand towel in the bottom of the tub.

Catch a thief with a comb. A comb helps you part your hair – but it also makes sure you don't part with your wallet. Slide a comb into the fold of your wallet and put your wallet in your front pocket, with the teeth of the comb facing up. A pickpocket will have a tough time stealing your wallet because the comb will catch on your pants pocket.

Secure your wallet with safety pins. Safety pins actually do provide safety. Use one to pin your trousers from the inside to make the pocket's opening smaller. Leave enough room so you can barely squeeze your wallet in and out – but you'll definitely notice if someone else tries to.

Guard your life with three essentials. Remember to pack three key items, and they might save your life. Always travel with a flashlight, a battery-operated smoke detector, and a roll of duct tape. In case of an emergency, you'll be prepared. Keep your flashlight on the night stand by your bed in your hotel room. The flashlight can guide you, the smoke detector will warn you, and if you're trapped in your hotel room during a fire, the duct tape can protect you. Just use it to seal off the vents and cracks in the door so no smoke gets in.

Track down belongings with matchbooks. You don't have to smoke to take advantage of hotel matchbooks. Take one from each hotel you stay in during your trip. That way, if you leave something behind, you'll have the name and address of every place you've been.

Safeguard valuables in resealable bag. Protect important travel items from rain and dirt. Make sure you bring a resealable plastic bag to hold your passport, binoculars, camera, film, and maps.

Protect your home with bright idea. The lights are out, and burglars know nobody is home. If you have lights connected to timers, make sure you put in new light bulbs before you leave on vacation. That way, they'll definitely come on when they're supposed to. Save the older light bulbs and use them when you're home.

Take special precautions if you're female. Women traveling alone should take some extra precautions to avoid unwanted attention. Label your bags "Mr. and Mrs." or just use your initials. Don't carry anything personalized with your name on it. That way, people will know as little about you as possible. Wear a costume-jewelry wedding band or engagement ring. And walk like you know where you're going.

Diabetics – stash syringes in plastic jar. If you have diabetes and take insulin, you have special travel concerns. In addition to the usual traveler's worries, you have to deal with syringes and medication. You can bring along an empty peanut butter jar to dispose of your used syringes. Any plastic jar with a screw-on lid should do the trick. While you're at it, get a note from your doctor saying you need to carry syringes because of a medical condition. That way, you won't get hassled by airport security. Also, buy a small thermal insulated lunch bag to keep your medication cool.

'Watch' out for tricky time zone changes. Just because you change time zones doesn't mean you have to change your medication schedule. Instead of struggling with any confusing adjustments, bring an extra watch set to the time zone where you live. That way, you can take your medicine at familiar times without any problems.

Super solutions for
better pet care

Fly beside your pet. If you must travel by plane with your beloved pet, don't assume she can't stay with you. Many airlines allow small, caged pets to fly in the cabin with their owners. But always call first so you'll know exactly what the rules are and what it will cost you.

Be direct when booking flights with pets. You know large pets usually must travel with cargo, but you also know how often luggage gets lost or misplaced. To keep this from happening to your pet, be sure to book a direct flight. That way, you and your pet will arrive together at your destination.

Watch out for your pet in cargo hold. For your peace of mind and your pet's protection, ask to watch your animal being loaded into the cargo hold. When you finally lean your seat back on that long flight, you won't have to keep wondering if your furry friend made it or not.

Travel safely with pug-nosed pets. Certain breeds of dogs and cats should never be placed in the cargo hold of a plane. Chow chows, Pekinese, and Persian cats can easily become overheated or low on oxygen because of their pug noses. If you aren't sure about your pet, check with your veterinarian before flying.

Time flights with temperature. Think temperature when you're taking a pet on a flight in the summer or winter. Your pet will be most comfortable if you book early morning or late evening flights in summer and midday flights in winter.

Coax your pet to love his carrier. If you know in advance that you and your pet will be flying, let him spend time in the carrier you plan to take him in. Set it up in your home and put a few of his toys inside. You can get him to go in to investigate by leaving small treats in it. Before long, he'll think of the carrier as a cozy hideout and not a scary box.

Put ice cubes in pet carrier. For obvious reasons, you shouldn't feed your pet for several hours before traveling by plane. Give her a little water beforehand, but don't bother filling the water tray in her pet carrier. It will likely tip over and make her wet and miserable. Instead, try putting a few ice cubes in the water tray. As they melt, they'll supply just enough water to keep her content.

Put pet pictures in your purse. A photo of your pet can be a great conversation starter on an airplane, but if the pet is traveling with you, it can be much more than that. On the off chance that your pet becomes lost or misplaced, you'll be able to show airline employees a photo for quick identification.

Sneezing and wheezing not fur related

You might think your animal allergies are caused by your pet's fur. But it's really dander, saliva, and urine particles that make you miserable. When tiny bits of these substances drift into the air and eventually your lungs, they can trigger allergic reactions, like sneezing and asthma.

Breathe easier with pets and asthma. Even though most pets are happier living inside with you, asthma sufferers may have to keep pets outside. If you allow your pet in occasionally, be sure to clean him first with a damp cloth. This will get rid of some of the dander that would otherwise float around your home. If your pet does stay inside with you, never let him sleep in a bedroom. A laundry room or basement makes a better choice. Ask someone without asthma to bathe and groom him each week to keep dander to a minimum. Grooming should always be done outside.

Run errands without your pet. You're planning to make several stops for errands on this beautiful summer day, and you'd like to bring your pet along for the ride. Hold everything! Even if you leave a window cracked open for air, your car can reach very high temperatures in just a few short minutes. And don't forget your pet can't remove his fur coat. Never leave a pet alone in a car for even a short time.

Secure pets in a truck. Never put your dog in the back of a pickup truck – no matter how fun it looks. He could be injured if you stop short, or even thrown from the truck bed into traffic. Let your dog ride in a pet crate secured to the truck bed, or in the cab with you. Use a dog harness, which is like a seat belt for dogs.

Throw in the towel when traveling with pets. You would probably remove your fur coat for a long car trip, but your pet doesn't have that option. To make him more comfortable, put a damp towel over his travel cage. Not only will it make him cooler, it will also cut down on static electricity in the car.

Teach pets to love the car. If you know you must take your pet on a long car ride, take him on several short trips beforehand. Dogs especially will love riding with you if you seem enthusiastic about it. In addition, the short trips will help your pet adjust to the car's motion, so he'll be less likely to get sick traveling. Start the process several weeks before the long ride, and your pet will be a veteran car rider by trip time.

Protect pets from thieves. You would never leave your pet in the car on a hot day, but what about a cool day with the windows open? This is still a bad idea. Your pet could be stolen by people who resell animals for profit. You don't even want to think about where your pet might end up. So keep pets at home or stay with them at all times.

Pack a little litter tray. When traveling by car, you can stop at rest areas for bathroom breaks, but what about kitty? Tuck a litter tray and some litter into a large plastic bag, and you'll both be set for the trip.

Drive away Rover's fear of traveling. If driving in the car makes Rover whine and drool from nervousness, take a few practice runs in your driveway. Open the car door and invite him in with a biscuit. Then let him settle in with you and enjoy his treat. Do this until he looks forward to hopping in the car with you. The next time you take him for a ride, he should be a happy camper.

Plan for disaster with pets in mind. When disaster strikes, pets frequently get lost in the mad dash for safety. But with a little planning, you can save yourself and your pet. Keep your pet's immunization and health records in the same place you keep your valuable papers. If you have to leave home suddenly, you can grab one box and go. Most emergency shelters won't take pets so you'll have to make arrangements at a kennel, which will require your pet's medical records. As an alternative, locate in advance a motel that allows pets.

Catch a cat quickly in an emergency. Buy a pet carrier for your cat and keep it handy. In an emergency, transporting pets quickly and safely can be a life or death situation. In a pinch, you can tuck a cat into a pillowcase, but it won't want to stay there very long.

Picture your pet safe. Keep a snapshot of your pet with your valuable papers. During an emergency, your pet might run away in fear. But if you have a picture of the animal, you'll be able to make fliers to help find it.

Make fliers for lost pet. As soon as you realize your pet is missing, have fliers made up with your pet's picture and contact information. Post them all over your neighborhood, and while you're tacking them up, ask people if they've seen the animal.

Put papers to work on lost pet. Lost your pet? Don't just sit there worrying. Put an advertisement in the local newspaper. Describe your pet's breed or mix, coloring, weight, and where and when you saw her last. Also mention her name so if someone sees her, they'll know what to call her. And don't forget to scan the papers regularly for animals that have been found.

Keep in touch to find missing animal. Don't give up on a missing pet. Call the humane society in your town and surrounding towns. Contact animal shelters and veterinarian offices. Keep in touch with all of these people because your pet could show up at any time.

Supervise pets outdoors. Even if you loved the movie "Born Free," don't be tempted to let your cat or dog stay outside without supervision. Very young or old animals are especially at risk since they can't always help themselves out of a jam. Short-haired pets should never be left outside in winter, as they cannot adapt to very cold temperatures. In fact, a short-haired dog might even enjoy a tasteful doggie sweater when you take him out on a very cold day.

Invite pets inside. Your dog is a pack animal, and the day you brought her home she identified your family as her pack. Don't deprive her of your companionship by keeping her outside. She'll be happier if you let her live inside with you but take her out for frequent walks. Cats are sociable, too, although they're often too cool to let it show. If they could talk, they would tell you they feel safest inside with you.

Put a lid on food poisoning. Keep indoor and outdoor trash in sturdy containers with lids. The smell of meat scraps is too tempting for many animals, and they'll pay a steep price if the meat is contaminated. Some bacteria don't give off a bad smell to warn them away. You could save your pet from a nasty case of food poisoning by keeping him out of the trash.

Save your cans and your pet. Keep your recyclable bin away from your pet. Tin cans can be dangerous because of their razor-sharp edges, and a pet foraging for food can severely cut her nose and mouth. In addition, the scraps of food left in the can can give her food poisoning or even lead poisoning.

Protect your pet from sunburn. With all the warnings about skin cancer, you wouldn't think of going outside in the summer without sunscreen. But what about your pale pet? Animals with light-colored coats and skin can get sunburns and skin cancer, too. If your pet is light-colored, put a bit of sunscreen on his nose and on the tips of his ears when taking him out in strong sun.

Spare your furry friend's feet. Your pet relies on you for relief from summer's heat. Don't let him down by walking him on a sizzling sidewalk. He could burn the pads on his feet and become overheated in the process. Keep him in the shade and on grass whenever possible, and move quickly if you must take him on the sidewalk or road.

Give your dog a cool haircut. You can help your dog beat the heat of summer by shaving her long, thick fur to about 1 inch in length. You'll also be able to easily see any fleas or ticks. Just don't shave off all her hair since it's her natural protection from sunburn.

Help pets with heatstroke. People aren't the only ones who get heatstroke. Your pet can be overcome by hot weather as well. If your pet pants rapidly, twitches, barks for no reason, or stares with a crazed look, he may be experiencing heatstroke. Pour cool water on him every few minutes, but don't try to place him in a tub of water or put ice on him. That could send him into shock. Offer him water to drink, and let him rest near a fan while you call your veterinarian.

Weatherproof your dog's home. If you're someone who prefers to keep a pet outside, be sure he has a good shelter for winter weather. Doghouses should be built off the ground and be sturdy enough to block the wind. Make sure the house is only a little larger than the animal so it will hold his body heat well but is large enough for him to stretch out. Cover the entrance with a piece of waterproof burlap or plastic to keep the elements out, and put straw or cedar shavings on the floor for added warmth and comfort. And remember, if it's freezing cold, your pet would really appreciate it if you invited him inside with you.

Watch pet's food and water in winter. Outdoor pets need extra food during the winter because they burn extra calories trying to stay warm. If your pet isn't overweight, and he eats all the food you give him each day, talk with your veterinarian about increasing his portions. Also, keep an eye on your pet's water dish to be sure he has fresh water that isn't frozen. Frozen water is of no use to him, and he could quickly become dehydrated. Remember to put his water in a plastic bowl instead of metal, which could stick to his tongue in very cold weather.

Protect paws from chemicals. If you take your pet outside in the winter, beware of chemicals used on driveways and roads to melt snow and ice. Your pet's bare paws could be injured. Wipe his paws before he comes in the house, too. He might try to lick his pads clean and irritate his mouth, as well.

Safeguard paws from road salt. You can protect your pet's paws from irritating road salt in winter. Simply spread a thin covering of petroleum jelly on the pads of her feet before you take her out. Wipe her paws on a soft towel before coming back into the house.

Fix your pet instead of the fence

Are you constantly repairing the fence your pet is destroying so he can rendezvous with the pet next door? Having your pet "fixed" might take care of the problem. Animals are less likely to run off once they are spayed or neutered.

Treat your pets to a safe Halloween. Kids everywhere love Halloween. Pets are less enthusiastic. Scary-looking strangers coming to the house all evening can cause them more than a little anxiety. Some pets will even try to escape when you open the door for trick-or-treaters. Treat your pets right by keeping them in a secure, quiet area during the festivities. And skip the adorable pet costumes. Animals don't usually enjoy dressing up, and some outfits can even be a health hazard to them, causing them to trip or choke.

Trick or treat without Fido. It might seem like a fun plan, but don't let your kids take the dog trick-or-treating. Children who are already struggling with costumes may not be able to handle a pet. In addition, your dog is likely to fear passing "creatures" and noise. For safety, leave your dog at home.

Give your pet a healthy Halloween treat. For a pet, a piece of candy on Halloween is no treat. Chocolate ranks high on the bad idea list since it can be toxic to many animals. Instead, put some pet treats in a bowl and let your kids give a couple to your dog or cat. Just be sure they don't accidentally hand them out at the door.

Distract your pet during fireworks. If you're like most people, you enjoy the bright lights and noise of fireworks on the Fourth of July. But to your pet, it feels more like Armageddon. If you leave him tied outside, or even in a fenced yard, he could get hurt trying to escape. To ease his anxieties during the festivities, keep him inside with the shades drawn. Turn on a radio at normal volume, and leave it near him to help drown out scary sounds while you're out.

Deter pets from decorations. That flickering candle in the jack-o'-lantern looks great, but what happens when Fluffy sticks her paw in it to investigate? Keep pets away from candles, streamers, and other holiday decorations. Their natural instinct to smell, touch, and taste things can lead to injury if you're not careful.

Make a quick cat toy. Stuck in the house with a fidgety cat and no cat toys? Grab an empty film canister and put a few pieces of pasta or a few pebbles inside. Your cat will be as delighted as if you had spent a week's salary on a toy.

Combat fur balls with fish. If you've ever seen your cat hack up a fur ball, you probably don't want to repeat the experience. Your cat doesn't enjoy it much either. To keep both of you from suffering through another attack, feed your cat sardines packed in oil every three or four weeks. The oil helps the fur move quickly through the digestive tract so it won't clump in your cat's stomach.

Zap fur balls. Here's another way to help your kitty fight the never-ending battle against fur balls. Add a teaspoon of liquid paraffin to his food every now and then. Long-haired cats will need this tonic more often than short-haired cats.

Give your cat fair warning. On cold days, outdoor cats look for warm car engines to snuggle up against, and indoor cats hang around warm appliances, like clothes dryers. Either situation could lead to a disaster. Before you start your car, knock on the hood to shoo away any critters, and always check for Fluffy inside the dryer before you use it. If you find her there one day, close the door and bang loudly on the top a few times before you let her out. That will deter her from hiding there again.

Air condition your cat. You can get your cats to toe the line by blasting a bit of air at them when they misbehave. Buy a can of compressed air used for cleaning computers. You can find it at stores that sell computer equipment. The next time your cats start doing the cancan on the table or hanging from the chandelier, spray a bit of air at them, but don't overdo it. The air is quite cold.

Think out of the box about cat germs. You would never install a toilet in your kitchen, but many people have no qualms about keeping a litter box there. Since this is really your cat's bathroom, it contains all sorts of nasty germs you should avoid. Keep the litter box in an out-of-the-way place, and wash your hands thoroughly after cleaning it.

Screen windows for cat hazard. When warm weather prompts you to start opening windows in your home, check each screen to be sure it's properly secured and in good shape. Cats love to cool themselves in an open window, but they can fall out if a screen is not sturdy enough.

Make your trash can unappetizing to kitty. Sometimes the interesting scents wafting out of a trash can are just too tempting for a cat to pass by. If your cat is constantly into your kitchen trash, sprinkle a bit of chili powder in it. Your cat's taste for garbage will suddenly change.

Butter up a cat in a new home. Put an adult cat at ease in a new home by spreading a bit of butter on its paws. Cats love the taste of butter so much that they'll keep coming back for more.

Take a shine to your cat. Ever notice how some cats' coats gleam? You can get your short-haired cat to shine like that by rubbing her fur with a chamois leather cloth. A piece of silk or velvet will do the trick, too.

Feed cats cat food. If you have a dog and a cat, you might be tempted to buy one type of food in bulk for both of them. Resist the temptation. Cats need five times as much protein as dogs do, and they require more vitamins and fatty acids than dog food contains.

In addition, they must have the amino acid taurine, which is added to cat food because they can't make it themselves. A cat fed a steady diet of dog food will eventually show signs of illness, including heart disease and eye problems that can lead to blindness.

Don't give your cat a raw deal. Even though your cat is descended from wild animals, it would be a big mistake to feed her like one. Don't give her raw meat. It can harbor bacteria and pesticides that her immune system can't handle.

Protect your cat from food poisoning. Don't feed your cat raw eggs. They contain a protein called avidin, which can rob her of biotin, a vitamin needed for growth and a healthy coat. In addition, raw eggs can be hiding *Salmonella,* bacteria that can make her very sick. But she doesn't have to miss out on a delicious, high-protein snack. Just be sure to cook the eggs before putting them in her food bowl.

Cook fish for your cat's health. Never feed kitty raw fish, no matter how much she begs for it. Raw fish can harbor tapeworms, which will rob your cat of nutrients as the worms feed themselves. In addition, raw fish contain an enzyme that destroys thiamin, a vitamin cats need for good health. Without it, they can suffer brain damage. But all this doesn't mean your cat can't have her favorite food. Just be sure to cook it well. Cooking fish at a high heat destroys any harmful organisms and eliminates the harmful enzyme.

Deliver your cat from bone problems. Everyone knows cats love liver. But did you know that more than a couple of servings a week can cause bone problems in a cat? That's because liver is rich in vitamin A, which is toxic to cats in high amounts. If your cat takes vitamin A supplements, liver should never cross his whiskers.

Tame your cat's tuna habit. Some cats love tuna so much they eat it every chance they get. If this sounds like your cat, don't let that be too often. A teaspoon or two of tuna each day won't hurt, but more than that could cause mercury poisoning, since many of the fish are contaminated.

Ban mushrooms from cat's diet. Don't let your cat munch on mushrooms you've brought home from the store. Even though these are safe for cats, she might get the idea to start foraging for them in the woods. That could lead to trouble since many wild varieties are poisonous.

Don't let your cat 'pig out.' Never give your cat pork to eat – and that includes bacon. Pork fat doesn't break down into tiny particles, like other fats, and the globs of fat can block a cat's blood vessels. Bacon is especially bad because it contains sodium nitrate, a preservative considered hazardous.

Protect your cat from mothballs. Cats love to play in out-of-the-way places, like closets. But danger could be lurking there if you use mothballs. A chemical in mothballs called naphthalene is toxic to cats, even if they just smell the fumes. It can cause liver damage, vomiting, severe stomach pain, lack of coordination, and coma. Keep mothballs zipped in garment bags or in secure trunks. If you think your cat has come in contact with mothballs, call your veterinarian immediately.

'Shoo' cats from countertops. Keep your cat off kitchen counters for sanitary reasons and so he won't accidentally walk on the stove when you're cooking. You can protect overly curious cats by covering cooking foods and turning pan handles inward.

Don't let your cat take a powder. Keep your cat out of the bathroom when you use talcum powder. It might make her smell better, but the little bit she inhales can cause lung damage. And if she manages to eat any, it can cause damage to her internal organs.

Keep cats from cozying up to recliners. Ahhh. You love relaxing in your cozy reclining chair. But if your cat decides to relax behind it, she could be in for big trouble. The back of a reclining chair usually offers enough room for a cat to nap, but if someone sits in it, that space disappears as the chair reclines. Make a loud noise or spritz your cat with water if you find her in this dangerous situation.

Enjoy a pet and good health

Are pet owners healthier than other people? Could be. According to recent statistics, 70 percent of the people who frequent health food stores own a pet, and 61 percent of people surveyed believe having a pet leads to a healthier life.

Take a swipe at shedding pets. Does your dog shed hair all over you and your furniture even though you brush him outside regularly? Try this. Swipe a dryer sheet over his fur each day. The dryer sheet will pick up stray hairs and keep them from landing on your clothes and couch.

Wash your dog without water. Whew! Fido needs a bath, but it's below zero outside and he really hates to get wet. Don't suffer through the winter with a smelly dog. Use this trick. Take him outside or into the garage and pour plenty of baking soda on his coat. Work it into his fur, then brush his coat thoroughly. Much of the dirt will leave with the baking soda, and he'll smell a whole lot better, too.

Clean your dog's ears at home. There's no need to take your dog to the vet to get his ears clean. Make this simple rinse at home. In a small squirt bottle, mix equal parts water and vinegar, then label the bottle. Squirt the solution over the outer portion of your dog's ears, then stand back. It's best to do this outside, since most dogs will shake their heads to get the liquid out.

File this under toenails. Don't let your dog's ragged nails wreak havoc on furniture and hardwood floors. You can gently file them with a metal file for large dogs and emery boards for smaller ones. Distract the dog with a chewy treat and praise him for cooperating.

Keep shampoo out of your dog's eyes. Use this old hairdresser's trick to keep soap out of your dog's eyes when he's getting a bath. Dab a bit of petroleum jelly on his eyebrows and under his eyes. The soapy water should stay on his coat and out of his peepers.

Learn the best way to wash a dog. Don't dive right into washing your dog. A little prep work will go a long way to making him look his best. First, start by brushing his coat to get rid of tangled and matted fur. Now you're ready to start washing. Only use official dog shampoo or baby shampoo. Anything else could cause skin irritation. Lather him up with warm water, using a handheld shower if one is available. After toweling him off, use a hair dryer. Make sure it's set on warm, never hot. If your dog fears hairdryers, simply keep him inside until he's dry.

Walk the dog before washing. Ever bathe your dog, only to have him immediately run outside and roll in the dirt? You can avoid this frustration by taking him for a walk before bath time. That way, he won't have any reason to go out until he's good and dry.

Chase bad smells from your dog. Until dogs stop rolling in stinky things, pet owners will need tips like this. After washing a bad-smelling dog, add lemon juice, vinegar, or baking soda to the rinse water. And for a dog with long, thick fur, add a creme rinse with a conditioner to keep his hair tangle free.

Protect property with puppy pacifiers. Give your puppy rubber chew toys to divert him from carpets, furniture, and shoes. For a dog that chomps on wooden table and chair legs, rub a little oil of cloves into the wood. After a few tastes, he'll decide he prefers the chew toys after all.

Soothe a sleepless pup. Is there anything sadder than the nightly whimpering of a puppy newly separated from his mother? Help your puppy adjust by placing a warm water bottle next to him. Wrap it in a towel to make it more cuddly and to conserve the heat. If you add a ticking alarm clock and soft music, your puppy will quickly drift off to dreamland.

Don't give a dog a bone. Don't give your dog bones to chew on, no matter how much he begs. A bone can shatter while he's gnawing on it, leaving splinters that can cut his mouth and even choke him. Instead, buy him a rawhide chew at the pet store.

Put a lid on drinking from toilets. You might think it's cute when your dog drinks out of the toilet, but if you use chemical cleaners in the bowl, your pet could be poisoned. Keep the lid down at all times to keep him away, and be sure he has fresh water in his official drinking bowl.

Save furniture from dog slobber. If you have a Saint Bernard or other dog that slobbers, you'll be grateful for this tip. To clean dog saliva from upholstered furniture or other fabric, wet the material, then sprinkle a bit of meat tenderizer on the affected area. Let it soak in a bit, then wash as usual. Make sure you test this on a hidden spot first.

Trick your dog into losing weight. If Fido is having a harder and harder time fitting through his doggie door, maybe it's time to do something. You can put your dog on a diet without him even realizing it. Simply cut back on the dog food you serve him, and make up the difference with a portion of cooked vegetables, like green beans or carrots. Keep mixing this low-calorie grub into his regular food, and Fido will soon be slipping gracefully through his door.

Protect your family from dog germs. Be sure to clean your lawn daily of any "deposits" your dog has made. If you don't, he could track germs into your home, and you and your family could get sick. Bury the doggy-do in the woods or in a garden. And if he waters the lawn in the same place every day, spread some gypsum on that area to keep your grass from dying.

Amaze friends with this pet trick. You can make Lassie look like an amateur by teaching your dog this trick. Tie a cowbell to a string and hang it inside, near the back door. Before you let your dog out, take his paw and bat the bell to make it ring. Don't let him out without making him ring the bell. Before long, he'll start ringing it on his own to let you know he wants' to go out. This works best with puppies, but some older dogs catch on, too.

Teach barking dogs to 'can it.' Does your dog bark at anything that moves? To keep her quiet, put some coins in an empty coffee can. The next time she barks without good reason, shake the can near her face. Dogs hate the noise and will immediately hush. In time, just the sight of the can will remind her she's barking up the wrong tree.

Remove burrs with oil. Has your dog come home covered with burrs or sticky substances, like tar or paint? Before trying to wash him, pour vegetable oil on his fur. The oil allows you to brush out whatever is stuck to his coat. Use dog shampoo and warm water to remove the oil, and he'll be good as new.

Prolong pet's life with good oral hygiene

Did you know that keeping plaque off your pet's teeth can add two or three years to his life? And that's in people years! Experts say bacteria in plaque can get into an animal's bloodstream, damaging internal organs and cutting short his life. But brushing and checking your pet's teeth and gums regularly can keep bacteria at bay. Ask your veterinarian about keeping your pet's teeth in tiptop shape.

Give your dog a Hollywood smile. Use baking soda to keep your dog's teeth sparkling and free from ugly tartar that causes tooth decay. This inexpensive kitchen staple can also banish your dog's bad breath. If he'll allow it, use a toothbrush dipped in baking soda to clean his pearly whites. If not, try using a damp cloth dipped in the stuff. Just don't use toothpaste. Some of its ingredients are harmful to dogs.

Help your cat lick fear of medicine. You think you've tried everything to get your cat to take her medicine, but have you tried this? Squirt the medicine directly onto her coat with an eyedropper and watch what happens. She'll immediately tidy up by licking it clean.

Discourage fleas with garlic. If fleas are your cat's constant companions, feed him a garlic capsule every other day. Fleas don't care to have garlic breath, and they'll look for a better-tasting host.

Hang a 'no vacancy' sign for fleas. You wouldn't allow fleas in your home so chase them away from your dog's house, too. Fleas will vacate the property if you add some pine straw and pour salt in all the nooks and crannies.

Salt your dog to repel fleas. If you hate fleas and those chemical-laden flea collars for dogs, wash your pet in salt water instead. Fleas will quickly look for another victim. For added protection, rub some baker's yeast into his coat once it's dry.

Introduce fleas to rosemary. Don't spend a lot of money on flea repellents. Fleas will flee when confronted by rosemary, a very fragrant herb. In a small pot of boiling water, steep two teaspoons of rosemary. Once it cools, sponge it onto your pet's coat. When the smell starts to wear off, repeat the process to keep your pet flea free.

Evict fleas with fragrance. Make fleas feel unwelcome in your pet's quarters. Spread cedar shavings, fennel, rosemary, or eucalyptus under and around his bedding. You'll enjoy the fragrant smell, but fleas will flee from the odor.

Wipe out fleas with water. Do you hate fleas that attack your pet outdoors, but dislike the harsh chemicals it takes to do them in? Try this all-natural solution – water. During flea season, flood your yard, especially the parts where your pet hangs out. When the water dries, your unwanted backyard guests will be gone.

Tag your pet for safety. Invest in an identification tag for your pet. You can have your pet's name, your address, and phone number inscribed on a tag so someone can contact you directly. If your pet ever gets lost, you stand a better chance of having her returned to you with proper ID. If you find an animal that seems lost, don't keep it while looking for the owner. Instead, take it to an animal shelter. That's the first place an owner would check for a lost pet.

Make a temporary ID kit for your dog. You can make a temporary identification kit for your dog to carry on vacation. All you need is a film canister with its lid. Cut two slits in it about a half inch apart, and slide your dog's collar through it. On a small piece of paper, write your name, where you're staying temporarily, and the phone number or your cell phone number. Slip this information into the canister, and your dog will be all set for the trip.

Tame pet odor. If you notice a powerful animal odor when you open your front door, maybe it's time to do something about it. Try mixing brewer's yeast into your pet's food. Use a teaspoon of yeast for a cat and a tablespoon for a dog. Your pet's scent will become much less noticeable.

Rid your pet of skunk perfume. If your pet occasionally tangles with skunks, you'll be glad to know you can rid him of that horrible smell. In a bucket, mix one and one-half quarts of 3-percent hydrogen peroxide, one-quarter cup of baking soda, and one teaspoon of dishwashing liquid. Put on some old clothes and a pair of rubber gloves and start washing. Rinse several times and your pet's smell will be much improved.

Take two pets and call me in the morning

You always knew your pet was good for your health, and now there's proof. Studies show playing with a pet can lower your blood pressure, relieve stress, and put you in a better mood.

Choose a 'cheep' pet. If you would like to have a pet, but you're on a limited budget, a bird makes a great choice. Caged birds, such as parakeets and canaries, don't eat much, and you can buy bird seed in bulk for very little.

Clean your fish tank the easy way. You can clean a large aquarium without throwing out your back or getting soaking wet. How? Use a shop vac to remove the old water. First, put your fish in another container of water. Next, cut a leg off an old pair of pantyhose and work it onto the shop vac as a filter. This keeps the gravel in the tank from being sucked into the shop vac. When all the water is out, clean your tank, then refill it with fresh water. Now you can return your fish to their sparkling clean home.

Give your pet's coat a lustrous sheen. When buying dog food, look for quality ingredients. Vegetable oils are important because they contain fatty acids that dogs need. Corn oil, wheat germ oil, and linseed oil are good choices. There should also be some animal fat in your dog's diet, such as chicken or turkey fat. The combination of fats will keep your dog's skin soft and his coat shiny.

Pop pet food in popcorn tins. Don't throw out those giant tins of popcorn you get every Christmas. Recycle them. After you wash and dry them, they work great as containers for dog food or birdseed. Not only are they sturdier than a bag, but with the lid on, they don't attract bugs and rodents like an open bag of food does.

Hold the onion on pet food. Onions make your food taste so much better, you might think your dog or cat might want a bit in their food, too. But many animals, including cats and dogs, can't handle a compound in onions called disulfide. Eating just a few onion slices a week can cause your pet to develop a serious type of anemia. So keep the onions on your burgers, and off your pet's food.

Make a disposable pet bowl. Want a disposable bowl for your pet while traveling? Cut the top off a gallon milk jug, leaving a few inches at the bottom. When you return home, simply throw the already recycled bowl into the recyclable trash.

Help a runt get his rations. Help the runt of the litter get his fair share of the food by feeding tiny kittens and puppies out of muffin tins. Simply place equal amounts of food in every other space, and the littlest one won't have to fight for his supper.

Protect your pet from penicillin. Did you know penicillin can kill your pet? When you're taking this antibiotic – or any drug for that matter – keep it in a secure place your pet can't reach.

Prevent pet poisoning. Both indoor and outdoor plants can be toxic to your pet if he gets the urge to munch on them. Beware of rhododendrons, Japanese yew trees, and lily of the valley flowers. Also, don't let your pet chew on pits from fruit trees. Some of them, such as peach and cherry pits, can make him sick.

Have a heart about heartworm

Want your pet to be around for a long time? Protect his heart from an invisible killer – heartworm. Both dogs and cats can get this deadly illness, which is spread by mosquitoes and fleas. Ask your veterinarian about heartworm pills.

Have a pretty yard and healthy pets. Keep Fido and Fluffy away from newly fertilized lawns and gardens. That goes for pesticides, too. If possible, keep them in a fenced backyard and forego the chemicals there. Too many pets become sick and even die after eating plant food or fertilizer. And before adding ornamental plants to your yard, find out if they're toxic to animals.

Index

Index

Feather dusters 101
Felt 103
Fences 228, 271
Ferns 274
Fertilizers 273, 278
Fiberglass 5
File cabinets 75, 129, 130
Film canisters 286, 321, 335, 347, 352
Fingernails 144, 261
Fire hazards 250
Fire safety kits 251
Fireplaces 15, 123, 193
Fires 248-253
First aid kits 74, 148
Fish tanks, cleaning 372
Fishing supplies 111, 326-327
Fleas 232, 236, 371
Flies 236, 237
Floors 20, 21, 80, 96, 177, 248
Florist tape 114
Flossing 150, 152, 153
Flour 54, 232, 242, 264, 274
Flower boxes 115, 124
Flower pots 113, 122, 274, 275, 285, 301
Flowers
  African violets 278
  azaleas 272, 274
  bulbs 265, 271
  camellias 274
  chrysanthemums 242
  drying 272
  for pest control 262, 263
  fresh cut 114, 269-270, 299-300
  gardenias 278
  growing 271, 272, 279
  hydrangeas 272
  marigolds 262, 263, 266

paper 313
poinsettias 287
pressing 320, 321
rhododendrons 272, 274
roses 272, 273, 274, 276
Food processors 91
Food safety 29, 35, 40, 44
Food stains 37
Foot care 145-148, 338
Foreign currency 346
Fragrances 140
Freezers 8, 35, 79, 81
Fruit flies 236-237
Fruit trees 267, 268, 275, 276
Fruits 34, 36, 37, 40, 135, 136, 138
Frying 42
Furniture polish 7, 15, 96, 97, 99, 156
Fuses 181

G

Garages 23, 72
Garbage cans 11, 236
Garbage disposals 8, 83
Garden accessories 115, 121, 122. *See also specific accessories*
Garden hoses 335
Gardening tools 188, 260
Garlic 31, 40, 41, 147
  for pest control 262, 263, 266, 267, 371
Gates 121
Gelatin 35, 46, 137, 284
Gifts, homemade 301-304
Gifts, wrapping 295-297, 313, 321
Ginger 150
Ginger ale 150

Gingerbread 291
Ginseng 241
Glass, glassware 7, 86, 102, 111, 113. *See also Windows*
Gloves, mittens 310
  fabric 54, 144, 186, 228, 257, 309
  plastic 1, 283
Glue removal 180
Glue safety 318
Gnats 237, 258
Golf bags 261
Golf balls, clubs 328
Golf shoes 277
Gophers 237, 264
Grapefruit 36, 245
Grapes 267, 268
Grass stains 61, 62
Grass, lawns 240, 273, 276-277
Graters 177
Gravel 113
Gravies 31
Grease stains 14, 63, 64, 312
Greeting cards 127, 294-295
Grilling, grilled food 29, 31, 43
Grills 6, 274, 325
Grits 231
Grout 2, 5
Guitars 325, 326
Gum, chewing 13, 14, 65, 234
Gutters 186

H

Hair care 135-137
Hair dryers 81, 89, 121, 343
Hair spray 63, 136, 154, 162, 285
Hammers, hammering 179, 184, 188-189, 277